PRAISE FOR *THE STRANGER ARTIST*

'A landmark in Australian literature – a book written in gouache, acrylic, blood and tears: the story of the modern frontier, where high art, for a brief, magic time, was made from the trust and tension between two worlds.'

Nicolas Rothwell, author of *Quicksilver*, *Belomor* and *Red Heaven*

'Utterly compelling. Vivid and unflinching. Beautifully written. An exceptional and intimate portrait of artistic collaboration informed by a deep knowledge of place, people and culture, this is a story of how Indigenous art emerges in the Kimberley, inseparable from the Country itself, and the embers of history. *The Stranger Artist* captures the texture of everyday life in the Kimberley in a way no book has done before.'

Mark McKenna, author of *Return to Uluru* and *Looking for Blackfellas' Point*

'Quentin Sprague has written a grand cross-cultural tale of genius, co-dependency, brotherhood, mythmaking and hubris.'

Kim Mahood, author of *Wandering with Intent* and *Position Doubtful*

'Like many a fine work of art, *The Stranger Artist* attracts with a brilliant surface while fascinating with its deeper layers ... it is full of intense colour and eccentricity, while also permeated with great sadness.'

Luke Stegemann, *Australian Book Review*

'The absorbing origin story of a painting movement like no other. Quentin Sprague draws us into a world of heat, busted LandCruisers and community decay with a lyrical portrait of tragic hope, where art and cultural exchange come to life.'

Ashleigh Wilson, author of *Brett Whiteley: Art, Life and the Other Thing* and *On Artists*

'A gripping tale of hubris, the consequences of historic violence on an entire region, and glimpses of the redemptive possibilities of creative expression.'

John Kean, *Artlink*

'Sprague's hauntingly beautiful descriptions of Country, his deep understanding of two cultures in collision, and his sumptuous descriptions of the act of painting, mark this work as a literary gem.'

Judges, 2021 Prime Minister's Literary Award

'... lucid, moving, and bears the mark of first-hand experience. This book is destined to become an invaluable accounting of a ground-breaking art group that was also an audacious political gesture.'

Robyn Ferrell, *The Canberra Times*

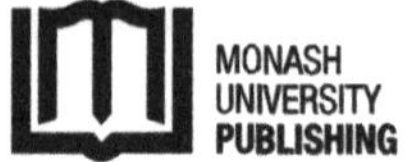
MONASH
UNIVERSITY
PUBLISHING

WHAT ARTISTS SEE

ESSAYS

QUENTIN SPRAGUE

MONASH UNIVERSITY PUBLISHING

For Leah and Djuna, my favourite artists

Published by Monash University Publishing

Matheson Library Annexe
40 Exhibition Walk
Monash University
Clayton, Victoria 3800, Australia
publishing.monash.edu
Monash University Publishing:
the discussion starts here

Aboriginal and Torres Strait Islander readers are advised this book contains written depictions of Aboriginal people who have passed away.

9781923192379 (paperback)
9781923192386 (pdf)
9781923192393 (epub)

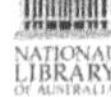
A catalogue record for this book is available from the National Library of Australia

Cover design and typesetting by Small Tasks
Printed in Australia by Griffin Press

The paper this book is printed on is certified against the Forest Stewardship Council® Standards. Griffin Press holds chain of custody certification SCS-COC-001185. FSC® promotes environmentally responsible, socially beneficial and economically viable management of the world's forests.

Contents

Introduction

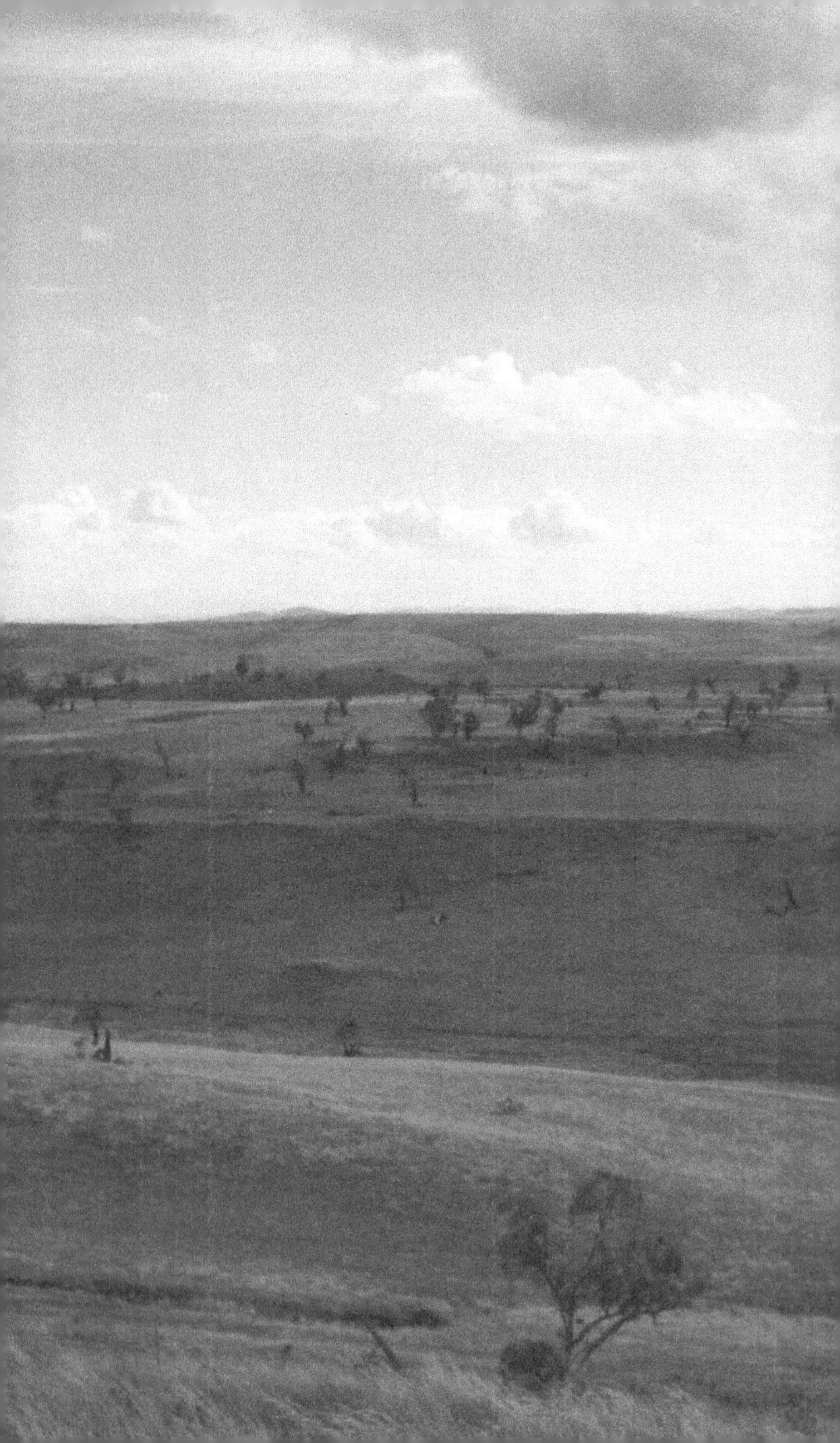

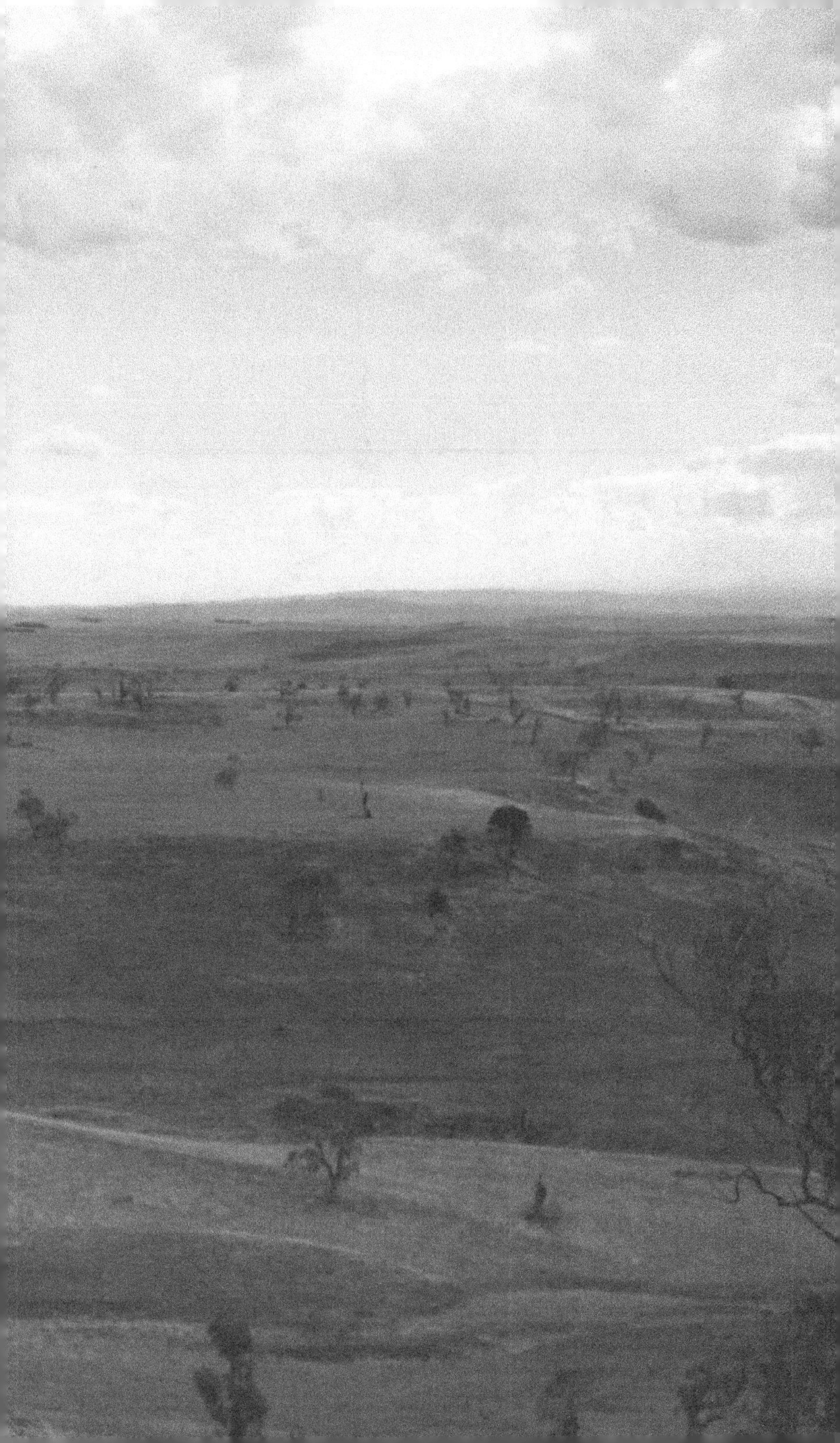

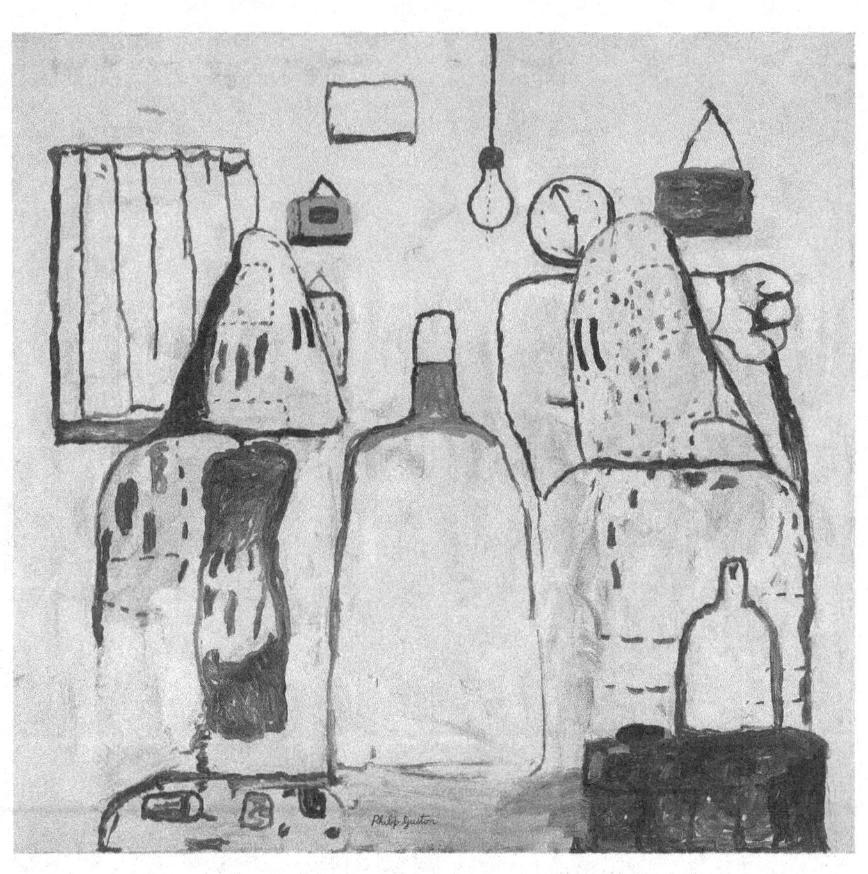

Philip Guston *Bad Habits* 1970

I Want to See This Place

From time to time, in the mid to late 1980s, we would drive from the farm to the city for the day, returning after nightfall. It was only a round trip of 300 kilometres or so, but as a child it was still among the longest journeys I knew. It was always an event: a passing from a familiar world into something altogether different.

We would start early, my single mother at the wheel of our white twin-cab Kombi utility, my sister and I strapped in behind her. The sun would only have just risen over the landscape: the sub-alpine plains and rolling hills in the southeast corner of New South Wales known as the Monaro. And what a landscape it was! Only recently have I truly understood how lucky I was that it was this place, rather than a place of suburban sprawl or inner-city clutter, that was my most formative. Maps will tell you that it begins as far south as the Victorian border and extends all the way to the outskirts of Canberra to the north. But for me its borders were far more subjective. Most days the Monaro of my mind consisted only of the view from our home, an angular house of weatherboard, corrugated tin and basalt rock that my mother had raised with a group of eager friends on a bare hillside in 1983. Crowned with a turret, its prospect took in the tussock-yellow plains and hills that ran all the way to the sawtooth horizon line of the Snowy Mountains.

Light in this landscape was often seen from afar, flooding through the gaps in clouds, but it could reach in an instant across open ground. In winter it glittered on the distant snow caps – a shock of white that rhymed with the white of gnarled snow gums far closer, their trunks bent groundward after a lifetime growing against wind. In summer, this wind would announce itself as a shimmer in the tussocks, or as an unexpected flurry of black volcanic dust – the topsoil that a mere two or three generations of pastoral grazing had rendered so vulnerable. Sometimes it would howl for days at a time.

To drive this country, as we did on those mornings that we set out with the just-risen sun, was to follow its undulations in long carving movements. Solitary willows marked creek beds – invariably dry, or just about – while remnant gums clustered on certain rocky hilltops and ridges. Only twenty or so minutes into this journey came another one of those subjective borders: a bend in the road where the view re-emerged after a shallow rise, and the grassland seemed to roll away with a kind of ecstatic grace. Just beyond it rose an odd hill. From the highway it appeared perfectly conical, its humble summit crowned with a single tree silhouetted just so against the sky beyond. We knew this hill as The Birthday Cake, a name coined by my mother and her two sisters decades before, when they had driven this road in the back seat of their family's Holden station wagon, my grandfather at the wheel. It was this hill that for me truly signalled either a departure or a return: a marker that even now occupies a space of iconic clarity in my mind.

—

The days in the city were for culture. My mother had returned to the place she'd been raised after spending some decades in Melbourne and elsewhere, and she'd brought back an enduring love for books, music, theatre, cinema and art. Canberra – which in the 1980s was a city only in name – didn't have a lot to offer, but it had just enough to offset the otherwise culturally isolated rural life she had embraced not long after I was born: live concerts, a handful of independent bookshops, a well-regarded cult-movie house.

All this undoubtedly left its mark, but it was visits to the National Gallery of Australia that truly imprinted on my young consciousness. Who that went there as a child in those years can forget the entrance to that grand brutalist building by the lake: the broad elevated walkway that led from the High Court like a giant's arm reaching through space; the revolving entrance doors that, although almost impossibly heavy for a child, couldn't help but appear insignificant against the huge façade? Inside, the high ceiling in the wide lobby was patterned by a honeycomb grid of cast concrete. Daylight was replaced by the even glow of some largely invisible yet presumably complex lighting system. Surfaces were hard and unforgiving, but footfalls nonetheless softened; voices hushed. This was the land of art as I came to know it.

In recent decades we have become inured to the strange idea that galleries are mere extensions of some vast industrial entertainment system and so must capture our attention immediately – hence the oversized foyer sculptures, merchandise-rich giftshops and brightly coloured children's zones. But back when I started to push my way through the National Gallery of Australia's revolving doors on a semi-regular basis, a sense of quiet awe – enveloping, gentle, deadly serious – was more than enough. It grabbed hold of me. And if, in the decades since, it has ever slackened its grip, it has done so only briefly.

It's hard to recall exactly which artworks I saw when. We moved to Canberra in 1990, where I completed school and, later, art school; throughout those years and since, my visits to the gallery only became more frequent. Yet, there are works I've always associated with the very first times I went there. The small carved figurine referred to as the Ambum Stone, for instance – a seated half-human, half-animal, its appealing elongated face crowned by sleepy eyes. A quick Google now tells me what I didn't know then: that it was collected from the Enga province of Papua New Guinea in the 1960s and has since been dated as at least 3500 years old. Not that such lack of knowledge bore any weight in my young mind. The encounter, and what flights of imagination it might set in motion, was everything. I could just as easily picture the Ambum Stone blinking slowly behind the glass of its display case as I could later walk among the 200 intricately painted hollow log coffins that constitute *The Aboriginal Memorial* – a visionary work commissioned by the gallery in 1988 – and see a forest extending to the horizon.

The main event for me, though, was the collection of twentieth-century American art – Warhol, Pollock, de Kooning, Frankenthaler, Rothko – and, standing tall among it, two masterpieces by the late, great Philip Guston. In fact, I now realise that these paintings of Guston's struck me so fully that they seemed to enact their own gravitational pull. I would like to say that I recall the very moment I saw them, that they drew me at five or six years old from across the gallery and held me transfixed. This may be true, but I have no memory of it. Instead, I just have an image of these works in my mind that is nearly as clear as any I can raise. This is partly because I still see them as often as I can. Don't get me wrong: I don't make a pilgrimage of it. It's more that, as someone who has since placed art somewhere close to the centre of my life, I often go to the gallery, and when I'm there, no matter what I'm there to see – perhaps a newly opened exhibition or a much-hyped recent acquisition – I can never resist the urge to seek these paintings out, almost as if they are talismans and I risk a run of bad luck if I don't.

Recently, I have begun to wonder what these paintings – *Bad Habits* (1970) and *Pit* (1976) – taught me. Not only what it is about the way Guston saw the world that resonated so strongly, but how this has inflected my own experiences with art. How have these two paintings – the images of which I have carried with me as long as any I care to think of – shaped my understanding of what artists do? Or, more to the point, how has it shaped my feel for what artists, as they follow the thread of their practices, are driven to see?

Like all great art, *Bad Habits* and *Pit* possess the quality of a whole life concentrated within them. Born Phillip Goldstein in Montreal in 1913, Guston was the youngest of seven siblings, their parents Polish Jews who had lived in Russia before fleeing rising antisemitism. As a child he was wide open to the world – he felt things intensely, as if he had no protective skin, a quality that would come to underwrite the significant emotional heft of his work. At seven years old, after the family had moved to Los Angeles, he experienced life-shaping tragedy: his father, a one-time boilermaker turned rag-picker, hanged himself in the back shed of the family home. Although his mother claimed otherwise, Guston would later recount that he was the one to find his father's body and cut it down. Either way, a noose would become a recurrent symbol in his work; so too the single naked bulb that hung (noose-like) in the closet where he would subsequently hide himself away for hours at a time, drawing and reading.

In *Bad Habits*, this bulb hangs down from the top of the picture, dangling above the incongruous figures of two Ku Klux Klansmen shrouded in hoods, both rendered in the disarmingly comic style from which Guston forged his brilliant late signature. He had first emerged as an artist in his early twenties with precociously complex figurative paintings, before turning to abstraction and making his name among the New York abstract expressionists. But by the time a major retrospective exhibition at New York's Guggenheim Museum opened in 1962, his brush was already taking him elsewhere. It had begun to pick out featureless head-like forms amid the daubs and cross-hatchings of his otherwise abstract paintings. Riven by anxiety and doubt, he spent two years making only drawings. Always central, his line now became everything. It shook and quivered but, as if possessed of a consciousness all its own, knew exactly where it was going. Guston – a sublimely intuitive artist – was emboldened to simply follow. More forms emerged, then figures. The world that *Pit* and *Bad Habits* are drawn from finally took shape: 'a forgotten place of beings and things, which I need to remember', as he later wrote. 'I want to see this place.'

I now realise that one thing those two paintings of Guston's taught me (and I like to imagine that I understood this in some inchoate way as I stood before them as a child) is that a real artist doesn't so much create the world of their work as uncover it. This is a process of chipping away at the stone face of something, finding a vein and pursuing it. For Guston it meant reaching back to his childhood – perhaps as far as the closet in which he once hid himself away. This was likely the first place where he could shut the world out as a means to look at it more intensely, which is to say, it was his first 'studio'.

In its ideal form, a studio is a place in which the mind can wander freely even as it pulls itself into ever sharper focus; the kind of place, as Guston surely knew, that children are so adept at cultivating and that becomes almost irretrievably distant for many of us as adults. I see this when I watch my young daughter drawing. Even though it's nearly two decades since I gave away my own nascent art practice, I can't help but feel a pang of jealousy for the ease with which she enters this state. The door is wide open to her: she effortlessly follows forms into complex-seeming narratives, talking away to herself as she goes. The process transfixes her. To break these moments of reverie is to cut an unspooling thread; it never feels less than callous to do so.

I don't want to suggest that artists must only work from some primary state of innocence. Or that 'innocence' is even close to the right word. But a state of something like unthinking thought – a state, to paraphrase the architect Juhani Pallasmaa, that allows the hand to think before the mind – is the place where most serious artists want to land. When Guston found a way to return there it allowed him to forge something entirely new: a visual language that appeared as far from outwardly 'consequential' or 'academic' art as one could get, and all the better for it. It was a language that lifted wholesale from fixtures of his childhood: syndicated cartoon strips like *Mutt and Jeff*, *Barney Google and Snuffy Smith*, and, above all, George Herriman's brilliant *Krazy Kat*. The results were deeply playful, but although satirical humour was a constant, they were never less than serious. Guston knew the world's true face. The narratives his work revealed to him were as complex as anything: amid the so-called American Century, he opened himself to the violence and social unrest that surrounded him. He let it in, and in doing so, fearlessly examined how he was himself implicated in the events around him. In this, he understood that the act of making has an ethical dimension. That this dimension presents an essential consideration for an artist is another lesson that Guston's late paintings firmly underscore. *Feel the world as fully as possible*, they say. *Don't turn away.*

The Klansmen of *Bad Habits* emerged at this moment. Guston most often depicted them in pairs or small groups, caught in in-between states of idleness and boredom. They linger and lurk, patrol otherwise empty streets; in *Bad Habits*, they simply sit in a spartan room, a large bottle of booze on the table between them, a butt-filled ashtray to one side. Did I know that the two hooded figures outlined in thick cartoon strokes at the painting's centre were Klansmen, or even what Klansmen were, when I first saw them? Probably not, but I'm not sure it mattered. Once that knowledge came, it made perfect sense – their vague menace had already been clear to me.

But although they provide caricatures for the darkness of American history, these unsettling figures also refer to Guston himself. The painting's 'bad habits' are his too – the drinking and smoking, the way he would isolate in his studio, beating himself up about the relative success or failure of his work. One Klansmen raises a small whip against the other, ready to strike, but neither of them betrays any hint of anger or fear. Instead, the two pairs of eyes – no more than vertical dashes on the otherwise blank face of each hood – stare at one another with the kind of docile implacability that will be instantly familiar to readers of *Krazy Kat*: it's the same implacability with which Krazy wanders Herriman's pages, overcome by his quixotic and self-debasing love for the psychopathic mouse, Ignatz.

Although Ignatz's response is always the same – a brick lobbed casually at his suitor's head – Krazy always returns.

—

Pit shows the same world as *Bad Habits*, but it is far more inward-looking. Painted six years later, it's all dark reds and black against the earlier painting's high-toned pinks and white. It depicts a figure that the viewer can only really see as Guston himself. He lies wide awake in the titular pit, his 'blanket' a jumble of nailed boot heels and cartoon legs – the weight of the world pressing down. A stone-scattered ground extends above the pit's edge. On the horizon, two fires burn; a framed painting leaning between them depicts a red landscape subject to an onslaught of thick orange rain.

For many years I believed that *Pit* was a painting of emotional torment, a literal picture of descent into precipitous despair. When I learnt that Guston suffered lifelong depression – unpredictable moods that, in his words, 'changed like the shape of clouds' – the tenor of the image only seemed clearer. Seen from this perspective, the painting is deeply unsettling. So much so that I can't help but wonder why, when presented with a small surfeit of pocket money during one of my early visits to the National Gallery, I chose to purchase a postcard reproduction of it. What was wrong with me? Perhaps my own lifelong tendency towards depression was already nudging me on its path, seeking points of recognition and contact in the outside world. Or perhaps it was simply the fact that the image spoke so directly that, for all its spiralling emotional complexity, it was readily understood by a child.

Either way, at some point the postcard came with me – slipped into a pocket or pressed between the pages of a new book – on one of those night-time returns to the farm. The highway leads up and away, the city retreats into a pocket of glittering lights; the road ahead is dark. If it was winter, the windows would have been cracked open to avoid our combined body heat precipitously fogging the windscreen, and the cold air would be rushing in. My sister and I would be wrapped in blankets. The familiar boundary marker of The Birthday Cake would eventually pass unseen in the darkness, and we would soon after pull into the long gravel driveway to the farmhouse, the sweep of the Kombi's headlights skimming the rocky paddocks. I pinned the postcard in an alcove above my bed, next to a small, trapezoidal window from which I sometimes stared across the night landscape, unable to sleep. It stayed there for some years, and eventually came with me to Canberra. I still had it, tattered and worn, during my initial studies at art school, after which I can only assume it was lost in some haphazard move from one group house to another.

Did the emotional rawness of *Pit*, with its seemingly restless protagonist failing to find sleep in a ragged hole in the floor, come to haunt me, pinned so close to where I laid my head to rest? I'm not sure. But if it ever did, I now believe it shouldn't have. I've recently come to understand it differently. Not long ago I found myself once again at the National Gallery, walking briskly down a corridor with a media staffer a half-step ahead of me. I was there to interview a visiting American artist whose newly acquired work promised to cause a furore. The galleries in which the permanent collection is displayed had recently been rehung during a kind of curatorial pogrom, and I'd heard that the two Guston paintings had finally been taken off the wall. But they hadn't.

As my companion and I made small talk, I glanced to my right and there they were. Seeing them was like recognising friends in a room crowded with unfamiliar people: an unexpected and complete reorientation of the moment. For some reason I murmured, 'What are these?', as if I were encountering them for the very first time.

I stopped briefly; I looked.

There was *Bad Habits*, as fresh as the day I first saw it – its white ground spread thick by Guston's brush, and the perfectly clumsy outlines of its two Klansmen almost vibrating with Guston's concentrated fury for the nature of the world.

As for *Pit*, it looked as dark as ever. But this time I found myself focusing on how alive with individual character each of the things in the painting is: each of the stones weighted just so, the nest of boot heels with their lines of cobbler's nails, the flames of each horizon fire rising like contained tangles of windswept hair. Guston treats all of them with profound sensitivity, brushing them into being, granting each of them the same attention.

By the time he painted *Pit*, Guston had returned to these kinds of things (and they are very much things, not subjects) again and again. They provided a base vocabulary from which he could thread together simple sentences and short passages of visual prose. In this, Guston's work, at its most fundamental level, concerned the act of looking. By which I mean it was about his insatiable curiosity for images and the strange power they can enact, a curiosity that often tipped into something close to compulsion. Sometimes it was about looking-as-bearing-witness – to himself, to the world around him – and sometimes simply looking-as-feeling.

What Guston achieved as an artist is the thing that most artists reach for and, if they succeed, what they too come to grasp. This is what this book is about: the process of reaching, holding and reaching again that propels an artist's practice – the pattern that ideally sustains them, and takes them forward. How they do it varies from practice to practice, sometimes radically, but there is nonetheless a common ground: it is formed by the interlinked acts of looking and seeing, acts the vast majority of us perform without a second thought but which for artists must be undertaken with a kind of concentrated attention and care.

Looking again at *Pit*, my gaze is drawn to the bottom-right corner, which is nearly filled by the blanketed figure's bulbous head. He lies face-down; his huge single eyeball, fringed by long lashes, is pressed against the base of the picture. I can't see this image now and not think of my child self, watching from the Kombi window as the landscape moves past in the middle distance, each familiar landform marking either a departure or a return to a place I then knew more intimately than any other.

In my memory, this act of looking is foundational. It provided me the visual vocabulary that began to shape me, indelibly, into the person I am now, especially the part of me that has made a life from looking at art and attempting to feel my way through it. And although I'm not an artist in the way that Guston was – nor, for that matter, in the way that any of the artists profiled in this book are – the fact that his painting can still so directly evoke this act and its effect for me lays bare its power.

For what I've recently come to see is this: *Pit* is not an image of despair at all, but rather an image of an artist at work, feeling their way forward; looking, always looking, for the things they are compelled to see. That oversized eye – the most delicate of organs, its fragile jelly centre protected only by the thinnest of films – is wide open, letting the world flood in.

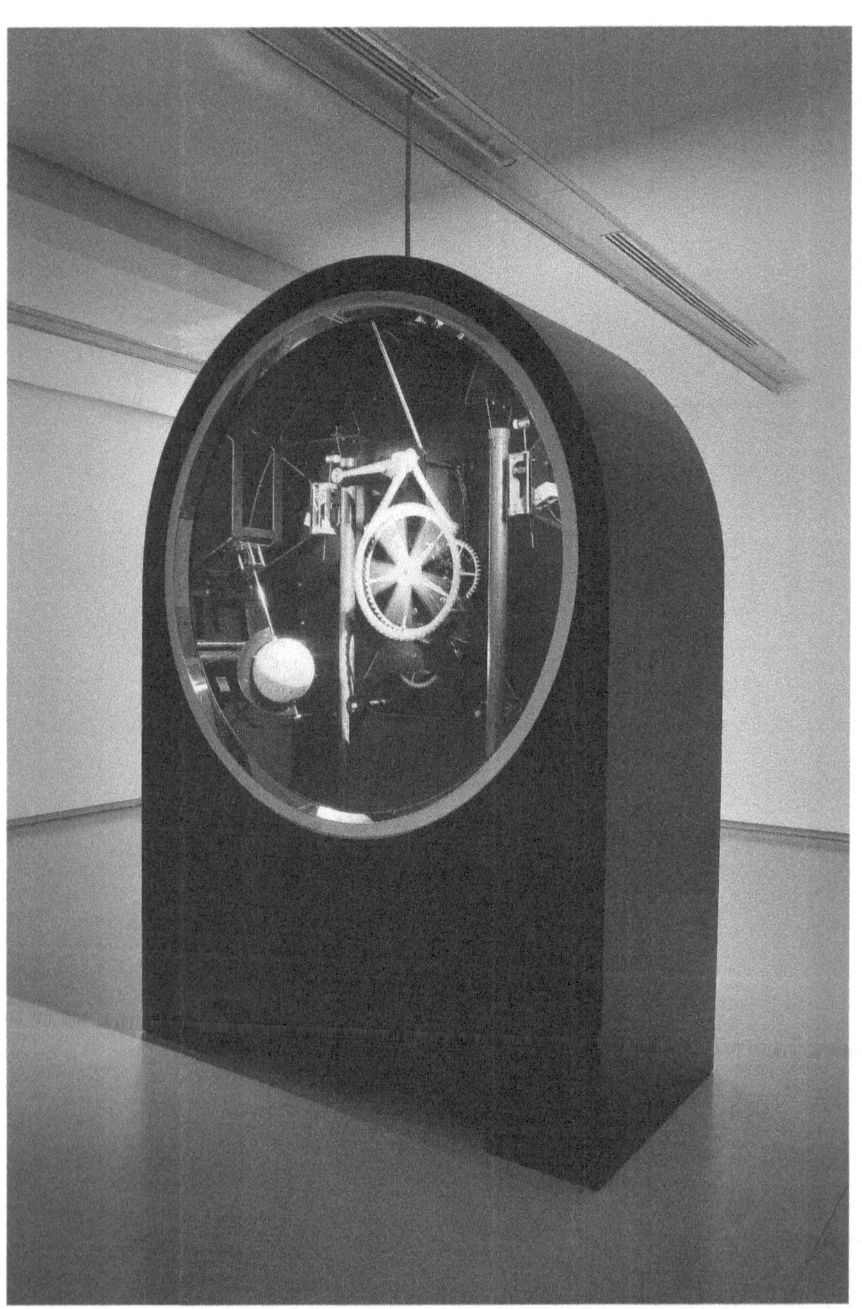

Stuart Ringholt *Untitled (Clock)* 2014

1

The Nuclear Clock

In an act of almost shameless foreshadowing, Stuart Ringholt's slim, propulsive book *Hashish Psychosis: What It's Like to Be Mentally Ill and Recover* – a firsthand account of, well, exactly what the title promises – begins thusly: 'One night, at the age of twenty-three, I wanted to have sex with my mother.'

Ringholt, who recently turned fifty, has in the years since his illness established himself as one of those oddly visionary artists who only comes around once every generation or so. Most serious viewers of his practice would be aware of his book in one form or another – it was presented in manuscript form in an exhibition of his work in 2005 and was self-published the following year. But even those who don't know it would not be shocked to learn of its subject, or its raw honesty. Ringholt has made his name as a performance artist and sculptor whose work is characterised by the kind of radical vulnerability that the book takes as its very raison d'être. His performances often ask viewers to engage in public displays of emotion (anger, fear or shame), while his sculptures and installations seek to make tangible such vaporous psychological states as anxiety, disassociation or euphoria. Even what may seem to the casual eye like minor entries in his oeuvre – such as his 2008 installation *Low Sculpture*, which consists of a scatter of seemingly worthless everyday detritus subtly and not-so-subtly reconfigured – prompt an odd psychological shiver. To view a work like that is to see familiar objects recast just out of reach: an aerosol nozzle is attached to the crushed can of an energy drink, as if the contents had been used as air-freshener; a plastic garden chair is reassembled with its middle section missing, thus rendered too narrow for its purpose; a polyurethane hamburger is crowned by the upswing of a dog's chew toy, whose phallic twin lies nearby, pierced by the aluminium shaft of a target arrow. Like this writer, many viewers will have no direct experience of the scrambled faculties that attend a psychotic episode of the kind Ringholt forensically documents in his book, but they will nonetheless sense that dismissing such objects as cheeky absurdities – as is the risk with much of Ringholt's work – does little to account for their hauntedness.

Hashish Psychosis, which charts Ringholt's descent into psychosis while travelling in India in the mid-1990s and the role that art played in his recovery back in Australia, was first written for the most pragmatic reasons. His illness eventually landed him in the locked ward of Perth's Graylands psychiatric hospital, and when he was released he had no contextual information at all. Questions pressed in – what had he gone through? How might he go about ensuring it never happened again? – but answers proved elusive. When he searched for a book that would offer the reassurance of shared experience and a narrative of recovery, he found nothing. He decided to write one himself.

But for all its value as a document of his illness, Ringholt's book also doubles as a means to understand, however obliquely, the unsettling qualities of his art. For surely the terrifying conviction that a psychotic breakdown delivers, at least in part, is that the world will never again take on its old, familiar configuration, or that when it does, the risk of irreparable collapse will always remain. With this in mind, a series of finely wrought fissures become apparent in much of what Ringholt creates: his art often takes recognisable forms, but there's always something just a little bit off – a skewedness, a logic that always appears a touch out of whack in how it attempts to tease order from the world around us.

Because of this, light can rush into the most unexpected places: strange, and often strangely beautiful, things are illuminated.

Due to Ringholt's experience with psychosis, one is initially compelled to view his work through that illness's lens. It's easy enough to do. Google *'creativity + mental illness'* and the results are many: links between the two have long been the subject of study, and are often compelling. Take this as one example among many: sufferers of psychosis often experience a perceptual disorder known as apophenia (widely believed to be an acute stage of schizophrenia) which can be understood, to borrow a phrase from Swiss psychologist Peter Brugger, as the 'pervasive tendency ... to see order in random configurations'. The human brain is already vulnerable to such flights of fancy: pareidolia names the far more innocuous tendency, shared to varying degree by all, to seek visual order where there is none – to see faces in clouds, or a crouching figure in a mountain's silhouette. But what distinguishes apophenia is that it's not prompted solely by the visual. Any input – a snippet of overheard conversation, a photograph, a flashing light, the way the sun hits a window, a certain song played on the radio – risks being spun into a narrative that becomes, for the psychotic mind at least, charged with revelatory meaning.

But lest we position apophenia too neatly within the borders of so-called insanity, research suggests that it occurs on a sliding scale. At the far end it heralds the onset of full-blown psychiatric illness, while at the near it's deployed by artists and other creative thinkers on a daily basis. The perfectly unexpected metaphor, the visual equivalence sought between one thing and another, the bringing together of the otherwise unrelated to create new meaning: all this lies at the centre of creativity. The fact that at a certain point such thinking might tip over into mental illness partially explains the long-running cliché that great art is made by madmen (and according to the myth, it is usually men) – like all clichés, there is a grain of truth. Mental illness of course has no direct correlation to creativity, but the particularly limber minds of creative thinkers may nonetheless court its attentions. The space between free association and outright delusion can, after all, be vanishingly small. The ability to mine that territory may well be an artist's most powerful asset, but it can be treacherous too.

—

When Ringholt and I met to discuss his book and the ways in which his experience of psychosis both did and didn't shape his work as an artist, I was particularly interested in his most recent sculptures: two huge, meticulously designed clocks that brilliantly distorted something that most would take as an absolute, the passage of time itself.

Ringholt, who is tall and sinewy, with intense eyes, freckles and straw-like hair, met me in his studio, a nondescript building set among a development tenanted by plumbers and video production businesses. He works in this large space alone, surrounded by a select clutter of past work, much of it in post-exhibition storage crates. My visit came on an overcast weekday morning, and as we made our way from the lower level to the mezzanine, where Ringholt has a desk and worktable, the light that bled through a handful of windows was washed-out and meagre.

He explained that writing *Hashish Psychosis* had been difficult: 'I'd write a chapter here and there, but then it'd just get too painful.' Doubts would creep in – *God, I just can't do it*, he'd think – and eventually he swept all his notes into a box, which soon filled up. 'I literally put it away in a closet,' he said with a laugh.

But no matter how hard he tried to forget about it, its unfinished presence would gnaw at him. Every so often, he'd bring the box out and continue work, but progress was piecemeal. By the time the manuscript was completed, a decade had elapsed since his hospitalisation, and he was well on the way to establishing himself as an artist.

Hashish Psychosis is not a great book, at least not by conventional measure. The prose is unremarkable, the description of events for the most part blandly procedural. Ringholt knows this, warning the reader at the outset that his is not a literary undertaking: 'I see the process as one of sweeping out the house,' he writes. Anything approaching poetic language is out the window; so too any literary flourish. Yet either despite or because of this, it works supremely well. The linear narrative gives the book the momentum of a thriller. There's also a touch of the experimental. When Ringholt is hospitalised in Perth, for example, the first-person perspective suddenly gives way to the blunt language of his psychiatric reports and patient-observation notes, both of which are included unedited. In dispassionate prose we read of Ringholt stripping naked in his room, of how his aggression and threatening behaviour led him to be restrained, of how on one visit a nurse discovered him standing, naked again, with his arms outstretched as if he were a cross-bound Jesus Christ, deep in the grip of the messiah complex that psychotics are often said to fall victim to. It has been suggested that Ringholt's use of nudity – both his own and that of others – in many of his performances is simply about courting controversy. But, as we sit together in his studio, he points out that the compulsion to strip naked goes straight to his experience of psychosis. 'Here's Stuart, naked *again*,' he paraphrases his patient notes, smiling thinly.

A series of photographs are reproduced in Ringholt's book. Two show him at twenty-three, sitting with first his father and then his mother on the portico of his childhood home. He's freshly returned from India and in the throes of psychosis. The wildly distorted thinking that characterises apophenia is present: the reader will learn that at the very moment he poses with his parents he wholeheartedly believes not only that they are the King and Queen of England, but also that his father is the singer Rod Stewart. The revelation sparks escalating joy in the young Ringholt: 'I have never won the lotteries,' he writes, 'but I imagine I was experiencing similar feelings to the ticket winners when they jump up and down ...'

The moment foreshadowed in the book's opening comes soon after. Ringholt is wracked by what he believes are telepathic thoughts, convinced that his neighbours, an elderly white couple he's known since childhood, are wordlessly informing him they are in fact full-blooded Aboriginals, many hundreds of years old, and he is their lost son. He makes concerted plans to carve a didgeridoo from a decommissioned power pole, and in the bathroom checks his penis for signs of encroaching blackness, which he's not at all shocked to confirm. One night Ringholt's father leaves the marital bed to let his son seek comfort there, and Ringholt, his mind churning as he attempts to settle, becomes convinced the woman next to him is his wife-to-be. For a moment the reader holds their breath, but Ringholt doesn't act on his compulsion: he finally falls asleep. 'Thankfully my inexperience and shyness with women most likely saved us,' he writes. Thankfully indeed.

—

The events leading to Ringholt's descent into psychosis will carry familiar contours for many, even if his illness and recovery remain foreign. A suburban Australian kid, Ringholt entered adulthood educated but aimless. His book reveals a character solitary, sensitive and stubborn: perfect raw material for the artist he later becomes.

He works odd jobs that lead him through the Kimberley region of far North West Australia, where he's employed at a roadhouse.

With some money saved, he travels on to Darwin, purchases a didgeridoo and settles into a backpacker's hostel. There he meets fellow travellers who inspire him to buy a ticket to India, and in a matter of days he finds himself in the disconcerting heart of Delhi. Again, he moves on, this time heading for the region of Himachal Pradesh, where the quiet hill town of Manali is renowned for hippie travellers and good marijuana. He rents a tiny room in a family home, where his window overlooks a river and a 'garden of dope'. For a period, this is how he travels, moving further and further from the beaten path, renting local accommodation for as little as a dollar a day. He joins his host families around tiny wood-burning stoves for meals of chapattis, dhal and rice; on the slopes outside, apples trees, marijuana and wild strawberries are abundant.

In Vashisht his downfall begins: he spends five dollars on half an ounce of good-quality hash – a soft, buttery and powerful concoction that he later pinpoints as a root cause of his mental unravelling. He then travels on towards the border with Tibet for a Buddhist sermon delivered to a throng of some 10,000 devotees on the slopes of an otherwise deserted valley, and sets about getting stoned among a crowd of fellow Westerners who have also arrived to watch. The sound of hundreds of monks chanting in unison will stick with him; so too will the stench of so much humanity packed together with no plumbing.

When his limited funds dissipate, Ringholt leaves the festival early and boards an overcrowded bus that winds its way over the 3980-metre-tall Rohtang Pass: the eastern end of the Pir Panjal mountain range, part of the Himalayas. From his window, the precipitous drop is all he can see. When hit mid-passage by a particularly bad recurrence of the diarrhoea that has been afflicting him since his arrival in India, he demands the bus stop one too many times: the driver leaves him squatting by the roadside with the few items that constitute his luggage, his stomach convulsing and buckling for an hour. ('The view,' he notes, 'was breathtaking.')

Briefly recovering, he hitches to Delhi, his butter-like hashish now stowed within the didgeridoo he has carried with him all the way. Once there, it's cheap hotels, good food, a flurry of strangers and fellow hashish-smokers who quickly become friends. He meets a young Russian doctor known for his intravenous drug use. A somewhat sinister Indian man introduced as George becomes a recurrent presence: claiming to possess great powers of healing, he has already corralled a loose group of Westerners around him, and Ringholt joins them.

Signs of his developing illness now arrive at a steady clip. When the setting sun glows through the smog one evening, he joins a crowd in the street, drawn to the way the light has turned everything 'a bright, transfixing yellow', the vivid description carrying more than a touch of unreality. One night he returns late to the hotel to find it locked. At a loose end, he sits down in the street with his didgeridoo and barks gibberish into it for hours, until a menacing group of men appear with sticks and he desists. All the while, hashish is consumed any number of ways – smoked in pipes, baked into cookies and mixed into the infamous bhang lassi. Ringholt begins to find that the more he imbibes, the less high he gets.

Full-blown psychosis comes not long after. Ringholt takes a meandering walk through the streets of Delhi with the messiah George and an unnamed man, where they encounter two men carrying a length of pipe long enough to span the entire width of the street. Ringholt ducks under it, and is overwhelmed by a rush of euphoria – 'feelings,' he writes, 'that I had never experienced in such magnitude.' It's as if he has crossed a threshold. A new reality as convincing as anything Ringholt has experienced is immediately apparent to him. Its revelation is sudden and irresistibly compelling: 'I was an action movie star and was being filmed – I literally believed this to be the case.'

Within days, the dissolution is complete. Ringholt's euphoria drops away precipitously, and paranoid delusions flood the void, the most vivid of them the belief that George now wants him dead. He flees his hotel, 'packing' his belongings by sweeping the detritus from the floor of his room and bundling it, dust and all, into a sheet. He makes a last-ditch effort to reach the Australian embassy but arrives outside the locked gates on a Saturday. Not to worry – he flings his makeshift luggage over the wall and follows it, coming to rest, catatonic, on the neatly manicured lawn.

After receiving basic treatment at a private hospital, he is back home in Perth within a week. He steps off the plane long-haired and wild-eyed, still gripped by illness. He's dressed in white, and is carrying his didgeridoo.

—

Before our first meeting, I'd been anxious that my focus on the link between Ringholt's experience of psychosis and his art risked oversimplifying things. The art world is supremely good at finding ways to make art seem complicated, and in recent decades Ringholt has moved in the kind of circles – international biennales, contemporary museums and high-end galleries – where such complication is par for the course.

I needn't have worried. Not only was Ringholt happy to discuss the subject, he was also eager to emphasise the link between his practice and his recovery: 'Healing is almost a dirty word in the art world,' he told me. 'But that's exactly what my practice did for me: it healed me.'

Before his trip to India, Ringholt's interest in art had taken him through a graphic design degree at Curtin University, and even in his darkest moments abroad he was sketching and drawing. A couple of such drawings survive and are reproduced in the book; although they are muddy and free-associative in a manner that betrays their drug-fuelled origins, they nonetheless display a striking sensibility: he's talented. Following two stays in Graylands – the first a week, and the second just shy of a month – he swore off drugs and, for good measure, alcohol. He rented a series of studios and began to make sculpture. Art moved towards the centre of his life.

By 1997, just three years after he'd been released from the psychiatric ward, he had been picked up by the well-regarded Galerie Düsseldorf in Perth. It took him some time to directly confront the experience that had overcome him in India, but by his third exhibition with the gallery he was ready. Titled *Yoga Art,* it consisted of a rambling mess of more than 500 objects scattered across the gallery's concrete floor. Half that area was overtaken by what he simply termed the 'rubbish pile', a collection of, as he later wrote in *Hashish Psychosis,* 'every drawing, book, sculpture, photograph, writing, and item of clothing pertaining to my experience of psychiatric illness'. He scrawled confessional texts about the experience of psychosis on wooden boards that he propped among the apparent chaos.

One morning he arrived at the gallery and undertook an impromptu performance in which he re-enacted aspects of his illness: he stripped off and dressed in an elaborate king's costume – a reference to the messiah complex that had for a period gripped him – before swapping it for an AFL uniform, dropping to the floor and doing push-ups; he waved a white flag, sat down cross-legged and played the didgeridoo. It was messy, coded, intended for only him. From there, he and his girlfriend drove to Graylands, where he revisited the grounds that had briefly been his home. She documented Ringholt as he posed, once again dressing as a king and a footballer. The experience was confronting: Ringholt would later recall being impatient and anxious as the photos were taken and the difficult memories flooded back.

But there was something there.

When he staged another, more elaborate performance two months later, it was in front of an audience of thirty or so. His parents were among it, and although he was once again anxious, he also felt 'an odd mix of liberation and joy'. The feeling acted to destroy the remnant shame and fear that was still attached to his memories of illness. Later, he discovered that techniques of regression are used widely in psychological treatment to assist patients in processing past trauma and realised that his own early forays into performance had delivered him the same.

By the early 2000s, Ringholt had turned this revelation towards less traumatic events, testing the theory that performance art could deliver practical benefit. This time, he confronted the kinds of minor, socially driven fears that can cluster together to constrict a life.

While travelling with a friend in Italy in 2001, he spent twenty or so minutes in Florence's popular Palazzo Vecchio, standing before the ornate fountain with a length of toilet paper hanging from the rear of his pants. At home in Perth he appeared in public with a tangle of white thread in his beard, or 'I am stupid' scrawled on a Post-it note affixed to his back. Once, he sat on a train chewing a pen so the ink spread over his teeth and lips; later, he wandered the streets of Melbourne wearing an odd-looking prosthetic nose. A quietly slapstick humour guided each action, but it was tempered by serious intent. The revelation, when it came, was simple: Ringholt realised that not only was he debilitatingly shy, but that the feeling of dread accompanying his moments of carefully orchestrated embarrassment was the same as that which accompanied his attempts, no matter how small, at romantic attachment. He drew on his performances to face the fear head-on, aiming, as he later wrote, 'to bridge the gap between my loneliness and happiness'. When he relocated to Melbourne and met the woman who would become his long-term partner, Lanie Stockman, he credited his performance practice with their successful courtship: 'Years later we remain in love,' he wrote. An earlier, much briefer, romantic success had already prompted him to imagine the triumphant newspaper headline that had now come true: 'Conceptual Artist Gets Girl!'

Ringholt then began to extend his focus beyond himself, wondering, following a well-timed question asked in a 2004 interview by the curators Františka and Tim Gilman-Ševčík, what benefit his art might deliver to others. That same year he set about organising what he termed 'Funny Fear Workshops' in his studio, events that asked participants to re-enact the kind of embarrassing moments that had prompted him to overcome his own fear of the opposite sex. A series of ongoing 'Anger Workshops' began four years later; 'Laughter Workshops' followed soon after. Both hit a nerve in the art world and were soon being commissioned by major biennales and museums around the globe. By 2011 he was leading a series of naturist tours of art exhibitions at a number of Australian public galleries, including the Museum of Old and New Art in Hobart and the Museum of Contemporary Art in Sydney: brave members of the art-viewing public arrived on the arranged day, signed a waiver and disrobed for a group tour led by a naked Ringholt. Although the benefits of the exercise likely varied from one participant to the next, Ringholt himself was drawn to the idea that public displays of vulnerability might help people to clear blocked emotions or confront hang-ups and fears.

While the workshops and tours took the DIY aspect of self-help at face value and played upon various quasi–New Age ideologies, they were, like everything Ringholt does – even the funny things – deadly serious. His anger workshops, for instance, encouraged participants to seek genuine and lasting psychological release. Usually undertaken in museum or gallery settings, they were characterised by what Ringholt saw as a 'series of compressions' that allowed for deeply embodied stress to find release. Participants in a workshop would begin by standing in a samurai-like pose: fists clenched, legs apart, knees bent, feet pressed hard against the floor. For a full five minutes, abrasively loud techno would play over speakers as the group screamed together in ragged chorus. Participants have described the sound as becoming increasingly 'guttural and intense'. It's also physically demanding: those with heart conditions or similar medical concerns are barred from taking part. Then the pulsing techno would be replaced by the symphonic lull of Mozart's *Eine kleine Nachtmusik* and participants partnered off in hugs, pressing their bodies together for another full five minutes. 'The workshop is hyper-emotional and hyper-compressed,' Ringholt explained in a 2014 interview. 'There is a lot of living done in this short ten minutes alone.'

The desire to live intensely – to be present in and aware of the moment as it unfolds – may well be another theme that courses through Ringholt's work. Again, it's possible that this links back to the heightened (albeit disordered) nature of reality he experienced during his mental illness all those years ago, but even if that's the case, it's a more general characteristic that allows his work to resonate. It speaks to a common human drive to seek what the American psychologist Abraham Maslow termed 'peak experiences': the kinds that allow one to briefly transcend the mundane limits of everyday life and to feel integrated into a larger, more meaningful whole. The British neurologist and author Oliver Sacks similarly described a desire for this kind of transcendence: 'To live on a day-to-day basis is insufficient for human beings,' he wrote not long before his death in 2015; 'we need to transcend, transport, escape; we need to see overall patterns in our lives.'

For Maslow and Sacks, humans seek to rise above the everyday in a variety of ways, meditation, prayer, travel, drug-taking and communion with art among them. Presented with Ringholt's workshops, one might be tempted to add the snake-oil charms of the self-help charlatan to this list if it weren't for Ringholt's deeply felt belief in art's ameliorative potential. It's a belief that lies at the root of much of what he does. Even *Low Sculpture* – the scattered multi-part installation in which disparate forms are writ strange by Ringholt's calculated interventions – can be understood to reorder what would otherwise be seen as disordered thinking into something resembling sense, however foreign a sense it might be. It seeks to create something transcendent from the most ordinary of things. Put simply, it seeks a pattern. I first saw *Low Sculpture* in 2014, when it was installed as part of Ringholt's survey exhibition, *Kraft*, at the Monash University Museum of Art in Melbourne, and well recall not only its compelling oddness but the way in which this same quality almost imperceptibly shook the world into new and surprising configurations.

As we sat together in his studio, Ringholt explained how he'd used that work to make sense of a patchwork of feelings, memories and sensations. He recalled how, after his stint in the locked ward at Graylands, he was released to the open ward, where security seemed lax by contrast. 'People were leaving and going to the pub and coming back,' he said. Wandering the grounds by day, he'd found ready evidence – a scatter of empty bottles, cigarette butts, even used condoms – that spoke of their nocturnal excesses. *Low Sculpture* took that form and ran with it: random-seeming ephemera spread across the ground in a manner that prompted speculation. What events had occurred? What strange gatherings?

But it was more than that too. Once his illness had compelled him to give up alcohol and drugs for good, Ringholt spent much of his remaining twenties attempting to negotiate a culture in which inebriation too often forges the social bond. For a period he stopped attending parties altogether. 'I thought, *Oh well, maybe this is what I experience,*' he said. '*I don't experience the party; I experience the detritus, what's left afterwards.*'

Bringing together the disparate parts of the installation allowed him to make sense of the apparent chaos, almost as if he were a forensic detective picking his way through a crime scene: the residue of a suburban bacchanal gone awry. He was compelled to join things in the simplest of ways – identifying two apparently unrelated parts and bringing them into some kind of relationship. As he went, the resulting objects gathered unsettling meanings. Narratives emerged: an aerosol can thrust into the top of a pumpkin was, in his conception, a 'rape scene'; the arrow-pierced dog toy was a 'retribution'; the too-thin chair was a body wracked by anorexia or bulimia.

It's likely such inner connections are what made the work so compelling. I recall picking my own way through the various floor-bound components and identifying as I went, if not narratives, then at least formal resonances and visual rhymes: my very own patterns coming to light in the artfully strewn chaos before me.

—

Yet the work that many consider Ringholt's very best, and which would usher in for him a years-long obsession, was yet to come. As much as I'd been struck by *Low Sculpture* in Ringholt's survey, the exhibition's true centrepiece was the first of his two clock sculptures, *Untitled (Clock)* – a huge, fully-functioning clock that sat squatly in a darkened gallery all of its own.

I remember my encounter with that work: how its illuminated face seemed to draw me across the room; how the sound of its ticking was not only heard but felt. I may or may not have been there for the chimes that sounded on the hour, but they were readily visible through a glass panel at the clock's rear, hanging on each side of the slowly spinning gears and wheels of its pristine mechanism, tiny spring-loaded hammers poised to strike them. It was not yet clear in 2014, but this work would be the first of two hugely ambitious undertakings, the second of which, *Nuclear Clock*, would stretch Ringholt's belief in art to its very limit.

Built in collaboration with a Sydney-based horologist, when it was first exhibited, *Untitled (Clock)* stood out among Ringholt's practice: it signalled another, more elaborate register. At three metres tall, it takes the form of a classic mantle clock, its circular face adorned with Roman numerals and framed by an owlish and faintly Art Deco black casing. Ringholt set it to run purposefully fast: as its thin red second hand sweeps along, a minute is gone in only forty-five seconds; a day disappears in eighteen hours. As he told the art historian Amelia Barikin in 2014, the clock's 'fictional proposition' is this: 'What would be the biological reality of planet earth rotating once every eighteen hours instead of twenty-four?' It sounds a touch random, but there's a sense of poetic wondering to Ringholt's question. 'You have less time, but you have more days in the year,' he told Barikin. 'So there's a sense of losing something and also gaining something. With an eighteen-hour day, there's many more yesterdays.'

The origins of *Untitled (Clock)* can be traced to a series of altered wristwatches that Ringholt had begun a decade beforehand. They remain in a crowded display case in his studio, alongside a jumbled gathering of disparate components and pieces from his long practice. Some of the watches are full of a tangle of mechanisms that obscure their faces, while others have additional hands or disordered or inaccurate numbers. On the first of them, which for a time he wore on his wrist, he simply painted over the glass face: the mechanism inside still worked, but whether it told accurate time was elevated to a matter of embodiment rather than witness. Time shifted from being something prosaic by which one measures a day or keeps on schedule to being an inscrutable power held by the body, talismanic and mysterious.

In an essay on Ringholt's work, Barikin imagined *Untitled (Clock)* sitting in a primordial swamp, beamed back from the current day to a time when the Earth was closer to the moon and was rotating faster – a time when its eighteen-hour day would have been accurate – but Ringholt sees it in simpler terms. He told me that he first intended it as a kind of mechanical organ inserted into the depths of the museum, where it would not only measure time in its own ever-so-slightly-diminished fashion but also provide a kind of beating heart where previously there was none. It was the relationship with the body that drew him, the way its ticking could be felt as much as heard.

Afterwards, he began to notice other large clocks in bell towers and at train stations; in the digital age, many of them had been superseded and allowed to stop altogether. He sought access to a working clock in the Yarrawonga Shire Hall in regional Victoria but was denied. He had more luck at a parish church in the Melbourne suburb of Malvern, where a robed priest was happy, if a little perplexed, to guide him up a series of ladders to a dust-covered room in the belfry, replete with the carcasses of pigeons lying in the dried remnants of their own shit. After hearing that clock up close, he wondered what it would be like to work on a clock as immense as London's Big Ben, to stand in that tower as the vast mechanism thundered away and the passage of time was writ viscerally.

Working on *Untitled (Clock)* with the horologist had convinced Ringholt he wouldn't have what it took to build an accurate clock at a similar scale, but building an inaccurate one was a different matter. He was soon ensconced in the minutiae of clock-making, determined to construct one himself. As complex and involved as *Untitled (Clock)* had been, the second clock that Ringholt embarked upon – to be titled *Nuclear Clock* – made it appear simple. On commission, he'd received $40,000 towards the construction of *Untitled (Clock)*, to which he'd added around $20,000 of his own money: a lot, but a manageable amount. This time, costs quickly spiralled. Even though he was essentially building the new clock by hand, he needed to outsource key aspects. He brought an industrial fabricator on board for three months to develop computer renderings of the intricate parts; these then needed to be laser cut. There was a team of painters and welders and metal polishers, each of them turning their particular trade towards aspects of the overarching project. Once the clock's mechanism was built, electrical engineers were needed to get the thing running. Whereas the form of *Untitled (Clock)* was familiar, albeit at a dramatic scale, *Nuclear Clock* would eventually look like something from the distant future, its function instantly recognisable but its form nearly alien. The vast illuminated dial shows four numerals (03, 06, 09, 12) in a crisply modern font, and is set in a deep circular casing that hangs cantilevered at head height from an industrial-scaled steel pole. The reverse consists of a window that looks onto a neat array of immaculate inner workings clearly visible through a triple internal aperture cut into the shape of the nuclear hazard symbol.

Ringholt had conceived of this second clock as a far more complex machine. As its mechanism turned, the clockwork set in motion other effects: on each hour, for instance, one of a collection of store-bought foam stress balls printed to look like globes or mini moons would drop from a feeder in the clock's rear chamber. These balls would gather one by one in its depths, where they rolled around a large yellow sphere which Ringholt conceived of as a 'sun' or a 'neutron'. When an opening in the outer casing aligned with the inner, they would spill out onto the floor, coming to rest in random configurations that Ringholt eventually conceptualised as imagined galaxies aligned by chance. He built in a grinding mechanism so that a viewer could secretly feed something – such as a piece of material, placed into a gel cap – which would be slowly ground to dust by the incessant momentum of the cogs and wheels. Ringholt explained that the idea it could in turn generate its own kind of 'cosmic dust', the composition of which was unknown to him, struck him as profound.

He chose the title *Nuclear Clock* in reference to the notional idea of a clock in which accuracy is defined by the precise frequency of a nuclear transition, which is to say in increments smaller than a nanosecond – an idea that theoretically improves upon the current most accurate time-keeping method, an atomic clock, by a factor of ten. The theory is guided by propositional physics – how it might be further explained is, to me at least, unclear – but it wasn't the scientific detail that resonated for Ringholt, but the way it encouraged poetic and metaphoric speculation. The title, he explained as we sat together in his studio, was also intended to evoke notions of time beyond human comprehension: among them the half-life of certain nuclear material, which is measured in tens of thousands, even hundreds of thousands, of years.

Other references soon came to shadow the work, some intended, others not. As Ringholt laboured away, the world changed, often for the worse: disgraced-businessman-turned-reality-television-star Donald Trump unexpectedly seized the American presidency; global fossil fuel emissions reached one record high after another; catastrophic weather wreaked havoc across the globe. A new word emerged for checking newsfeeds: doomscrolling. The work-in-progress couldn't help but evoke the symbolic timing device known as the Doomsday Clock, maintained since 1947 by the *Bulletin of the Atomic Scientists*, poised at one hundred seconds to midnight: as close as it had ever come to an anticipated human-driven global annihilation.

Ringholt had designed the nuclear hazard apertures to be large enough to climb through so the clock's inner workings could be reached. As the world outside turned, he crouched within it, tinkering away. He eventually settled on a slow rhythm that stretched the eighteen-hour day marked by *Untitled (Clock)* to thirty-three hours, evoking a time in the far distant future – 900 million years, to be precise – when the Earth's rotation had slowed accordingly. The acid yellow Ringholt chose for the clock's colour scheme made the whole thing hum with radioactive menace, but the beauty of it – the pristine cogs and wheels, the shining surfaces, the odd patterning of ideas that Ringholt had sketched through it – was almost impossibly seductive. A more apt symbol for our troubled times would be hard to imagine.

But works of great ambition are rarely, if ever, straightforward. Ringholt has long refused to work to either budget or deadline – 'I'll produce the work as best I can,' he told me, 'but if it takes longer, I'm committed to that' – yet the clock tested even his limits. One problem gave on to another, in a sequence that soon seemed endless. The project became a sinkhole into which he poured both time and money. He confirmed to me that it cost him 'well beyond' what the first clock did, but would not discuss figures. Ringholt's partner, Lanie, was supportive, and in hindsight he is confounded by why she allowed him to spend as much on the project as he did; his decision to self-fund it now struck him as 'stupid'. There was also the creeping sense that he'd placed all his creative eggs into one basket: he began to fear that the gamble might not pay off. 'To expend that much energy on one idea is, I think, dangerous,' he said.

Until that moment Ringholt's art practice had given him far more than it had taken. 'I liken it to another partner in some ways, whether that's a good thing or not,' he said. 'It's something that only ever loves you and is generous and nice.' Art had helped deliver him from his psychosis beforc granting him a focus, but as *Nuclear Clock* spun out of control, it seemed as if it might now turn against him. A shadow of betrayal fell across the relationship.

The final push came five years after he embarked on the project, when Ringholt was invited to exhibit in the 2019 Aichi Triennale in Japan, one of the largest international art festivals in the country. The curators, initially interested in an anger workshop, were impressed enough by the clock to partly fund its completion. But even then it remained a source of great anxiety for Ringholt. The work weighed three tonnes, a good portion of which was cantilevered into the air: what if it fell on someone? Exhibiting it required extended conversations and contracts covering safety, public liability and insurance.

When it was finally installed in a darkened, vault-ceilinged gallery, it looked stunning, but Ringholt was not quite able to see past the trauma it had caused him. 'I feel like I lost a few years,' he told me. 'It was scarring. But sometimes you make works and you know what direction not to head in again.'

When we met, the feeling was yet to settle. On arrival at Ringholt's studio I'd navigated my way through a jumble of wooden crates still plastered with the freight stickers marking their return passage from Japan: the components of *Nuclear Clock*, not yet unpacked, let alone assembled.

Ringholt explained that he occasionally gets requests to view it, but no gallery has yet understood the level of commitment it takes to exhibit. Even to show an interested curator or art collector the work in his studio would require weeks of labour to assemble it. His first clock had found a permanent home at the Museum of Contemporary Art in Sydney, and for a short while after *Nuclear Clock* was exhibited in Japan it appeared a major Australian gallery might purchase it, but they were eventually put off by the weight: they decided their floors were not strong enough to safely display it.

If he hadn't known it before, *Nuclear Clock* had made one thing achingly clear to Ringholt: obsession is a complex thing. It both gives and takes. When I think of recent Australian art, I can think of no single work that underscores this idea so firmly, nor one that embodies it with such grace. In the weeks and months following our initial conversation, I often returned to images of the clock installed in Japan and imagined walking around its pristine exterior, just as I had done with Ringholt's first clock, and peering through its rear aperture at the mechanism inside. I thought of Ringholt in India, overcome by the exhilaration and by the spiralling fear of his illness, his disordered mind essentially robbing him of time hand over fist. No matter how much he saw it as a folly, I couldn't see *Nuclear Clock* as anything but an act of absolute dedication and control. Its construction, I came to understand, had – bit by incremental bit – demanded of Ringholt the kind of sustained focus and clarity that had once threatened to fall away entirely.

—

In Perth there was once a dance club, overseen since the 1970s by a group of sannyasins, devotees of the controversial guru Bhagwan Shree Rajneesh. It was called, somewhat incongruously, Club Zorba, and was open each weekend until midnight. In the years immediately following Ringholt's psychotic break, it was another tool in his recovery.

Zorba's attracted people of all ages. Some parents even brought along children. A large picture of Bhagwan with his diamond-studded wristwatch surveyed the proceedings. The venue was licensed, but it was dancing, not drinking, that drew punters. Many danced barefoot; no one, it seemed, cared what anyone was wearing, or whether they were good dancers.

'Everyone was shaking and moving. No rhythm, including me,' Ringholt recalled. 'There was no judgement.'

Prior to his performance practice, Ringholt found at Zorba's the beginnings of a way to move beyond his anxieties and fears. He could be himself while surrounded by strangers. It may sound a touch glib, but that doesn't mean it wasn't true. He'd go there and dance, and even though in those days he was not yet fully confident in his recovery, he nonetheless felt in those moments at Zorba's that everything would be okay.

It turns out he was right.

Although he has for now set aside the ambition of *Nuclear Clock*, art is still at the centre of what he does. When we meet, he is in the midst of a series of paper collages, a form he has turned to often throughout his years of practice. It's a strikingly different approach to art-making than that which brought his clocks into being, but both share a common thread. Collage disrupts existing images; it allows strange juxtapositions, teases forth new meaning from otherwise familiar or innocuous material. Ringholt has used all kinds of material for his collages – art books, niche-interest magazines, vintage pornography – and was now meticulously taking his scalpel to a stack of 1940s textbooks that he sourced on the internet, full of black-and-white images of just about anything.

'I can finish one or two works in a day,' he tells me – clearly a relief after the trials of *Nuclear Clock*. He arrives at the studio enthused by the prospect of where each new collage might take him. It's the kind of energy that all artists need to somehow maintain, but Ringholt sees the shadow of his psychosis in it too.

'You have these skills,' he said, 'these heightened ways of thinking and seeing and doing.' He knows that much of what his illness revealed to him – the messiah complex, for instance, or the belief in superhuman strength or power – was unreal, but that's beside the point: it's the belief that matters, the way that it feels in the moment so unshakeable. As he established his practice in the years after his breakdown, he brought some of that belief with him: he became a workaholic, and now readily characterises himself as an art obsessive. He's aware of the negative connotations of both terms, but doesn't care, at least not in light of the alternative: 'Art's really healthy,' he tells me. 'Psychiatric illness is really dark: I wouldn't wish that on my worst enemy.'

He also understands that what compelled him to get high in the first place, which he knows is what sparked his illness, is the very same thing his work often seems to riff on: the desire to shift one's consciousness. As I leave Ringholt's studio, I realise it's a desire that relates to a very human awareness of time – the exact thing he captured so viscerally in his epic clocks. The knowledge that time is finite creates the yearning to slow it down, to stop it altogether, to somehow create the space for more. In this conception, time is fluid. It shifts and changes in a way that aligns it far more closely with how we actually perceive it, which is to say the way in which it's actually lived.

For Ringholt, art is the thing that makes this possible, the channel by which he mediates his relationship to the world. In this, he quietens his otherwise overactive mind. What has resulted is a practice of carefully wrought contrasts and echoes, one that, in coupling irreverent humour with deadly serious introspection, brings both darkness and light into momentary focus.

It's a practice that intones something both simple and profound: *here it is,* it tells us, *more life: do with it what you will, but don't waste it.*

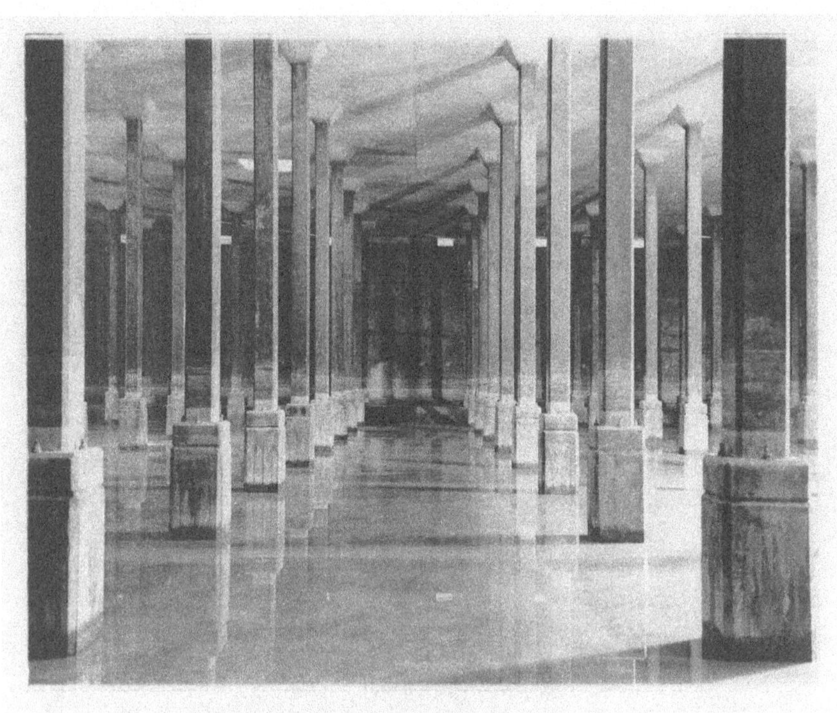

Simryn Gill *Pawn #2* 2019/2022

2

The Artist in Space

The first point that Simryn Gill wants to make is that an artist's biography should not be trusted, at least not as a means through which to understand their work. Yes, an artist's life provides the frame within which their character and sensibility finds form, but good art is always far more than the simple sum of these parts. She'd said as much on our very first phone call, and now, some two weeks later, as we settle at her simple studio table at her home in Sydney's Marrickville, she reiterates her position with a smile: 'I've got a great story,' she says. 'As long as you don't write it down.'

She's teasing, of course. But she's also not. Gill's practice is full of biographical breadcrumbs that together trace her history from Singapore, where she was born in 1959 – the first child of Indian parents – to the Malaysian coastal town of Port Dickson, where she grew up in her paternal grandfather's grand house, and on to Australia, where she has lived in Adelaide and Sydney. Today she divides her time between Port Dickson and Australia; both places indelibly shape her work. To look at Gill's practice is to gain an intricate feel for what fuels her art – her motivations, the unique quality of her eye, the thinking that has resulted from a life forged between the relative poles of 'here' and 'there' – but she wants me to know that none of this equates to biography, at least not in conventional terms.

'As an artist you get asked this question: what are you doing? What is your work about? And it's a really perplexing one, because the work is actually about figuring out being: if I knew why I was doing it, I wouldn't do it.'

Her biography, she explains, provides her less of a subject than it does a ground upon which her work finds form. 'I work *from* the ground and *with* the ground,' she says. What truly motivates her are far more abstract ideas: repetition, time, return. She aims for a certain density in what she does. Pinned to the otherwise blank wall behind her are a number of relief prints she has taken from the inked body of a dead ibis – one small part of a cascading sequence of works (photographs, prints, photograms and an artist book) that comprise a recent major commission, *Clearing*, for the Art Gallery of New South Wales. The prints show the ibis's individual feathers with exquisite clarity. It's like seeing a bird anew. Perhaps Gill notices my attention settling there, because she adds, 'I work from closeness as well; I work from detail.'

There's something faintly daunting about writing on Gill's practice. It's not just her resistance to a biographical frame; it's also the dizzying variety of what she does. Since she began exhibiting in the 1990s, she has exercised a pronounced talent for shapeshifting. She goes where each work demands, choosing materials and forms as needed. Everything is linked, but a casual viewer could be forgiven for asking: just what kind of artist is she, exactly?

Although she has consistently used photography, to call her a photographer misses much of what she does. As the ibis attests, a good deal of her output in recent years could be loosely characterised as printmaking, but only in the most expanded sense of the term. She's just as likely to create meticulous collages from the pages of antique books or to make small sculptures. One recent series – a favourite of mine – saw her cast the flesh cavities of fruits and vegetables in Plaster of Paris, a process that made permanent that which usually rots away. At times she has simply presented her viewers with the prismatic results of a life spent combing the mangrove-fringed beachfront of her childhood home – eschewing the shells and pebbles that might draw the eye of most in favour of pieces of sea-worn plastic and other materials of human origin renatured by their subsequent life in salt water. During our time together she referred to herself as a gleaner – the term popularised by the late French documentarian Agnès Varda, who used it to describe a particular kind of intuitive gathering, not only of objects, but of the thoughts and feelings they might spark.

Gill's process is often elliptical, both heavy with labour and light with poetic wonder. The motivations that guide her are difficult to put into words, but she is drawn to the challenge. Over her long career, she has managed to forge something all too rare in the art world: a gracefully open-ended way of writing about her work that illuminates what she does yet leaves its central mysteries intact. 'Making something out of nothing,' she wrote in 2012,

> order out of emptiness, through the labour of doing, redoing, and redoing again. Because. It's as if all of life is in that because, which stops just there and doesn't go any further. An unattached reason. A floating specificity: whimsical, empty and very full. I have been able to call the actions of this urge 'art'.

For her 2013 exhibition *Here art grows on trees*, which she presented as Australia's representative at the 55th Venice Biennale, the many threads of her art drew together. Australia's exhibition pavilion, designed by Philip Cox and opened in 1988, had always been intended as temporary, and it was finally poised to be replaced. Gill had the entire central roof section removed so that the works she installed within – a series of large unframed photographs; a scatter of sculptural parts; a long paper collage, also unframed – were exposed to the elements. To represent one's country at Venice is surely among the highest-profile opportunities on the international stage, and many artists would meet it head on, seeking to make an indelible, career-defining mark. But Gill's approach was far more oblique: for her, the driving heart of the project lay in making the ultimate impermanence of her work tangible. With no roof to shelter it, it was made vulnerable to what would otherwise be understood as catastrophic damage: drizzling rain, humidity, pollution, falling leaves, dust and, eventually, creeping mould.

Don't think Gill isn't a perfectionist, though: she is, famously so. When I ask about this, she refers to her Venice exhibition in terms of an offering. That's why the works were so meticulously presented; why she insisted that her preferred team of art installers were flown in from Australia; why she engaged the expertise of Venetian plasterers to prepare the walls before soaking the paper-like plaster surface in a wash of velvet-black India ink. 'So much needed to go into it to make it just right, so that it was ... what's the word I'm looking for? A *sufficient* offering to the gods,' she says. Her eyes dance, suggesting she's aware of the ego involved in such a notion, but also of the fundamental truth. 'If that's your primary audience, it has to be perfect.'

—

As a child, Gill was drawn to liminal spaces, in the way that children often are – spaces that suggest an elsewhere or provide an imaginative link to another world.

Beyond the mangroves in Port Dickson lies the Strait of Malacca. The passage is an infamous maritime chokepoint between the Pacific and Indian oceans: the 90,000 or so vessels that pass through each year constitute between 30 and 40 per cent of global trade. The volume was far less in Gill's childhood, but she still vividly recalls the view from her childhood home as a horizon traced by a constant stream of ships. With their father, Gill and her siblings would look out through binoculars and read the names painted on each hull, trying to identify where the vessel was from. Both her father and grandfather were keen amateur photographers, and the family subscribed to magazines such as *LIFE*, *National Geographic*, *Newsweek* and *Time*, which all, in varying ways, turned upon the power of the photographic image. The young Gill would pore over them. She did the same with the many books in her grandfather's library. Although she cautions me against making too direct a link, she concedes that 'a lot of my eye, or my visual training, or my thinking, came from that library – just my grandfather's books, or the magazines that came through'.

In step, her lifelong habit of beachcombing took hold. She became so familiar with the nuances of the intertidal zone outside her family home that when a large power station was constructed next door in the early 1970s she was able to identify resulting changes in the marine ecosystem: a tiny shift in water temperature or in the numbers of certain shells. More recently, she has been approached by an ecologist who lives in the area. 'He often brings things to me,' she says. 'He asks, *Tell me, did you see these as a child? When did you start seeing them? Do you think the number of them have shifted?*' They go for walks and discuss what's changed. Again, it's the same idea: looking closely, working with fine detail.

Gill moved to Adelaide in 1987 with her husband, Souchou Yao, a Malaysian-Chinese social anthropologist who had previously studied there. In Malaysia, both public and private life spilled into the streets, but Adelaide seemed by comparison deeply guarded. Gill and Yao already had a young son, and a daughter soon followed. A sequence of thirteen black-and-white photographs, titled *A long time between drinks* and shot by Gill during a return visit to Adelaide in the early 2000s, captures something of their early life there. They show the places she walked with her children: glimpses of the once-familiar routes she'd taken between home and school, to friends' houses and beyond. In her photographs, there's not a soul in sight – just trees, streets, buildings and skies. Fences are tall; doors closed. One image is of the garden she planted in their suburban backyard, but you wouldn't know it unless told: devoid of the human figure, it too is inflected with a kind of elegiac emptiness.

It was in Adelaide that Gill had begun carving out a life as an artist. She enrolled briefly in art school, but it was 'too slow': 'my mind was already galloping'. Even so, it left her with little doubt she had found her vocation. She discovered a selection of artists' books in the school library, including a number by Ed Ruscha, the American Pop artist acclaimed for his mundane-yet-soulful serial photographs of his Los Angeles surrounds: apartment blocks, swimming pools, gas stations. He once threw a vintage typewriter from a speeding Buick and drolly documented its shattered pieces. *This is art?* Gill wondered. *But I've been thinking like this my whole life.*

Ruscha's influence on Gill isn't often noted, but it is nonetheless clear. Any number of her photographic series recall not only the coolness of his eye but also his capacity to allow his photographic subject, no matter how nondescript, to speak, to emanate character.

Around the time Gill made the Ruscha-esque *A long time between drinks,* for instance, the power station next to her childhood home in Malaysia transitioned from oil to gas. By then it had towered for three decades over the family garden, which her mother and grandmother had planted with the mangoes, neem trees, jacarandas, tamarinds and gulmohars that characterised the Indian regions in which they had grown up. Gill speaks of the station, ruefully, as a 'strange blessing'. Since her youth, much of Port Dickson's beachfront has been sold off to developers, and the mangroves and tidal zone she loved have been razed and built over. But her childhood home and garden, now owned by her brother, is so close to the power station that it's within what's termed a security zone: there, the beachfront remains, and with it one of her most valued sites – it still often features in her work.

During the station's transition, Gill talked her way inside and photographed its sprawling control rooms and corridors, framing them as dispassionately formal panoramas: vast switchboards, forests of pipework, empty desks and chairs. She took the same approach to her family home and exhibited the resulting series in 2004 at Shiseido Gallery in Tokyo. She shows me the small catalogue from the exhibition. Each double spread is comprised of a domestic image and its industrial counterpart: the familiar and the unfamiliar, the soft and the hard. It's tempting to read the series as an indictment of industrialisation, but it's also simply about proximity. The transition to gas reduced the air pollution, yet it made the turbines considerably larger. 'Imagine living in that electrical flux,' Gill says. Look at her photos and you can.

Part of Gill's talent lies in her resistance to categorisation. She explains that she has always been careful to avoid being pigeonholed as 'a little banner for this version of being in the world, or that'. She realised early on that in the Australian art world – which in the 1990s was self-consciously questioning its regional and cultural context – she could be 'very boxable'. Her work can appear to cleave easily to themes such as displacement, migration and globalisation – key art-world preoccupations – but on closer inspection it often directs viewers elsewhere. Put simply, Gill always manages to wriggle free.

This is why she was initially sceptical of the invitation to represent Australia at Venice. 'I work well in an invisibility,' she explains. 'I'm visible, but I'm also not really in the stream, as it were.' The idea of representing the nation – a place that she was simultaneously both part of and not – was confronting, and the project left her drained. Not long afterwards she returned with Yao to Port Dickson, where she has a house not far from her childhood home. She stayed for four years. And although she was partly there for family reasons, it was a productive time: she developed various bodies of work, much of which remains unseen. In 2016 she was joined there by the Melbourne-based printmaker Trent Walter, and the two developed the relief-printing process that has since underpinned much of Gill's work. They started with a large collection of driftwood – unidentified planks and timbers, intriguingly shaped formwork from fishing boats – that they inked and printed on long sheets of paper as unwieldy, stacked compositions.

The two remain close collaborators; when I spoke with Walter, he jokingly referred to Gill as 'one of my best students'. Although they work on discrete projects together, she often takes an idea discovered along the way and runs with it. 'Once Simryn's got something in mind, she goes deep,' he said. The point where one thing ends and another begins is often purposefully diffuse. She picks at the edges, he explained, looking for the loose thread. She makes things hers. 'What makes her a great artist is that she doubts. And through that doubt she gets to the core of things, the centre.'

—

Gill's recent project, *Clearing*, which was commissioned as part of a series inaugurating the Art Gallery of New South Wales's newest wing, grew directly from the work that she and Walter began in Malaysia.

The ambition of it had rapidly expanded beyond taking prints from driftwood: on a subsequent visit that Walter made in 2017, Gill was intent on taking a printed impression from an entire palm tree, a quixotic-seeming undertaking that grants *Clearing* its most obvious touchstone. It hinges around a similar printed investigation of a displaced date palm, but that's not to suggest that she accepted the commission with this in mind. Or, for that matter, with anything much at all in mind. 'You say yes even though you might not know what you're doing,' she says. 'You just have to deal with it, and trust. It's like being a writer: you have a blank page and you think, *Do I have anything in me still? Can I find the first line, have I got a way in?*'

The pavilion-like structure of the gallery's new wing, which was designed by the Prizker-winning Japanese architectural firm SANAA, extends across the parkland of the Domain, towards the harbour. It combines walls of rammed earth, concrete and stone with great swathes of glass. But it's what lies underneath that first sparked Gill's imagination. In the wake of the fall of Singapore in 1942, two vast concrete tanks were constructed under the Domain to store oil, emergency fuel for a naval fleet should a feared Japanese invasion eventuate. The new building's pristine white access ramp spirals into one of them, now converted into a huge, patina-rich exhibition space. Gill had heard that a tangle of tree roots, most likely from a Moreton Bay fig, had at some point in the tank's history broken through the walls, seeking water. She requested access to the in-progress renovations so she and another long-term collaborator, Alex Robinson, could take photographs. 'That was my way of saying I need to slow down and stand in the vicinity of these things,' she says.

The two of them photographed the cluster of errant roots, from which she would also later take relief prints in her studio, but for the most part they ended up simply documenting the cavernous interior. The stench of fuel remained strong. Sentinel-like columns rose from the darkness at regular intervals, their bases seared white with lime residue. Thin beams of sunlight made their way inside: just enough to illuminate long photographic exposures of ten or even fifteen minutes.

When a friend at the gallery alerted Gill that a 110-year-old Canary Island date palm had been removed to make way for the new building, she turned her attention to that. At first it was hoped the tree could be saved, so Gill worked onsite with a team of assistants to take two graphite rubbings on paper, both over twenty metres long, of the trunk and fronds. Then, in 2020, just before Sydney entered the first of its COVID-19 lockdowns, the palm was found to be infested by coconut weevils and, instead of being replanted, was sawn to pieces for disposal. She sprang into action, contacting a friend with a ute and directing him to collect as much of the tree as possible: the sections of trunk, the bundles of fronds, the seed heads. She took this to a storage unit, and then to her studio, where she and Sydney-based printmaker Marcus Dyer-Harrison worked throughout lockdown to make a sequence of relief prints.

The two took impressions of the fronds in various subdued colours; they cut the trunk and did the same with its circular cross-sections. Gill took the seed fronds and worked with Sandra Barnard, her long-time photographic printer, to make photograms of them (a process in which an object is placed against photographic paper before it is exposed to light, leaving a ghostly silhouette). Gill and Dyer-Harrison even sawed the seed heads into pieces and printed those too. In the resulting images one can see the gaps and absences where the weevils made their home.

The final work would eventually occupy an entire gallery of the existing building. One of the original graphite rubbings of the palm was unfurled like a vast scroll on a purpose-built table, while the surrounding walls each held the various groups of prints and the sequence of photograms. The whole thing hummed with a compulsive energy that came directly from Gill's apparent drive to capture something in its entirety. But beyond that it was harder to pin down. The palm was revealed as the simple sum of its parts – the trunk, the fronds, the seed heads – but the mystery of how these parts once formed a complex, living thing was left intact.

Although we meet only a week after *Clearing* opens to the public, Gill has already moved on. In her studio, she reaches for the artist's book she has produced as part of the commission: a large, loose-leaf black-and-white publication that places the project within a wider constellation of images and thoughts. She refers to it as 'a folio of associations', a perfect description. Books have always been central to her practice, both as an enduring inspiration (she is, and always has been, a voracious and broad reader) and as something she herself has made, usually to pair her photographs with short writings. She tells me that this nexus between image and text may soon become her 'primary mode' – her recent work with the Sydney-based writer Tom Melick, with whom she edits a proudly DIY publishing imprint called Stolon Press, has become a particular focus. She chooses her words carefully, aware that the opportunity to realise a work as far-reaching as *Clearing* is vanishingly rare for Australian artists. 'I'm not saying this, but you *could* say that my entire Art Gallery of New South Wales project, everything that's on the walls – that's the meal on the plate that you throw away, but which was necessary to make the book.'

She begins to leaf through the pages, pointing out the various images and explaining how they relate. There are the roots that found their way into the oil storage tanks, and an image of tangled hair, a tiny, folded paper boat tucked in among the strands. A sequence of three found photographs shows a departing passenger ship draped in a flurry of streamers. An accompanying caption, written by Melick, spells out the connection: 'Look at how the bunting tethers boat to wharf, like hair to a head.' The printed ibis is in there, gracing a double-page spread (the birds often nest in palm crowns), while another typically striking page juxtaposes photographs of an ancient temple overcome by tree roots with the body of a giant squid laid out on a beach, the once-glorious torsional beauty of its limbs tangled by death and gravity. Gill pauses at a photograph from 1942 that shows the oil-storage tanks under construction and points to a palm tree in the background: the same one that she so meticulously disassembled eight decades later as the basis for *Clearing.*

Alongside the images, the book contains a brilliantly digressive essay that wends its way around, through and beside *Clearing.* It is likely the most comprehensive statement Gill has yet written on her practice. If viewers of *Clearing* were left wondering why she was so enamoured by the palm, the answer is in the detail:

> Think of the tree as a very slowly upward flowing waterspout (in the same way that glass is a slowly downward sagging fluid), the sap travelling up through the trunk and outwards to the tips of each twig and each leaf, like a vertical water jet falling to earth in a 360 degree back-flip.

It's this sense of barely contained life that draws her – the softly vibrating force of it, the twined threads of grace and power that grant the tree its form. She describes how the first palm she attempted to take a printed impression from – the one in Malaysia, when she was assisted by Trent Walter – seemed to actively resist her attentions. It was on a farm in the southern state of Johor. Gill had purchased the tree so she could cut it down, before erecting a simple shelter over it to shade her and Walter's labours. She writes, 'The energetic life of the tree fought back; pounced at us; whipped us when we let down our guard; tore the paper, strong as it was; soaked it in sap, made it limp.' Afterwards, the farm manager shared a stew made from the sprouting heart of the palm crown: a rare delicacy that Gill notes is called *hati*, the same word for liver, in Malay.

In her studio in Marrickville, Gill asks me a question: 'How do we get to the things we need to get to?' She's still thinking through the connection between the work on display at the Art Gallery of New South Wales and the book open on the table before us, but she's also broadly referring to how an artist might negotiate the demands of the art world while staying faithful to the inchoate urge that drives them. 'What are the things that we have to do to be willing to say, *Okay, I'll do that: if you'd like a beautiful thing from me, I'll give you a beautiful thing. But can I have my unbeautiful thing at the end too?*' It's the book that fulfils the ideal: the unbeautiful thing that forms the ground from which new things – not yet known, let alone planned – will rise.

It's how Gill has always worked, at least since she found her footing as an artist. Back in 2012, when she accepted the invitation to show at Venice, she did so with what she now insists was a healthy dose of naivety. She was offered a decent-sized budget, and she found herself wondering what it would be like to photograph the many open-cut mines that mar the Australian landscape. She only understood the urge in the barest of terms: 'I just wanted to look in. Just stand at the rim and record the void.' The mining companies refused her access, so she did the next best thing: chartered a small plane and photographed the mines from above.

Working with a production manager – a friend and ex-journalist from Malaysia, Mary Maguire – Gill eventually shot mines in Tasmania, South Australia, New South Wales and Western Australia. She rugged up against the wind and literally hung out of the plane window, snapping away. Something came full circle; she thought of her child self in Port Dickson, hunched over photographic magazines in her father's library. She recalls saying to Maguire, 'Hey Mary, it's my chance to be a pretend, wannabe *National Geographic* photographer, hanging out of a plane. I can pretend to be one of those boys, and they're going to pay me for it!'

The photographs formed the series she offered up unframed to the Venetian elements. They are silent, regal images; a long way from the wind-buffeted, high-wire challenge of capturing them. They are also beautiful in a fashion that belies their subject. But as with much of what Gill does, including her near-forensic examination of the palm tree in *Clearing*, the resulting tension is not strictly the point. Nor are the environmental readings that she knew the photographs would evoke. All that is good, she tells me, but, as with so much of her disparate-seeming work, she was motivated by something different: the drive to carve out space at the edges of things, to grant attention to what might otherwise go unseen, the simple fact of bearing witness.

It's this that provides her practice both its impetus and its ultimate justification. 'Art lets you do things that you've had fantasies about since you were a child,' she'd told me earlier. 'That's the best thing about it. It's like, *Why are you doing that? It's because I'm an artist.* It's such a great answer, right?'

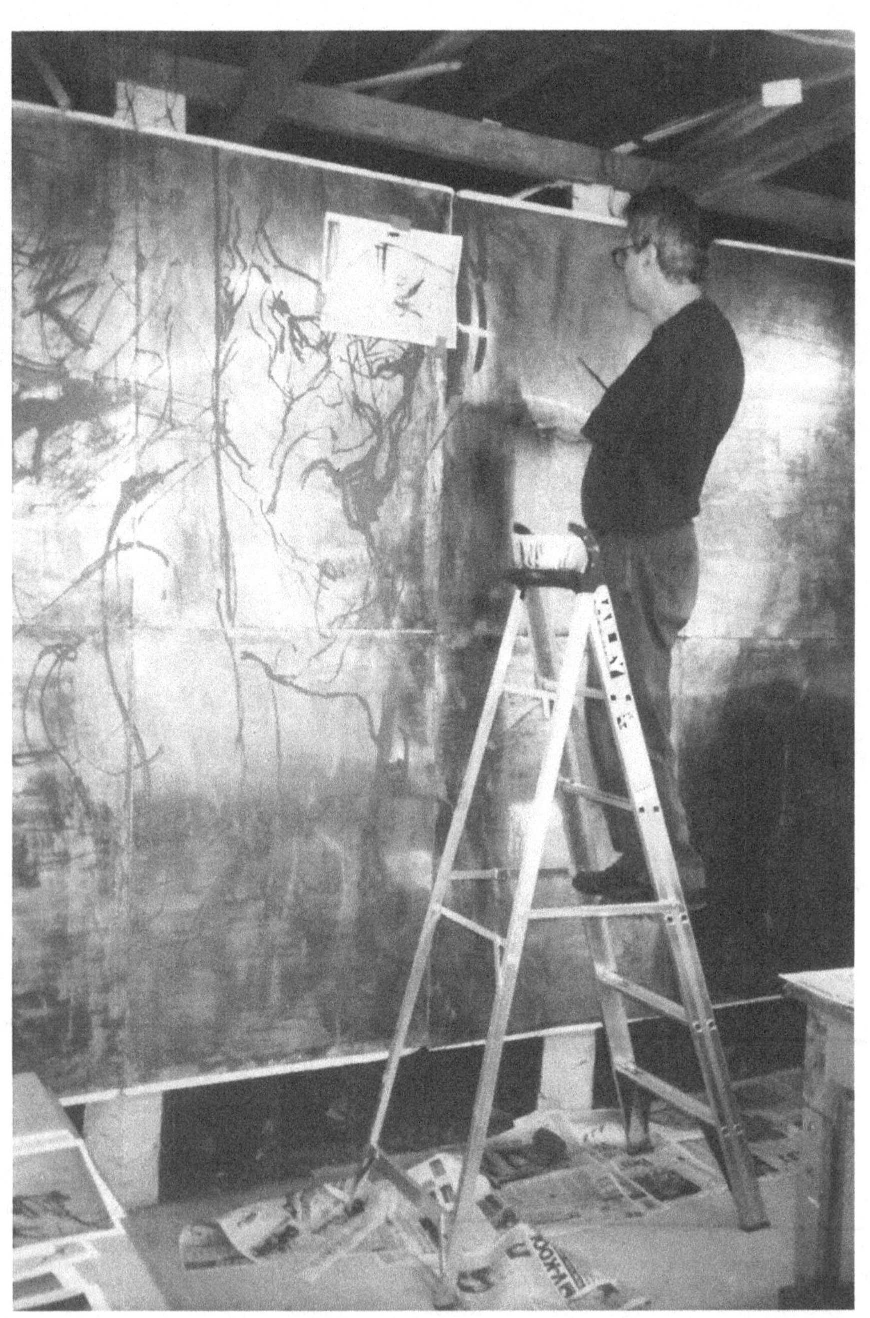

Mike Parr working at Viridian Press, Olinda c. 1997

3

Maps and Mazes

The Dandenong Ranges, which fan out in great ridges and gullies to the northwest of Melbourne, is a place of pronounced seasonal contrasts: hot summers, in which the bush dries out with crackling energy and the threat of fire hangs heavy, and long winters, in which the region's towering forests of mountain ash, messmate and grey gum are often wreathed in fog and drenched by frigid rain. For the master printmaker John Loane, who relocated his one-man operation, Viridian Press, from Melbourne to the ranges in the late 1990s, it was the relative extremes of this environment that made the move worth it. It seemed to reflect something of the practice he'd spent years refining: the elemental and physical qualities that, for a certain kind of creative mind, grant printmaking its allure.

Loane had grown up in Melbourne, but as a child had often visited an aunt who had a flower farm at Olinda, the highest village in the ranges and one-time home to the postwar Australian impressionist Arthur Streeton. The young Loane would spend his time there chopping wood and exploring the steep, wooded slopes and rainforest gullies that surround the town. At the time he relocated, Viridian Press was based in the suburb of Thornbury, where he lived with his partner and two young children in a property with ample room for a printmaking studio, but one day, driving around Olinda, he saw a big bush-shrouded block for sale, with an old weatherboard house on stilts. It sparked his imagination.

'It was great,' he told me when I visited him in his Canberra studio, as he cast his mind back to what proved to be one of his most productive periods as a printmaker. 'But it was cold and wet.'

Loane, a rangy man in his early seventies – hands creased and ink-stained with his life's work – is not someone prone to unnecessary elaboration: there is a marked inwardness to him, which, combined with a clear comfort in silence, speaks to a professional life spent in quiet labour. Printmaking is usually done in meticulously controlled environments – most master printmakers, the somewhat regal title applied to those who work side-by-side with artists to translate their practices into editioned prints, leave nothing to chance. But up in the bush, things were different by necessity, and all the better for it. Although Loane eventually built a large shed to serve as a studio, the set-up was at first far more haphazard: for six months or so after the move, all sorts of printing equipment sat cluttered on the drive under tarpaulins. He moved his printing press in under the house, which offered some protection from the elements, but still the weather came in: in winter it was wild and cold; at times, sleet would blow through his workspace. Once, when the rains had loosened the earth, a huge mountain ash came crashing down in the bush nearby. 'It was primitive,' Loane said. 'But I like primitive.'

Working in the face of such difficulty is part of Loane's raison d'être. After becoming the founding director of the Victorian Print Workshop (VPW, now the Australian Print Workshop) in 1981, he struck out on his own. He chose the name Viridian Press in reference to Luis Buñuel's darkly scandalous 1961 film *Viridiana*, but also for the fact that viridian – a particularly deep shade of green – is a challenging colour to use successfully in art. To Loane, who has made his own prints throughout his career, this offered an analogy for the challenge of printmaking itself, especially when one attempts to make a life of it.

His departure from the VPW came during a 1987 portfolio project that drew together twenty-five high-profile luminaries of the day, among them Brian Blanchflower, Susan Norrie, Jenny

Watson and Robert Rooney. Each was tasked with creating a print marking Australia's looming bicentenary. One by one, they worked alongside Loane or one of the technicians he engaged for the project in the VPW's Melbourne workshop. To put it mildly, it was demanding. 'We could spend up to two weeks with each of them,' Loane recalls. The resulting prints each employed as many as four colours, separated into different plates, and were printed in editions of eighty. Loane didn't do all the editioning, which ultimately amounted to 2000 prints, but he suspects he did most of it. It was all-consuming, and concurrently running the actual workshop – applying for grants, managing staff, developing plans – proved impossible. He resigned his directorship halfway through and completed work on the portfolio under the journeyman title of 'printmaker'.

Loane found all the artists interesting, but it was Mike Parr, a famously uncompromising performance artist who had already represented Australia at the 1980 Venice Biennale, who most caught his attention. The two would go on to establish something extraordinary: an intimate working relationship that would deeply mark much of their subsequent careers.

Parr, who was born with a left arm that ended at a stump before the elbow, is still most often linked to a particularly confronting 1977 performance – typical of his practice – in which he sat before an audience and proceeded to hack off a false arm with a butcher's cleaver. He'd stuffed it with raw meat, and as he hacked away, the meat spilled out upon the table before him. Those unaware of Parr's congenital physiology (that is, much of the audience) were, understandably, shocked. But although that work, which was titled *Cathartic Action: Social Gestus no.5 (The 'Armchop')*, would become Parr's most notorious, a series of far less elaborate performances that he'd undertaken in the early 1970s had already set the tone. Two are captured in a short film from 1972, which documents

Parr grimly carrying out the prompts of the film's title: *Hold your breath for as long as possible / Light a candle. Hold your finger in the flame for as long as possible.* As he completes the latter task, the skin of his finger begins to blacken, and the viewer can't help but sense the central character of his entire practice: his artistic medium comprises his own body, a canvas onto which trauma – past or present, individual or collective – can be re-played through coded, ritualistic-seeming actions. The resulting discomfort and pain, whether it is Parr's or that of his audience, demands to be understood as a form of catharsis.

Parr's performances had quickly propelled him to the leading edge of the small but influential tide of avant-garde Australian art in the late 1970s. But a series of what he deemed failures – including a work he presented in Adelaide in early 1980, in which he sat in a room in the Federation-style mansion Carclew House and attempted to smile for twenty-four hours – had snuffed out his momentum. Performance lost its pull: 'I thought maybe my mind had let me down. I had nothing left,' he would tell *The Sydney Morning Herald* three decades later. For a number of years he found himself suddenly an artist without a medium.

Drawing eventually filled the gap. After rudimentary beginnings, he arrived at a labour-intensive process in which he gridded photographic self-portraits into ever-more-minute coordinates before copying them out in graphite and charcoal. He scaled these up, strategically manipulating the grid into anamorphic distortions that pushed and pulled his features across the picture plane in a manner that couldn't help but evoke the bodily exertions he'd made in his early performances. This was the beginning of what he would term his 'Self Portrait Project', a soon-to-be-relentless flood of work that would come to define his creative output almost as much as his performances. Yet no matter how many times he took his own face as a subject, not once were the results the same, at least not really. He would eventually introduce Jacques Lacan's notion that 'repetition produces difference' to articulate the compulsion that drove the self-portraits: the idea that, by playing out set notions of ourselves, the infinitesimal stitching of our psyches can't help but be altered. Compulsive repetition was mirrored in Parr's case by what he would later refer to as the 'unstaunchable devaluation' of his subject that resulted: this was not self-portraiture as a means to lionise the artist, or to exercise the fidelity of their observational skills; it was a process of pulling his likeness apart to reveal the tangle of often contradictory psychological pressures that constitute a self. The results were unflinching, often verging on brutal. Once again, he was holding his finger to the candle flame and keeping it there as long as possible.

By the time he met Loane in 1987, Parr had returned to performance with vigour, but Loane was aware of his drawings, and found them highly charged. Any fruitful collaboration in the print studio, though, demands more from a printmaker than a simple appreciation for the artist's work. When the two first came together, there was something about their characters that clicked immediately. 'He's formidable, and I'm not; he's intellectual, and I'm not,' Loane says now, but it was likely more complex than a melding of opposites. Master printmaking requires an artful dance: an ability on the artist's part to forego some of the absolute control they exert over their practice, and on the printmaker's to use the resulting space to gently engineer something new.

The master printer draws upon a range of often arcane-seeming techniques, each of them bound by their own histories and conventions. In Japan, the practice of printing sacred Buddhist texts from carved wooden blocks dates to the eighth century, and it was used in Europe by the fifteenth. The wide use of intaglio printmaking – a European method in which a metal plate, usually copper, is treated through a variety of different techniques before being etched in acid – dates to the sixteenth, while stone lithography, the foundation of modern commercial printing, dates to the late eighteenth. Other methods, such as screen printing – similarly old but famously elevated to a high art by Andy Warhol's screen-printed multiples – add to the printmaker's toolkit.

Yet as much as exacting process and knowledge bring to the equation, it's the core relationship between artist and printer that really counts. There has to be trust. At times, perhaps more often than not, it doesn't work: prints can often appear as pale echoes of an artist's primary practice. But when a meaningful relationship is present, the results can be beautiful. In this, certain master printers play a role not unlike the most talented literary translators, who manage to inflect the text with their own sensibilities while remaining invisible to all but the most attentive reader.

—

By the time he met Parr, Loane had already established a practice as a sensitive printer, deft at responding to the varying needs of artists. But with Parr, who Loane found almost overwhelmingly ambitious from the very first moment, things stepped up a notch. 'His head is burning on all fronts, all the time, for whatever he's working on,' Loane said.

The portfolio print – a densely lined self-portrait elongated vertically through the picture plane and titled *Map* – was completed quickly, and before it was even editioned Parr was all in. He asked Loane for a further twenty etching plates that he could work on in Sydney and send down to Melbourne for editioning – a group that became a tortured-looking series titled *Organon #1–#20*. When Loane left the VPW to establish Viridian Press, Parr went with him. Over the following decades, Loane would work with a vast array of Australia's most acclaimed artists, but Parr would prove the most constant.

Loane likes to think it's his own subtly unconventional approach that made the relationship work for as long as it did. Before his directorship at the VPW, he undertook a tour of printing workshops in Canada and America. He was ostensibly looking at open-access models – workshops that hired print space to local artists – but it was the acclaimed high-art workshops of America, like LA-based Gemini G.E.L. (Graphic Editions Limited), that really interested him. Founded in 1966 as a publisher of flashy, convention-shaking artist editions, Gemini was then the gold standard of the newly reinvigorated art of master printing. It echoed the ambition of the artists it worked with, among them Robert Rauschenberg, Roy Lichtenstein and Claes Oldenburg. Large-scale prints were common: Gemini's first edition, a 1967 collaboration with Rauschenberg titled *Booster*, had for a time been the largest print ever made, a record that the workshop would go on to regularly break.

Loane simply visited Gemini's Melrose Drive gallery and talked his way into the printing studio that was discretely tucked behind. It was well worth it. The first printmaker he met there was the lithographer Serge Lozingot, a diminutive Frenchman who was hard at work printing white stars onto a signature Jasper Johns image of the American flag. Loane stood there astounded as Lozingot chattered away, flicking his ink roller across the image in a manner that struck him as both casual and precise. Later on the same trip, Loane visited Ken Tyler – a co-founder of Gemini who had gone out on his own – in an upstate New York farmhouse that Tyler had recently converted into his own genre-busting workshop. It was similarly impressive. There was a Robert Motherwell edition piled on the lithography press; Roy Lichtenstein's famous *Entablatures* series – large-scale horizontal images inspired by classical architectural mouldings and enlivened by gold and silver foiling – were underway; so too was an exquisite small etching by the acclaimed abstract painter Helen Frankenthaler.

Yet although he returned to Australia with a deep admiration for American printmaking, Loane would soon come to feel that the self-consciously ambitious innovations of such studios risked becoming as conventional as anything else. He now characterises the laborious process that underwrote them as 'overcooked and mercantile'. He sensed that working with Parr might allow him to draw another quality to the fore, one more forceful and immediate, closer to the antic possibilities of Parr's broader practice. Following Parr's print for the Bicentennial portfolio, Loane recalls that he suggested a soft-ground etching. This technique – in which a fragile ground is applied to a copper plate, covered with a thin paper such as newsprint, and drawn over with pencil or biro before being etched in acid – records a drawing's finest detail: even the lightest surface impression, intentional or otherwise, can lift the acid-proof ground beneath the paper, and thus transfer to the resulting print. Parr was working with his sleeves rolled up, and as he drew, rested his left arm on the newsprint-covered plate, shifting it as he went. Loane knew immediately that if the resulting impressions weren't erased from the plate (a process of using bitumen to block it out on the plate before it is etched) it would be legible on the final work.

Most printmakers would alert the artist to such an issue, but not Loane. He sensed that Parr tacitly trusted the process and he stayed quiet as he placed the plate in the etching acid as it was, as many as eighteen distinct stump marks punctuating Parr's finely detailed image. It was the right choice: when Loane inked the plate and printed an initial proof, Parr was enlivened by how the impressions had carried through. 'Mike calls that the "rough edges",' Loane said. 'I like to think it was at that moment that he became totally entranced by the potential of printmaking.'

The Olinda studio served to draw such qualities of discovery and experimentation further out of Parr and Loane's working relationship, intensifying them as it did. Even as they worked together in the limited space under the house, open to bush on all sides, the prints grew larger and more unwieldy. Multi-plate works constructed from as many as twelve or fourteen panels, each as big as 90 x 120 centimetres, were hung from the balcony on a makeshift plywood wall that allowed Parr and Loane to see them in their entirety. Parr would stay in Melbourne with his gallerist, Anna Schwartz, and make the hour-long drive up into the wilds of the hills each day. It wasn't an ideal arrangement – the commute at times threatened to disrupt their momentum in the studio – but it nonetheless worked: 'Mike thrived on it in his own peculiar way,' Loane said. He recalled Parr referring to it as his 'Gulley Jimson' period, after the Irish writer Joyce Cary's 1944 novel *The Horse's Mouth*, and subsequent film adaptation, in which the character of Gulley Jimson (played by Alec Guinness in the film) is an irascible artist who creates his paintings – at times on walls – in a state of uncontrollable creative ecstasy.

Olinda was the place where their most important innovation took shape: a shift away from editioning the works and towards what they would come to term 'unique states' – one-off images that freed their printmaking from the restraint of mechanical repetition. Loane had never seen himself as much of an editioner. He did it for other artists, but in his own work he'd always played around with one-off prints that were impossible to replicate due to post-printing additions like over-drawing or painting. He'd long been drawn to the resulting tension between what were usually treated as distinct mediums. As a student in the 1970s, he had studied at Melbourne's Prahran College, where he majored in painting, but he'd found the directness of the medium confronting. 'I think I was afraid of painting, in a way,' he said.

Nor did he feel he was a natural draughtsman, at least not in a conventional representational manner. When he later transferred to the Gallery School at the National Gallery of Victoria, printmaking offered him a productive alternative. Bea Maddock, one of Australia's most acclaimed printmakers, was then teaching there, and whereas it seemed to Loane that most students followed Maddock in her own practice by making photo-based etchings and screen prints, she encouraged him to follow his own sense of mark-making. He found himself drawn to the singular material characteristics of printmaking – its capacity for erasure and reveal, its indirectness.

With Parr, Loane had at first followed established convention and editioned many of the early prints they made together. Eight was the most common number, plus a printer's proof and an artist's proof. Occasionally they also pulled a *Bon á Tirer*, a French printmaker's term that means 'good to take', which refers to the final proof before an edition is made, the one against which the subsequent prints are compared for consistency. In the early years he would go on to print the entire edition, but once he and Parr set to work in Olinda, that became far less important. Process became everything; the resulting prints were all about pushing the medium in directions that met Parr's ambition head on, or at least came as near to that ideal as possible.

Soon, most prints were realised as unique states that allowed the two to embrace the beautiful happenstance and accident that the diligent printmaker usually spends a lifetime avoiding or carefully controlling – the ink bleeds and washes, the smudges and blurs – which both fitted with Parr's existing graphic sensibility and pushed it forwards. By the time Parr sat down in Sydney in 2002 and wrote Loane a long letter ruminating on how to most accurately describe the works, they had stopped editioning altogether. '[T]he whole point of repetition in the self-portrait project is to produce a kind of disorder,' Parr wrote. '... we need to get people to think of repetition as just repetition in order to make disorder signify.' He underscored the need to arrive at an eloquent tension 'between seeing handwork and printed image', a tension between the immediacy of touch and the mediation of this touch through printmaking.

Loane commissioned a printmaker friend to build a large-scale press, which he and Parr used for immense woodcuts: composite images printed from large plywood sheets, cut and gouged by Parr into chaotic compositions. They were rough and immediate, full of feeling. *The now schizophrenic* (2000), in the collection of the National Gallery of Victoria, was printed in deep red, the white linework cut away in forceful gestures that tangled into purposefully unresolved images: turbulent flashes of an unruly consciousness.

No matter how confronting, Parr's performances were known to be meticulously staged – one understood their intent by way of their often brutally deployed symbolism. In his 2002 performance *Close the Concentration Camps,* he sat in a gallery for six hours, during which time an assistant sewed shut his mouth and eyes. Viewers who gathered to see Parr slumped in a chair as blood and iodine solution seeped down his face were also presented with their own reflection, staring back from a large mirror on the wall behind Parr. In this way, they were implicated in the performance at a time when a ruthless new chapter in Australia's history of draconian immigration policies – indefinite onshore and offshore detention – had prompted detained asylum-seekers to similarly sew their eyes and mouths shut in protest.

Parr's prints were by contrast more obscure – political, yes, but never overtly so: they refused to be tied into the news cycle in any but the most oblique manner. Yet they too were confronting. Turmoil roiled the surface of each. The recurring images of Parr's face staring back at the viewer only served to underscore a feeling of psychic dread. Increasingly, they appeared to depict nothing less than the most unsettled manifestations of a self, breaching the mind's inner boundaries and tumbling into the world at large.

—

At first Parr would prepare the woodblocks in his Sydney studio and freight them down to Olinda, but as the unique-state works developed, he began to labour on them in Loane's studio.

It was a subtle but significant shift, one that drew Loane even closer to Parr's creative process. He would watch as Parr brushed out a guiding composition in ink, before clamping the block to a studio table, where the two of them would hack away at the linework with Stanley knife and chisel. Soon the process became more involved: driven by Parr's restless mind, one form of printmaking would come crashing into another. For a 2002 work titled *Introjection of a horse*, which showed a truncated head spewing forth a tangle of vaguely equine forms, Parr mopped a large pigment-laden brush over four wood panels. Instead of cutting the resulting linework away, as per a woodblock print, Loane meticulously traced it with glue, to which he applied abrasive carborundum dust, a little-used technique that enabled Parr's brushwork to be inked and printed as a positive impression. Just before the finished panels were printed one at a time, the two brushed a turpentine-thinned stain across the areas of raw wood that would otherwise have printed clean. It imparted a washy ground: 'blood-like', in Loane's conception.

At times, Parr still worked on plates in Sydney and sent them on to Loane's studio ahead of a visit. To quicken the process,

Loane took to proofing them and pinning the results to the wall before Parr's arrival. 'Mike would walk in the door, and he'd read an image in a flash, more or less: it was that quick. He'd say, "Fantastic. Take it down, let's get on with something else," or, "No, we have to work on that,"' Loane said.

Sometimes prints would gestate for long periods and would occasionally become overworked in the process. When this happened, they would be put away for later use, destined to eventually be cut up and reworked. But for the most part things were always urgent and immediate. The printmaking was adapted accordingly, becoming ever more attuned to the force of Parr's practice. Early on, he had used an angle grinder to carve out a series of smaller woodblocks, and he and Loane had inked up the resulting gouges and printed them like etchings. By doing that, they found they could get up to three images out of a block without re-inking, each slightly more depleted than the last (more conventional woodblocks, by contrast, are re-inked for each impression). Once again, a judiciously applied wash of coloured stain would cause the image to dissipate and bleed: perfect for the overarching tone of the work.

From then, Parr made the angle grinder something of a signature, later using it on copper plates, which the tool would dig out in deep grooves. The printing technique of 'dry-point' – which involves incising a drawing directly onto a plate and printing it without etching in acid – roughly captures the process, but does little to communicate the near-violence of it. Loane found it astonishing to watch Parr guiding the grinder to the metal surface with his truncated arm, sparks arcing as it made contact. 'When you see it, you'd swear, *Holy smoke! So that's how he lost his arm,*' Loane joked. 'But really he doesn't miss a trick: his concentration is phenomenal.'

Later, for a 2012 exhibition titled *Mike Parr: Brain Coral*, at the National Art School in Sydney, Parr created a work from twenty-four angle-grinder self-portraits he'd made in Loane's studio. Loane had moved with his partner to Canberra in 2006 and was in the final year of a six-year stint in a studio far smaller than in Olinda. He had cut the twenty-four plates down from larger sheets of copper that had previously been used for other works, and offered up what was once the verso for the new works. Reusing the material was partly about thrift – copper is expensive – but it was also perfectly in-step with Parr's idea that the self-portraits comprised a vast image bank. The repetition of what was held within was part of the point: as images recurred, they shifted and changed; disorder was the order of the day. Parr had brought with him an A4-sized rubber stamp he'd had made of one his self-portrait drawings, which he inked in white paint and pressed onto the plates. As Parr went, Loane re-inked the stamp as needed. The steady speed of his action added to the work's propulsive flow: some impressions pulled and smeared; others stamped cleanly. Once Parr had stamped all twenty-four plates, he took up his angle grinder, improvising in the moment a range of touches to roughly cut each portrait image into its metal ground.

Loane watched, but not for long. 'I just had to leave the room,' he said. 'It was a small space, and there was copper flying everywhere. But Mike did them in one hit: twenty-four of them with the angle grinder. Very precise: it's a wonderful work.'

—

Throughout their work together, Loane came to recognise Parr's keen sense of humour: he could be incredibly funny. From the earliest days in the studio, Parr displayed a deep feel for language that expressed itself in the titles he chose for his work – Loane particularly enjoyed the play of irony and ambivalence that seemed always to resolve into deadly seriousness. The series of twenty-four angle-grinder self-portraits titled *Brain Coral*, for instance, was subtitled *Recrudescence of a Head*. 'A phenomenal thought,' Loane said, laughing, 'just this brain that keeps growing in a horrible way!' One pictures unchecked thoughts solidifying together into clump-like growths, but the word 'recrudescence' – the re-emergence of undesirable behaviours or symptoms after a period of dormancy – immediately adds a darker touch.

Yet while words helped land the intent of finished works, in the studio everything was usually far more non-verbal. As far as Loane recalls, conversation was kept to the bare minimum. 'I just seem to have known what he needed to do,' Loane said. Often this meant working at a cracking pace: Parr urgently drawing, carving or grinding; Loane pulling proofs from the resulting plates in real time. Together they'd forged something that couldn't simply be understood as a friendship. The art historian Charles Green chose the title *The Third Hand* for his book about artistic collaboration. It may take on the contours of a bad pun in relation to Loane's work with the one-handed Parr, but it is nonetheless fitting. Green meant it to evoke the energy that can bloom unexpectedly between artists who work together, the way that their combined labours indelibly alter, even surpass, what they might do alone. This is not to suggest that Parr's work is also somehow Loane's. Far from it. 'All these developments just happen: some were his and some were mine,' Loane said, referring to the many unique methods and approaches they'd forged during their decades of shared work. 'But I think it's academic to start to break that down: the work is his, clearly.'

In the catalogue published to coincide with the *Brain Coral* exhibition, Parr explained how reassuring and calming Loane's presence in the studio often was. He used as an example his recently completed work *The Golden Age [Choking]*, a large composite print that began with a dominant, heavy, dry-point portrait of his father. To this he added a smaller and far gentler image of his brother Tim, who had died suddenly after a long struggle with alcoholism and mental illness two years before Parr created the work. It was a sensitive and difficult piece to complete: Tim's death had hit Parr hard. As he worked, technical challenges intertwined with complex family memories. Parr's mother had attended art school in the 1930s, but his father's view of art as useless and irrational had devalued it to such a degree that his mother had largely repressed her drive to create. As Parr put it, this 'made the idea of art, its threat perhaps, a very strong undercurrent in the family that was deeply implicated in the fears and social separation that the family imposed on itself' (the fact that Parr's sister Julie would also go on to become an acclaimed artist suggests that the repression was far from successful). By the time Loane arrived at Parr's Sydney studio to look at the plates in progress, Parr had added a ragged self-portrait that he initially saw as a kind of death's head, but which he came to understand more as 'a charred, abstracted tree trunk'. Looming over the whole composition was a 'peculiar scarecrow image' that Parr framed, in inverted commas, as 'family hysteria'. The pieces were there, but they had not yet settled into place.

Initially, Parr had incised the image of his father deeply into the plate, then used an orbital sander to partially bury it beneath a 'caul' of roughened metal – 'I rather liked the idea of the old man being reborn in this way,' he wrote. It was a tenuous moment: an act like that can easily go awry and the underlying image might be destroyed beyond recognition. Parr recalled Loane brushing his hand across the plate's surface and telling him that the sanded areas were 'terrific'. Little more was said, but Parr was reassured. Later, once Loane had proofed the plates in his

Canberra studio, Parr reworked them, seeking the right tension between the various image components. Loane quietly kept himself busy in the background until, once Parr had scraped back and re-drawn elements before finally pushing sandpaper blocks across his brother's image in a rhythmic subdual, it was done.

The work was full of difficult feeling – the kind of outpouring that as a viewer is hard to turn away from – but with Loane on hand its final passage was calmly deliberate. 'The key to our working relationship is this now well-established pattern of both being able to be interested at the same time,' Parr wrote in the catalogue for *Brain Coral*. 'It's an inspectorial, assessing quality. Something like the ruminations of a medical board.'

Loane made his own, far shorter, contribution in the same pages – an impressionistic, largely unpunctuated paragraph that attempted to capture in shorthand the vagrant energies of their creative relationship. 'You had to run with Mike's obsession straight out of the blocks,' he wrote. 'Do not second guess just make as you would and some excellent prints would be made.'

—

Loane's short text was titled 'The End of the Road', but although it quoted the final sentences of Cormac McCarthy's grim literary masterpiece *The Road* (2006), the choice was more than a simple pun.

By the time *Brain Coral* opened in 2012, the work that Loane and Parr had undertaken together was poised to enter a final, irrevocable phase. Prints had always formed a parallel thread to Parr's performance practice – no matter how each had inflected the other, they had for the most part remained materially separate. This changed in 2015, when Parr presented a solo exhibition at Anna Schwartz Gallery's grandly scaled Sydney space. Titled

Deep North, the exhibition brought together two photographic works alongside a sequence of six unique-state prints. One, called *Foreign Looking*, measured more than three by five metres, and was constructed of a grid of murky, clouded etchings that formed a ground for two obscure logo-like forms. For Loane, it was one of two 'masterpieces' in the exhibition, a kind of pinnacle of their work together, the ambition and scale of which had been enabled partly by Loane's move to a warehouse-sized studio in the industrial Canberra suburb of Mitchell. But if Parr had once shared this enthusiasm, it was no longer the case. By the time the works were installed in the gallery he'd gone cold on them, even come to resent them: they seemed to represent a dead end, an expression of an artist he didn't want to be. Some had already sold for as much as $100,000, but, as Parr told *The Sydney Morning Herald* a year later, his impulse was clear: 'I've got to get rid of this stuff.'

The decision wasn't easy, but once it was made, a new performance began to take shape in Parr's mind. He decided that, on 25 August at 5.00 pm – the last day of the exhibition's two-week run – he would systematically obliterate each of the six large-scale prints. This would be achieved by painting over them in red paint, one by one.

On the appointed day, with the help of a wheeled ladder, he would do exactly this. He chose as an accompaniment a soundtrack of a Chinese choir singing the communist anthems 'The East is Red' and 'The Internationale', as if the act were a riff on the collective amnesias of nation-building and history-making.

Although he didn't alert Parr of his intention to attend, Loane was there. 'It was difficult for me,' he said, with what by the time we spoke seemed studied understatement. He meant it was hard to see works like that disappear – that it was almost as if he himself were being obliterated, erased, hidden by the rough red strokes of Parr's brush. But he also meant it in terms of Parr's manner.

'It's just the decisive way he announces these things, and virtually unapologetically: *I'm going to paint them out.* But that's how he is. I completely understood why he wanted to do it. I think. It was shocking, but I understood the idea.'

Beforehand, Loane had entertained a kind of counter-action of his own: stepping out unannounced from the crowd of spectators and positioning himself wordlessly between Parr and the works, a protestor putting his own body on the line. He imagined his point would have been forceful and clear: *Paint over me too!* But he didn't do it – partly because he felt Parr would have gone ahead and painted over him without missing a beat, but partly, one suspects, for the simple reason that as painful as it was to witness the destruction, he inherently trusted the precision of Parr's creative judgement, just as he always had.

Either way, there was little choice: as integral to the creative process as Loane had become, the driving force of the work was Parr's, and always had been. Now, after almost three decades, that force was directing Parr elsewhere. The following year he would lay a grid of 120 smaller prints – mainly unsold editions from early in his work with Loane – across a concrete car park, cover them with fuel and ritually set fire to them; a subsequent exhibition would comprise solely of paintings. Another large-scale unique-state work would also be painted over, this time in black. When in 2016 Parr was honoured with the largest career survey of a living artist ever staged by the National Gallery of Australia, examples of his work with Loane recurred throughout, but it was those Parr had overpainted into large monochrome fields that occupied the final galleries. Few viewers would have been truly aware of the shared labour that underlay their surfaces.

So even as Loane imagined disrupting Parr's 2015 performance, he knew he wouldn't. Instead, he stood there listening to the swelling clamour of the soundtrack as Parr set about his work.

It would add to a growing disconnection between the two, which would in turn lead to a complete professional and personal estrangement. But Loane couldn't help but marvel at the surprising physicality of it: Parr – the artist who had so indelibly shaped Loane's own creative life – labouring away with the big brush, climbing up and down the ladder as each vast print slowly but surely disappeared under its new red coat.

Loane left before the performance's end, but Parr of course kept at it, his focus as fierce and unwavering as ever.

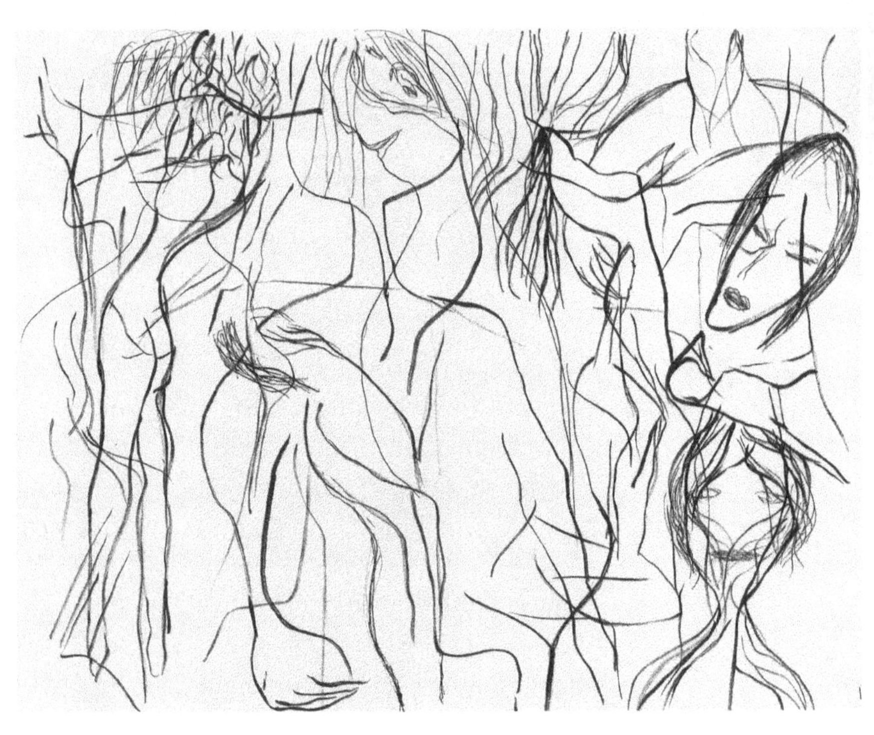

Ken Whisson *A part of the forest* 2006

4

Yes, Google Knew Immediately

The artist died only a year after he and I first met. He lived alone, and one day – no one is sure exactly which – hc simply dropped to the floor of his kitchen. He was ninety-four, but death, it seems, was sudden. There are many horror stories of elderly people lying in pain after a fall, unable to move, but although he hit his head on the way down, it was likely that by then he was already gone. It was the kind of thing that doctors refer to as a 'catastrophic medical event', by which they mean that life was gone as quickly as a light being flicked off: movement and thought one moment, the next nothing at all.

Did I know him well enough to say, as people so often do when someone elderly dies at home while still enjoying some level of independence, that it was the way he would have wanted to go?

Yes and no.

Yes, because that was clear to me, even though we'd only really met in person four or five times. It was clear because even at a casual glance one could see how much he valued his independence. Although famously retiring when it came to anything approaching the social machinations of the art world, he was by then one of the most respected painters in the country. His practice traced more than seven decades of Australian art, and his reputation among a certain small but influential coterie of fellow artists, collectors and afficionados had reached cult-like status. To meet him was to understand that independence in both art and life was for him the kcy.

It coursed through his wiry frame, which verged on bird-like, and glittered in his eyes, as if threatening to overspill. You didn't even need to know anything at all about his paintings, which he somehow gathered far from the edge of the conventional world, and which were as a result about as unconventional and independent as one might imagine, to see it. You didn't even need to know he was an artist. In fact, I'm sure if you'd passed him in the street at any point in his final years, perhaps as he made his weekly trip by mobility scooter to the supermarket – his long snow-white hair blowing unkempt and wisp-thin, his face so determined and proud (even, dare I say, set with a touch of arrogance that you likely wouldn't realise at a glance was hard-won and thus completely justified) – you would have thought something like this: there's a man who wants to die at home alone, independent as ever.

When he died, he was about as old as someone might hope to be. The beautiful thing was not just that he was painting to the very end, but that he was painting with a full grasp of the skills he'd honed over a lifetime. He still constantly surprised himself with the unexpected things that could emerge from his brush. This is what mattered.

—

On one of my first visits to his spartan Sydney home and studio – a two-bedroom 1970s flat tucked among the far older apartment blocks of harbourside Elizabeth Bay – I brought along images of a sketchbook of his from 1968.

It was June 2021, midway through the Covid pandemic, which the artist referred to with some relish as 'the plague', and we hadn't been talking long. I hoped the sketchbook would provide a prompt. He had made it during travels in Morocco and Spain, and in 1975 it was purchased by the National Gallery of Australia, where it can now be accessed online: one can look through its pages – there's less than twenty – and, if desired, print them. This is what I've done:

printed the images of his half-century-old sketches and brought them with me.

What do the drawings show?

They show the kind of thing to which the artist's eye was then attracted – for the most part little more than glimpses – but what overall picture they offer is at best fleeting. There are forms I take to be cloaked figures, their faces shadowed to blackness under wide-brimmed hats. But look again and they could equally be piles of clothing in a market, or even views of far-off mountains, the sides of which are folded and creased, and therefore only look like clothes and hats stacked messily, one on top of the other.

Another image shows a dog-like form of the abbreviated kind recognisable from the artist's later paintings; yet another, a tree line in the distance, rendered in black ink on cream-coloured paper. What is a drawing but something fleetingly observed, a memory recorded that would otherwise be lost?

My eye goes to a recurrent form, something between a plant gourd and a multi-stemmed vessel. It could be a seedpod, I think, or the root stem of some tuber, or even a wind instrument made from clay. On the back cover the artist has jotted the price of drawing paper and canvas in Tangier, and the address of a gallery in Paris that no longer exists: *Rue de Seine – Gallery Raymond Duncan – Open Saturday evening 5 or 6.*

I hand the artist the printed pages, and he leafs through them slowly.

'I don't know if they're drawn from memory, or directly from the subject,' he says uncertainly.

He keeps leafing.

'That's imagination,' he says, tapping an image of unarticulated forms that disperse across the picture frame. But once again he doesn't seem at all sure.

He stops, taps another. Recognition. 'Oh, that's obviously done in the little place I was living in.' This one – a pen-and-ink drawing only slightly less abbreviated than the others – consists of a handful of loose vertical and horizontal lines that sketch the interior of a room: here is where the floor meets the wall; there is where the wall meets the ceiling. The wall is broken by the deep aperture of a window; the floor, by a shallow step. There are three vases – one holding a branch of flowers – and two cats that seem to be suspended in mid-air, as if added after the fact, and with total disregard for the image beneath; one sits cleaning itself, its back legs splayed. Outside the window are the tiered stacks of apartment blocks, and a sky crossed by powerlines. The whole scene clearly took just moments for the artist to catch on paper, but it's enough for the viewer to fill in the gaps: the simple accommodations, the window-sectioned view from above the crowded city, the vertical cluster of houses. There are stray cats drowsing in the sun, and sounds rushing in from the open window.

Now the artist thinks back to that room, held almost irretrievably distant by the passage of more than five decades.

'At my age you can't remember back that far,' he says. 'You don't remember so very much with clarity – you don't. You can have vague memories of that place, and vague memories of moments there – when this happened, and that happened, and the other thing happened – but not details of the place.'

He speaks haltingly, and continues looking at the picture, more amused than perplexed.

'I remember there being quite a bit of space there – there was a bedroom, a moderately large bedroom, and a moderately large kitchen.'

In 1984 the artist sat for a long interview with a well-known poet, who was hard at work capturing the memories of those who'd been close to the birth of Australian modernism. Back then the experiences of those travels were much closer to him, the memories denser. He would recall for her the kind of things that would seep into his paintings – either from Tangier or Marrakesh – for decades after his time there: musicians drumming at the edge of the labyrinthine city centre, the rhythms of the music, the clowns and jugglers performing on the street. I'll remind him of this, and many of these things will briefly return to him, along with the memory of acrobats who, although clearly stoned on hashish, managed to pull off the most daring feats.

But for now most of that has left him: dispersed into his drawings and paintings, mostly as unattributed glimpses combined with other unattributed glimpses of other places and other memories. For now, sitting in his simple flat – removed from Morocco by half a century – this is what he musters: a memory of how, to access the three or four rooms he was staying in, he had to first signal a gatekeeper, who would unlock the gate onto a long external staircase. He would then climb all the way to the top, past what he can now only assume were other rooms, and other people, until he reached his own quarters. The drawing I've brought – the one with the cat, and the view to the city outside – shows what waited for him there.

—

Later, once our conversation is done for that day, I find myself thinking about the nature of memory, about how, as much as the past might appear to us like some smooth spool of fabric, it is in fact made as much from gaps and omissions as anything like verifiable fact.

I think of what I recall of my own life, and of my travels in Italy when I was twenty. I think of this because I had vaguely hoped to cross the Mediterranean to Tunisia, Algiers and then Morocco, but never did. As I write, those experiences in Italy are two decades in the past, and I find them, if not as fleeting as the artist's sparse recollections, then surprisingly thin: sequences of bright images linked by passages of near-complete absence.

What had drawn me, I wonder, to visit the island of Sardinia for what could have been a handful of days, or a number of weeks? What itinerary had I followed – what line had my movements sketched across the island? When I arrived in Cagliari, was I with a friend, or alone?

Either way, in the two memories that most readily return to me, I am travelling solo. I sense that it was at the end of what time I spent there: I was poised to board a ferry to the mainland in the coming days. The first thing I recall is a tumble of Roman-era ruins in the city centre, reached from cobbled streets by wide stone stairs. I discovered it at night and was impressed not simply because the ruins were so old, but because they were still alive: there was recent graffiti on the walls, and an outdoors café at the top where a DJ was playing.

The other memory is simpler still: I went to see wild flamingoes in the salt marshes near the beach. I recall it was close to the city's outer limits, but far enough away for me to now wonder how I got there, and whether or not I walked around there, or simply stood and looked.

The flamingoes were a much softer pink than I'd imagined. Of this I am certain.

—

The artist called me a few days later. It was a Sunday afternoon, and he wanted to thank me for prompting him to remember Morocco, which in turn prompted him to recall his travels in

Spain. 'It's nice, lying there at night as I go to sleep, remembering things I haven't thought of forever.'

Over the phone he recalls his visit to Toledo, which he thinks must have come in the weeks or months after Tangier. He tells me in the broadest of strokes how he searched out the beautiful works by the master painter El Greco, who for much of his life lived there by the banks of the Tagus River. El Greco's paintings moved the artist more than three centuries after their creation: the softly brushed groups of elongated figures reaching for the heavens, the emaciated saints, the lace-collared self-portraits on sepulchral grounds.

After viewing them, he went on to Barcelona, where he was similarly moved by Gaudí's turreted architecture. But it was Toledo that would lodge in his mind as a particularly magical place. When he first visited, it was yet to be marred by the rising development – the rings of factories and outer suburbs – that for him was evidence not of progress but of regression: the industrial complex, which he despised, reaching even the most beautiful of places.

But he tells me not to worry about that, at least not for now. 'It's just nice to remember,' he says in his declarative, slightly abrupt manner. 'That's all.'

On another phone call soon after, he tells me he's just finished a painting, and he'll now take a week or two off. He says it's a painting of a car, but that no one would recognise it as such. He painted cars near constantly, especially for a period in the 1970s, when they marked the beginning of a loose theme. Back then they were crumpled, ungainly things set against simple landscapes. When writing about the artist's work, critics still comment on the fact that he chose to paint cars: that the landscape for him was something always touched by human habitation. It came at a time when his contemporaries were making their names with a new take on the old Australian standard: the unpeopled landscape, beautiful, vast, at times underscored with a touch of menace. *Domestic Machine* was the perfect title he gave one of those early paintings. 'No one thinks I still paint cars,' he tells me. 'But I do.'

At first he's dismissive of the new work. He suggests it's a simple thing, even 'dumb'. I press him on that, as I'm drawn to the idea of a 'dumb' painting, at least in terms of something that can't speak, rather than something that has little or no intelligence. One of the qualities that draws me to paintings is exactly that: they are mute things, but communicate nonetheless. The mode of this communication – the way they can describe feelings and memories and scenes in fine detail – is mysterious, even if it appears to be simple.

But the artist quickly walks back his initial assessment, and instead takes the opposite position entirely. 'No, no, it's a complex thing,' he says of the new painting. His tone suggests self-admonishment. 'It's like a piece of music for a string quartet. If you can imagine the sound of all the instruments playing at once, if you can picture that as musical notation, that's what it is: a complex thing.'

I later realise that this too is a theme in his work, and whether it has recently emerged or not, it has threaded together the artist's recent paintings in a way that causes them to stand out amid his oeuvre. On another visit, just before the pandemic once again renders Sydney inaccessible to me, he introduces the idea of *passacaglia*. This is what he means by musical notation – this particular form, which originated in seventeenth-century Spain, and is used for dense, seriously toned pieces written in triple metre.

I search on the internet for an example of the notation of passacaglia and find one easily: it is marked by dense clusters of ascending and descending notes. It pictures a great volume of sound; a swelling and receding, a swelling again. The word is of course Italian, which is why the artist – who moved to Italy on a whim in the late 1970s and settled for nearly four decades in the northern city of Perugia – pronounces it with such evident pleasure. But there's another reference, too, and it's in this reference that the artist's thinking on the matter of cars and musical composition draws into focus. It comes from Henry Miller's 1945 collection of essays and stories, *The Air-Conditioned Nightmare*, and, in particular, from a comic essay contained within titled 'Automotive Passacaglia'.

Miller's book is a brief masterwork of that particularly modernist concern with the ways in which machines seduce us into seeing the world anew. It provides a loose account of his travels across America in the early 1940s in a used 1932 Buick coupé. Miller had only just learnt to drive, but he was compelled upon his journey by the oft-heard claim that the only way to see America is by automobile: 'It's not true,' he writes, 'but it sounds wonderful.'

In the essay, Miller waits at a service station in rural Albuquerque as a mechanic works on his car with the opaque authority of a surgeon. Miller gazes upon its engine, transfixed: 'It was the first time I'd ever seen what makes a car go. It was rather beautiful, in a mechanical way. Reminded me of a steam calliope playing Chopin in a tub of grease.' The whole thing remains mysterious to him, but he clearly prefers it that way.

Elsewhere, while stopped in Ohio, Miller thinks about cars in far less positive terms – their seductive qualities, he realises, veil something much darker. 'The automobile stands out in my mind as the very symbol of falsity and illusion,' he writes. 'There they are, thousands upon thousands of them, in such profusion that it would seem as if no man were too poor to own one.' He thinks that people less fortunate than the average mid-century American might look with wonder at such a proliferation, as if it spoke directly of a land of plenty – a veritable paradise – but they'd be wrong:

'They don't see the bitterness in the heart, the skepticism, the cynicism, the emptiness, the despair, the hopelessness which is eating up the American worker.'

So it is that the artist's paintings of cars are revealed as further proof of his preoccupation with what he'd memorably termed on our very first phone call 'the ugly face of the world'. In his flat he shows me the recent painting he'd referred to on the phone as 'dumb'. He tells me that he has now decided to title it *Automotive Passacaglia*: 'If it's good enough for Miller, it's good enough for me,' he says as he turns the painting away from the wall against which it leans among a few others.

Like all his recent work, the painting is relatively small. Its background is provided by the white primed canvas; the scene he has daubed and smeared upon it is green and brown and blue, with high points of red and yellow. It's anchored by two chairs, both standing empty on a russet-red ground. There is a yellow bird – rendered as a flurry of pointed movement – and the vertical slashes of eucalyptus trees, their oversized, teardrop-shaped leaves drifting downward.

At the top are four cars, clustered together. The artist explains that the whole thing is intentionally backwards, with the bird flying up towards the cars, which appear to float mid-air. The eucalyptus leaves are far bigger than they would be in real life, but this is the point of them: they cascade through the picture plane like descending notes.

He had just been telling me of concerts he used to attend in Perugia, so the theme of music is already hanging between us. The concerts were performed in an old church, and a musician the artist had watched play there once told him how difficult it was to perform under the gaze of whatever centuries-old religious icon hung behind the altar. Whether it was there or somewhere else he saw 'the famous Russian pianist' whose name eludes him is unclear, but that memory immediately rises up.

'Do you know the one I mean?' he asks, frustrated at his faltering recall. 'The one who broke it all apart, who decided the early Beethoven must be played in the same way as the late Beethoven? With the same passion and energy and violence?'

I do not, but not to worry; he continues, nonetheless. The famous Russian pianist looked like a crazed peasant as he stalked his way across the stage, all wild hair and fierce demeanour. 'He refused to do an encore, like he didn't care for such things,' the artist says, making for emphasis a dismissive sound on the pianist's behalf. 'Just walked off – but brilliant, bloody brilliant.'

Later, the artist will send me a rare text message: *Yes, Google knew immediately: Sviatoslav Richter.* I'll look at Richter's photograph on the internet and see how accurate the artist's description of the pianist was.

Soon the pandemic will once again close the border to me, and, although I don't know it then, I won't ever see the artist again. For a time our conversations will continue over the phone, ranging ever more freely. We'll touch on everything from daily Covid case numbers to Osama bin Laden, Seymour Hersh and *Harry Potter*: pretty much everything, that is, except painting – from that subject he always moves on quickly, as if talking about it for too long or in too much detail risks ruining its true pleasures. And then, one evening a mutual friend will call to say that the artist is dead.

But before any of that we stand together in his bare-bones flat and look at the painting of cars.

They no longer look like the cars of his early paintings, which were angular and fractured. The new ones are long and ropey – they stretch out across the canvas in muscular, sleek shapes, far more human than machine.

They're perfect, I tell him. Just perfect.

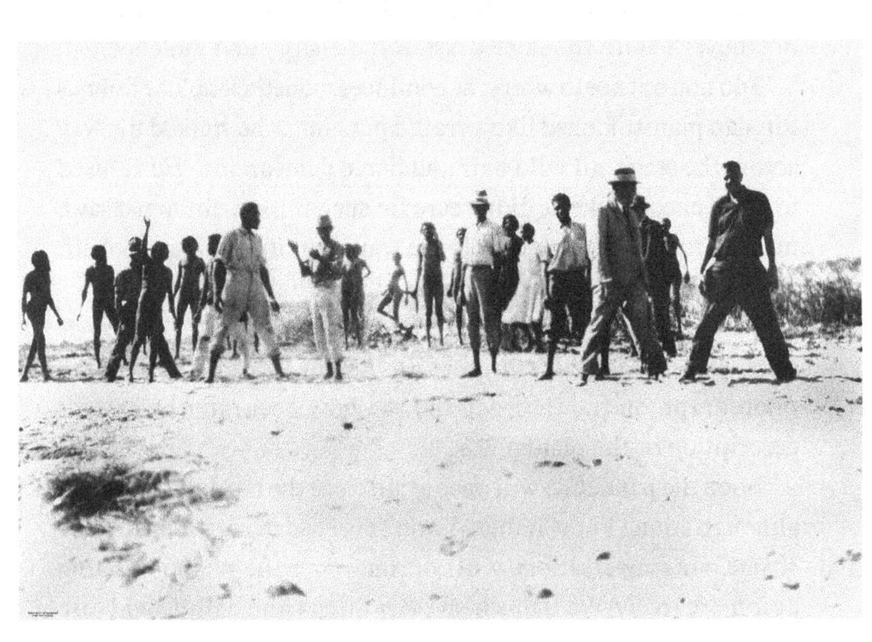

Gathering on Bentinck Island 1934

5

The Extraordinary Mrs Gabori

It was in early September 2014 that I met with the linguist Nicholas Evans at the Australian National University. I was seeking to find out more about an artist who had recently caught my attention and not let go: the Kaiadilt Elder Mirdidingkingathi Juwarnda, a painter then aged somewhere in her early nineties who was known more commonly in the art world as Sally Gabori. Evans, who had forged a significant reputation for his decades-long work with the Kaiadilt people, reportedly knew her story well. He welcomed me to his office warmly, if a little distractedly. It was just past six and outside the window an early spring day, crisp and clear, was slowly fading towards evening; over the course of our conversation, the book-filled room would darken around us.

I already knew the broad contours of Gabori's story: she had lived much of her life on Mornington Island, part of a tiny scatter of islands known as the Wellesley group in the southern region of the Gulf of Carpentaria, and had burst onto the art scene less than a decade prior. Her star had risen rapidly: within just months of her bright, discordant and apparently abstract paintings first being exhibited in 2005, some commentators were already hailing her as a genius. The intervening years had seen her achieve the kind of sustained visibility, not to mention market success, that most Australian artists can only dream of. Evans had watched it all, from time to time offering what interpretation he could. It was he, for instance, who first explained to the art world that Gabori's Kaiadilt name identified both the place of her birth – a site on Bentinck Island, the smallest and furthest-flung of the Wellesley group – and her totemic ancestor, the dolphin. In this way, it rooted her identity in place, intoning each time it was spoken a message at one with her art: *This is my Country, this is me. The two are indivisible.*

To understand this is to understand something fundamental about Gabori herself. In the late 1940s the Kaiadilt – a young Gabori among them – had been compelled by Presbyterian missionaries to leave Bentinck for the mission settlement on Mornington. It was a short yet treacherous trip, and would prove akin to exile: a return wouldn't be made for some four decades, and even then would only be partial. When Gabori first picked up a paintbrush, it was to Bentinck – flat, near featureless to the foreign eye, and fringed by a loose patterning of oyster-encrusted reefs and ancient stonewalled fish traps – that her mind immediately returned. When one looks at her paintings, which are most often large and loosely executed, this is what one sees: a particular reef glimpsed through the waters; a deep channel that flows towards the ocean's depths; the great cursive loops of the stone fish traps cutting through the island's littoral edges like some functional version of American sculptor Robert Smithson's famous *Spiral Jetty*. Look at an aerial view of Bentinck and, although the colours are far more subdued than in Gabori's paintings, the forms are all there.

Evans, speaking with the careful yet contagious intensity of a career academic whose true passion lies in fieldwork, explained how he first met Gabori when he arrived as a graduate student on Mornington in the early 1980s. The two hadn't been close, at least not initially. 'The irony is that I've turned into something of an interpreter for Sally's art,' he said. 'But because of the way the kinship system works I was at first given a certain role, and she was my mother-in-law, which meant that under the tribal system I couldn't speak to her.'

Even without this barrier, the two might not have spent much time together. Their initial encounters left Evans with the impression of a quiet and self-effacing woman, and in the early days of his fieldwork there was a large group of far more voluble Kaiadilt Elders from whom he began to learn the intricacies of their language, Kayardilt. By the time he began visiting regularly, they had carved out their own distinct space alongside Mornington's two other tribal groups: the Lardil, for whom Mornington Island provided an ancestral home, and the Yangkaal, from nearby Forsyth Island, which was close enough for the two groups to be partially governed by shared kinship and obligation. By contrast, the relative distance of Bentinck Island had historically isolated the Kaiadilt from all but the most fleeting – and often violent – intertribal encounters: on their arrival on Mornington they were widely seen as outsiders of fierce reputation and were at first generally shunned. In coming decades many would marry within their new community, but the distinctive status of the first wave of Kaiadilt to arrive would nonetheless endure. Eventually, they established their own satellite encampment: 'A little enclave of eight or nine humpies on the beach,' Evans recalled.

This was on Mornington's southern shore, facing across the water towards Bentinck. I would later come across an old photograph of the camp: a handful of ruptured-looking tin structures set among sand and low-hanging acacias; groups of old men and women seated cross-legged around cooking fires. 'I think they felt the severing from Country very profoundly,' Evans said. 'But my first impression when I got there was just of this incredible liveliness: totally ribald, outrageous humour; incredible emotional directness.' He would come to understand that he was lucky that his first professional engagement with Aboriginal Australia came via the Kaiadilt: 'Some communities can take years and years to get into,' he said. 'But there, you were just in.'

Over the following years, Evans worked away, drawing on ever-strengthening bonds. He learnt Kayardilt and compiled a grammar of the language for his doctoral thesis. In 1995 he published his research as a book; a Kayardilt dictionary followed soon after. As with many linguists and anthropologists of his generation, he also turned his newfound expertise back towards where he'd forged it. He worked alongside the Kaiadilt on a successful Native Title claim for Bentinck Island (it was transferred to the group in 1992), and then on a related sea claim. Those tasks required he interview the older women for genealogies, and in this way he stepped directly into Gabori's orbit. 'Whitefella rules crept in,' he would later write in *The Australian*, 'and we were able to converse.'

But one era was moving into the next. As Evans flew back and forth between Mornington and the mainland, the years began to unfurl into decades, and the ranks of Kaiadilt Elders thinned considerably. During his initial time there, he'd heard Kayardilt spoken all around him – as many as forty-five people were fluent, their social nucleus the beach encampment presided over by the ribald old women and handful of old men. All that was soon gone. When he and I met, I asked Evans the fraught question of how many truly fluent speakers of Kayardilt remained. 'Four or five,' he said, among which he was counting Gabori and himself. She would pass away a few months later.

—

Evans wasn't the first outsider drawn to study the Kaiadilt; nor would he be the last. His first years on Mornington came only a decade after a psychiatrist called John Cawte undertook a series of short-stay assessments and published a study on the mental health of the island's Aboriginal population. He titled it *Cruel, Poor and Brutal Nations*, after Dutch explorer Jan Carstensz's questionable assessment of a group, wrongly thought by some to have been Kaiadilt, that he came across when he passed through the region in 1623.

The picture Cawte painted of the Kaiadilt is bleak. He goes so far as to characterise them as the 'sickest' among the community, by which he meant the group most impacted by the degradations of colonisation. 'It is the little Kaiadilt nation,' he wrote, 'that exemplifies the extremes of rapid exposure to Western influence, ecological hazards, social disintegration, and mental disorder.'

The description stands in contrast to Evans's recollections – the warmth and conviviality of the beach enclave, the raucous humour of the old women – and suggests that the fleeting nature of Cawte's short-stay visits blinded him to deeper currents of social cohesion (during our conversation, Evans went as far as characterising Cawte's conclusions as 'bullshit'). But the darker legacies of contact and settlement brought to bear upon the people of Mornington – not just the Kaiadilt, but the Lardil and Yangkaal too – have nonetheless been well documented, perhaps most compellingly in the bluntly titled 2002 book *From Hunting to Drinking*, by another outsider drawn to Mornington Island, the British anthropologist David McKnight.

I first came across *From Hunting to Drinking* during my own two-year residence on another far-flung northern Australian island: Melville Island, one of two that make up the Tiwi Islands, which lie fifty kilometres north of Darwin. I moved there in 2007 to work in the northern Aboriginal art industry, drawn by a mixture of curiosity and naivety, and was quickly confronted by the stark fallout of Australia's colonial legacy: for the Tiwi people, crippling rates of suicide, domestic violence and alcoholism formed this legacy's most insidious and prominent features. Those things were a seemingly indelible part of daily life. Although specific to Mornington Island, the broad contours of McKnight's book – the transformation he traces from the complex ecological and spiritual demands of a hunter-gatherer society to one shaped by the social freefall of post-mission settlement – placed my own experiences, if not in full context, then at least in a far clearer light. As it had been for the Tiwi, McKnight describes how colonialism had been cataclysmic for the people of Mornington; its impact had metastasised through generations and could now be measured in any number of dire statistics: health, education, life expectancy. Against this backdrop, McKnight introduces the Kaiadilt and recounts their troubled history of contact in some detail. It is a story fraught with violence and distrust.

McKnight recounts that early visitors to Bentinck Island, both Aboriginal and non-Aboriginal, were often attacked, and sometimes killed. This, he explains, is what led to the Kaiadilt's reputation as 'fierce'. But the violence cut both ways, likely tracing as far back as skirmishes with Macassan traders bound for the northern Australian coast. In the early part of last century, the resulting distrust of outsiders had proven particularly fitting when it came to Europeans: the Gulf Country of northwest Queensland was an infamously lawless and violent part of Australia's frontier, and although the Kaiadilt were isolated on their island, they too were subject to its ravages. This delivered the most horrific consequences when a white pastoralist by the name of John McKenzie was granted a partial government lease on the southern side of Bentinck in 1911. He was later implicated in a massacre that left some eleven Kaiadilt dead, including children – a number that was estimated at the time to comprise 10 per cent of their population. McKnight recounts that when Queensland's Chief Protector of Aborigines, John William Bleakley, briefly visited the island in 1915, he noted that 'reports were received that skeletons had been found with what appeared to be bullet holes'. Nothing was done.

By 1941 Reverend J.B. McCarthy was leading a concerted effort to lure the remaining Kaiadilt away from what he referred to in his journals as their 'dark island', by which of course he meant their deeply held ancestral territories. McKnight includes excerpts from McCarthy's journals in *From Hunting to Drinking*. They chart a slow sequence of contact extending over a two-year period beginning in 1945 and eased all the way by an energetic Yangkaal man known as 'Gully Peter', who had long been inculcated to mission life.

The final push appears to have come in the form of a freak spring tide that inundated low-lying land throughout the Gulf and Torres Strait. It contaminated much-needed spring water on Bentinck, rendering it undrinkable. By October 1948, the last of the Kaiadilt had either boarded the mission launch for Mornington or been 'rounded up' by mainland police and taken to Burketown. Their long exile had begun.

In what Reverend McCarthy took as an effort to assimilate more fully with the existing population of Lardil and Yangkaal, the men burnt off their beards, but the impact of their move was nonetheless pronounced. For a period, no Kaiadilt child born on Mornington would survive; when they did, not one would learn the intricate tongue of their forebears.

—

McKnight arrived for his first period of fieldwork, his wife and children in tow, in 1966 – the same year that the Kaiadilt established the beach encampment that would later be so important to Nicholas Evans's early experiences on the island.

It was the final decade of mission life; its patterns had been set and were generally maintained. McKnight's research, which initially underpinned his thesis for University College London, at first unfolded in a relatively peaceful environment: the influence of the Elders remained strong, and decision-making still lay, at least partly, in the hands of a community council. It was the seismic shifts that he experienced when he returned just over a decade later, in 1977, that would provide the impetus for his book.

The mission had by then almost fully wound down – it would be disbanded for good a year later. In step, administrative control was ceded to a shire council, part of a network set up by the Joh Bjelke-Petersen government to help secure mining interests across the state's remote regions, particularly Aurukun, which boasted valuable bauxite reserves. Decision-making was taken out of community hands, and almost entirely outsourced to a revolving cast of non-Aboriginal bureaucrats. Further compounding this shift was the fact that the generation raised in the mission's dormitories had effectively been cut off from traditional practices. McKnight viewed this, along with the mission's practice of sending young community members to work on the mainland for extended periods, as a significant cause of the community's later social tensions. He argued that it constituted nothing less than a theft of identity, by which he meant a theft of the deeply held meaning that had once guided and shaped all relations.

Another devastating change had soon crashed headlong into the resulting void: the opening of a 'wet canteen' – a pub by any other name – in 1976. The island's post-mission order was tenuous, and the ready availability of alcohol only eroded it further. In 1982 the community was officially renamed Gununa, an alternative term for the Lardil language, but the symbolism of this act was offset by the new reality of the place. For many, drinking had become a way of life. Murder and suicide, both previously almost unheard of in the community, quickly reached epidemic proportions.

In documenting this shift, McKnight included a blunt statistic to underscore just how dire the canteen's impact was. During the sixty-four years of the mission's operation, there had only been one internally perpetrated murder; in the 1980s alone there were six, and in the 1990s seven, by which time the risk of a Mornington Islander being murdered was twenty-five times higher than nearly anywhere else in Queensland.

It only got worse. Over two months in 2000, five young Mornington Island men took their own lives. Three years later, an alcohol management program that was being rolled out in nineteen Queensland communities was met with stubborn resistance – police reinforcements were sent from Cairns to help quell the resulting unrest. A critical mass of community support finally forced the canteen's closure five years later, but a thriving black market – buoyed by locally produced moonshine – soon took its place.

This is the context in which Sally Gabori first started painting, and in which her star so quickly rose. McKnight, who died in Rome in 2006, likely heard nothing of Gabori's rise to prominence, but Nicholas Evans was watching closely. He found the whole thing unbelievable. Although he arrived after McKnight and had not witnessed the mission years, he knew the more recent ravages of Mornington life well. He recalled during our conversation in Canberra that patrons at the canteen had initially been limited to four cans of beer each, but this had soon changed. 'It just went up and up and up. The whole thing just exploded,' he said. 'By the mid-eighties it was horrendous.' Gabori was among a wider group of old Kaiadilt, most of whom abstained from alcohol. He recalled the women in particular – 'the classic women in the family, past the age of being too wild; holding it together'. It almost goes without saying that, like nearly everyone else, he never expected Gabori to so suddenly become a nationally renowned artist.

'I think it's a giant mystery, almost a religious mystery, what happened with Sally,' he said. 'If you were to ask me on my deathbed, *What are the three or four things in your life that totally baffled you and bowled you over?* That would be one of them.'

—

The only time I met Gabori had come a month before my conversation with Evans. Memories of our brief encounter had been clear in my mind as he and I talked over her story.

I'd flown into Gununa from Cairns. The tiny plane had stopped in the sun-blasted town of Normanton before skipping across the strait and descending towards Mornington Island's mangrove-fringed beaches just as a late afternoon sun bathed everything in a brief, golden light.

Although the community was new to me, much was familiar about my arrival. During the time I'd spent on the Tiwi Islands, I had flown back and forth between Darwin and the Tiwi community of Milikapiti numerous times: that passage had also crossed a glittering expanse of flat ocean before tracking similarly mangrove-fringed country below. There had also been the same vertiginous dip as the plane – usually nothing larger than a ten-seater – swung over a grid of housing, and down towards a roughly sealed airstrip where a handful of outgoing passengers were waiting in the heat.

I crossed the tarmac and entered the open-sided shed that served as a makeshift arrivals and departures lounge. Nearby, a faded sign advertised *Aboriginal and Islanders Artifacts – Nulla Nulla, Boomerang, Clap Stick, Spears, Painted Shells, etc.* An arrow pointed towards the low, red concrete bunker that lay little more than 100 metres past the airstrip's cyclone-wire fencing, which served as the Mirndiyan Gununa Art Centre. It was that small organisation's then CEO, Brett Evans (no relation to Nicholas Evans), who met me.

Brett Evans, who I'd only ever spoken to briefly on the phone, was a wary-seeming long-time resident – not the kind of idealistic young Aboriginal-arts worker I was more familiar with, and which I had once been myself. He was bald and sun-desiccated, and wraparound sunglasses hid his eyes – he might have been in his fifties or sixties, it was hard to tell. I would soon learn that he'd lived in Gununa for three decades and was married to a local Lardil woman; he'd first worked as a schoolteacher before cycling through a run of local positions that eventually led him to the art centre.

We climbed into his four-wheel drive and rumbled through the town's dusty outer streets. The art centre, Evans explained as he dropped me off at the simple workers' accommodation I'd booked before my arrival, was closed for the day, but he'd expect me there sometime in the morning.

As evening fell, I sat on the thin porch of my demountable and looked out across the strait. The sun was setting. I listened as the dry-season winds that had once brought Macassan traders to the northern reaches of the Gulf whistled and howled through the flimsy eaves, a sound that would persist for much of the night.

The next day I arrived at the art centre a little before 9.00am, where I was greeted by a small group of Gabori's family. We made our way to the old people's home where Gabori lived: me; her youngest son, Maxwell; and four of her daughters, Elsie, Dorothy, Helena, and Amanda, who had her own grandson, LeBron, in tow. En route in the art centre minibus, they explained that Gabori had outlived four of her eleven children and was matriarch of an extended family that included twenty-six great-grandchildren. 'She's like royalty,' Dorothy told me with a smile.

At the home Gabori appeared, unsteady on her feet and holding onto the arm of a white nurse. She joined us at a table in the sun and sat in near silence as the impromptu reunion flowed around her. Aside from the tall cyclone-wire fence and an imposing automated gate, our surrounds struck me as relatively idyllic – a few ancient-looking figures sat listlessly in the shade, while beside us a sprinkler lazily coaxed the parched grass to turn green. From time to time

Gabori leaned over to Elsie and spoke a quiet phrase or two, but her limited English clearly made conversation with even her close family difficult. Although her daughters did what they could to mediate, my own attempts met with little traction.

Perhaps sensing the impasse, Elsie stepped in. 'We are very thankful for what Mum has done for us,' she told me, her hand on Gabori's shoulder. Gabori's success had shifted her family's fortunes: this is part of what Elsie meant. But if it had changed her own material circumstances, it wasn't immediately clear. The only suggestion that the tiny, almost impossibly frail woman folded into a chair next to me was one of the country's most successful artists was a smear of garish turquoise paint that stained her dress.

—

Gabori began painting at a critical moment for Mornington Island art, not to mention Queensland Aboriginal art more broadly. For a time it had seemed as if Australia's much-celebrated Aboriginal art boom might bypass the sunshine state altogether. The majority of the movement's stars, past and present, hailed from the remote Northern Territory, Western Australia and South Australia, but beyond the notable success of a group of young women from Lockhart River, who'd taken to large-scale, abstract renderings of Country in the early 2000s, Queensland was largely absent from what had become a celebrated narrative of cultural and economic revival. The state's then Labor government, under Premier Peter Beattie, took steps to address this in 2004, when it initiated the Queensland Indigenous Arts Marketing and Export Agency (QIAMEA). Its remit was clear: create a new market.

Brett Evans described the resulting opportunity to me in his office back at the art centre, a simple room adorned with little beyond filing cabinets and a desk. The only nod to the art that had flourished in the adjoining studios was a small composition in primary colours propped casually on a shelf: Gabori's first-ever painting on canvas. Evans commenced his role at Mirndiyan Gununa just three years before QIAMEA appeared on Queensland's remote art landscape. The art centre had been in a difficult position, he explained. Core expenses were met by government funding, but regular income from art sales had proved elusive. Part of this came down to the market's taste: artists at Mirndiyan Gununa were for the most part still engaged with a tradition of figurative painting that had been set in motion in the 1960s and 1970s by two Lardil brothers, Goobalathaldin and Burrud – known more widely as Dick and Lindsay Roughsey – but the style had fallen out of fashion.

What tenuous links the art centre had with the lucrative southern market for Aboriginal art came mainly through artifacts, such as spears and painted shells, that local artists produced for tourist outlets in Sydney. 'We were basically a wholesaler of handcrafts,' Evans said. By 2005 the broader Aboriginal art market was, in his reckoning, 'like a golden goose'. He was familiar with the successes at Lockhart River and thought the artists of Mirndiyan Gununa might be able to achieve something similar. He gestured towards the studios and said, 'I started talking to these guys and saying, "Look, you've got to get into the painting, that's where the money is."'

With funding from QIAMEA in hand, Evans contracted a young arts worker called Simon Turner to deliver a series of painting workshops at the art centre. Turner, who was then co-running a small commercial gallery in Brisbane, Woolloongabba Art Gallery, came with a certain pedigree: as an art-school graduate in the late 1990s he'd accepted a position to set up and manage art centres in Utopia, a 5000-square-kilometre area northeast of Alice Springs. Over the previous decade, it had formed the epicentre of a particularly significant chapter of the Aboriginal art movement: the rise of one of Australia's most famous painters, the grand dame of desert painting, Emily Kam Kngwarray. Her success had catapulted her to the upper echelons of the art world, while also creating an unregulated market frenzy that at times had seen her paid in informal desert currencies like secondhand clothing and used vehicles. In 2017, her 1994 work *Earth's Creation 1* – an abstract rendering of her ancestral Country, Alhalker – would sell on the secondary market for $2.1 million.

The first of four workshops that Turner held at Mirndiyan Gununa in mid-2005 focused on a group of Lardil men. He followed a blueprint he'd already established elsewhere, encouraging them to think more strategically about what the art market wanted. This meant gently prompting them away from Roughsey brothers–inspired figurative images, and, in step with some of Kngwarray's most acclaimed work, showing them how the kind of designs that were once painted onto bodies for ceremony might be turned into 'abstract' paintings. By the end of the first week, they had a handful of works Turner deemed good enough for exhibition, but he still had Kngwarray's success on his mind. She'd passed away by the time he'd arrived in Utopia, but the shadow she'd cast there remained immense. As he told me over the phone in the weeks after my visit to Gununa, '[I was] looking for the old women immediately, but I was doing it quietly because I knew the men had to come first.'

Gabori had recently responded enthusiastically to an initiative at Mirndiyan Gununa aimed at reinvigorating traditional weaving practices, so it made sense that, during the second workshop, Evans introduced her to Turner. She took to painting quickly, and Turner was floored by the results: 'I just thought, *This woman is going to be massive*,' he said.

Evans would also recall Gabori's initial moments in the studio for me. He described how she first began on paper – a far cheaper material than canvas – but as her potential immediately became apparent, this changed: 'We just basically raced over and grabbed the paper ... and put a canvas in front of her,' he said.

Her earliest works were characterised by the loose, expressive touch she would soon become famous for, but they were also marked by a certain hesitancy: thick lines meandered their way through and around roughly brushed fields of colour as if she was feeling her way towards more definite imagery that would never materialise. By contrast, the content that would define her short career arrived fully formed. Although Gabori's images were not maps in the Western sense, they were certainly mnemonic devices that evoked specific places for her: her father's Country, her husband's, her own. The thick lines often referred to the ancient stone-walled fish traps – strategically piled stones bonded by generations of oyster growth – that Gabori had tended to as a young woman, while her fields of contrasting colour showed sandbars, tidal flats, schools of fish, deep water and shallow. For her advisers, the works suggested bigger would be better: 'The small paintings just didn't satisfy her,' Evans said. 'There just wasn't enough space for her to do what she could do.' In a direct echo of Kngwarray's celebrated large-scale paintings, such as *Anwerlarr anganenty (Big Yam Dreaming)* (1995), now held in the National Gallery of Victoria, her canvasses grew exponentially. Her inaugural solo exhibition, held at Woolloongabba Art Gallery in December 2005, featured the first of the epic works – which eventually reached eight metres in length – that quickly became something of a signature.

Gabori was in turn enlivened by her newfound status. In the catalogue accompanying the Woolloongabba exhibition, Evans described how, over the first months of her practice, he'd watched her demeanour change from 'being too shy to look at anyone' to 'interrogating anyone who comes into the studio'. She began to wear stylish hats, he noted (a photograph on the catalogue's cover shows her grinning from beneath the brim of a tartan bucket-style example), and if her transport to the art centre was too slow in arriving of a morning, she would set out purposefully on foot. A small group of female Kaiadilt artists almost immediately joined her in the studio, including her nieces Netta Loogatha and Paula Paul – but her position among them was soon clear: she was, as one commentator would later say, the art centre's 'Queen Bee'.

By then, Evans had already begun courting the southern art market more aggressively, and in late 2005 had sent an email to Melbourne's Alcaston Gallery with images of Gabori's early canvasses attached. Another high-profile Aboriginal art dealer had already passed up the opportunity to represent the Mornington artists, but Beverly Knight, Alcaston's director, recognised something in the brightly coloured works. 'I like artists who have a totally different view of the world,' she would later tell me. 'They were very raw, the first group of paintings, but I could see there was huge potential.'

Knight, an assertive former-restauranteur whose enthusiasm for Aboriginal art spilled over into a business in the late 1980s, is something of a major player in a small pool. Like Simon Turner, with whom she collaborated when he worked in Utopia, she is an advocate of being closely involved in the studio. At times she has worked directly alongside artists who she has represented commercially through Alcaston Gallery, either hosting them in Melbourne or, in at least one case, renting space closer to the artist's home in which she could undertake her own painting workshops, free from what she characterised to me as the demands and distractions of community art centres. She explained that this process allowed the space and time to both develop big paintings and to ensure that the superior art materials she provided were used correctly. Beyond that, she has often fulfilled a more intimate role with artists: 'rubbing their back and cleaning their brushes' was the example she volunteered. 'It's hard work,' she told me, 'but it was a one-on-one approach to really good artists. And I got the best work. I got great work.'

She soon visited Mirndiyan Gununa, and readily takes credit for steering Gabori towards higher-quality materials and closely advising other painting support staff employed after Turner's contract was completed. When I asked her what, if any, input she had beyond this, she was more circumspect: 'We were trying to get it to, you know, that level,' she explained.

As one of the longest-running specialist Aboriginal art galleries in Australia, Alcaston had existing relationships with some of the biggest stars of the movement. From the late 1990s onwards, luminaries such as the late desert painter Eubena Nampitjin, with whom Knight enjoyed a long association, had seen their prices driven rapidly upwards by a bullish primary and secondary market. Prior to the 2007–08 global financial crisis briefly flattening the market's top end, works by artists such as Nampitjin were commanding up to $75,000 in their primary dealer exhibitions, and occasionally more in the auction houses.

Gabori was yet to achieve the acclaim of her better-known contemporaries. Although her work had been widely collected, her prices still clustered around the $5000 to $10,000 mark: still accessible for collectors who had retracted from the market's higher end. Yet her foundation story – especially her first-contact status – was as near to perfect as anyone could imagine. As if on cue, the art world swooned.

Between late 2009 and early 2012, when declining health began to considerably slow her output, some 280 of Gabori's paintings were shown in upwards of twenty-two solo and group exhibitions in commercial settings. Fifteen of these were held by Alcaston Gallery, which had negotiated near-exclusive representation. Her prices rose quickly. This peaked between May and June 2011, when the gallery presented two major solo exhibitions – one each in Sydney and Melbourne – in quick succession, handling over half a million dollars' worth of work. Throughout, museum-scale paintings were sold into prestigious public collections including the National Gallery of Australia, the National Gallery of Victoria and the Queensland Art Gallery/Gallery of Modern Art. It seemed that, however briefly, acrylic paint and canvas had been transmuted into gold.

Alcaston Gallery's commercial acumen clearly underpinned this saturation, but it would not have been possible without what many described to me as Gabori's enormous work ethic. She was soon at Mirndiyan Gununa as many as five days a week: staff from either the old person's home or the art centre would collect her and other women from the home in the morning and return them in the afternoon. In a practice not uncommon at art centres across northern Australia, materials were not only provided, but pre-prepared: canvasses were primed with a black or white basecoat and colours either mixed on her behalf or squeezed straight from the tube. From the outset, the distinctiveness of her visual language was clear, but this level of control meant it could still be directly shaped by the distant market. Brett Evans told me, for instance, that when a gallerist expressed interest in black-and-white paintings, these were the only colours provided in the studio: 'I'd go in there and put black and white on her table,' he said. 'She used to hate it, but she used to do the most beautiful black-and-white paintings you'd ever seen. For a woman who loved colour.'

Gabori would often complete multiple large works in a single day, a volume that created its own challenges. 'Our biggest concern at the time was making it look like we weren't a sweatshop,' Evans continued. 'She just loved painting. But the good thing was one day she'd paint five absolute crackers and the next day she would paint five we would throw away, kind of thing. With the amount of work she was producing you always had a really good choice.' Knight concurred, telling me that in the early days they would 'go through hundreds of paintings to select a show'.

Unsurprisingly, this left many more than even the most enthusiastic market could absorb. With limited space at the art centre, a shipping container was soon required to store the overflow. These were perhaps best seen not so much as 'rejects' – the failed works that any painter might edit out – but 'outtakes': excess volume carefully edited to create a more contained and market-ready picture of Gabori's artistic vision.

Works that didn't make the cut were at times incinerated at the local rubbish tip. In a practice not unusual in the world of Aboriginal art, this was managed by a cast of art centre employees and other intermediaries, and largely occurred unbeknown to Gabori herself.

—

During my visit I was struck by the ragged energy of the Mornington community: the loose groups of children stalking Gununa's streets with ready smiles, the communal gatherings outside the well-stocked local store. There is a large school, a clinic and various service providers on the island, but there is also a darker edge that belies first impressions. Put lightly, the community is still gripped by well-documented internal struggles.

As with many remote centres, the island's economy is heavily dependent on welfare and the federal work-for-welfare initiative that was integrated into the Remote Jobs and Communities Program in 2013. In 2007–08 rates of diabetes were ten times that of the rest of Australia; assault-related presentations at the local clinic were thirty-eight times higher. Four months before I visited, a group of suspects in a high-profile sexual abuse case, aged between fourteen and sixteen, had been flown to Mount Isa for questioning.

Against this backdrop, stories like Gabori's are easily cast as a beacon of hope – a flash of good news to transcend the bleak cycle of media reporting that too often shapes the picture of Aboriginal communities held in the national consciousness. There is truth to this, but the reality is far more complex. In the broader art world, the healthy ambition of youth drives generational renewal; in Aboriginal art, by contrast, where old age is often aligned with outmoded notions of cultural authenticity, and in turn aligned with market value, the newest star is too often the oldest. Although younger artists are readily motivated by the success of those like Gabori, their own can be much harder to secure, and if it does come, far more moderate. From a local perspective the vagaries of outside taste that guide the remote art economy can seem confounding. 'I've been waiting a long time,' Elsie Gabori told me pragmatically when I asked her during my visit if she had been selling her own paintings. 'It's not like Mum's paintings: every time she paints, they go away.'

The resulting imbalance can have difficult consequences, especially when it comes to money. As elsewhere in remote Aboriginal Australia, Mornington's population is rising quickly; at the height of Gabori's success, in 2011, 39 per cent of residents were under fourteen, compared to just over 19 per cent nationally. Where once Elders like Gabori would have been supported by large extended families, for the stars of the painting movement the opposite is now usually true: their network of dependents can extend to vast proportions.

In the first twelve months that Gabori began painting, Brett Evans estimates that the art centre's income jumped from $12,000 to $300,000. 'It was like a drug to people,' he told me, referring to the market that flared up around Gabori's work. 'At the start you think it's a bit crazy and you've got a licence to print money.' Gabori's portion of this windfall quickly created immense pressure within the community. Recognising that the art centre, which takes half of the 60 per cent of the sale price that the gallery returns to the artist, was not only responsible for the creation of this income but also dependent on it, Evans struggled to make it work.

Following a series of meetings with Gabori's family, he helped devise a system of monthly payments to six nominated bank accounts. When there was a big lump sum, large purchases such as cars or boats were negotiated on a case-by-case basis. The pressure, however, remained intense; jealousies and recriminations flew. Eventually, in response to a third-party intervention (it was suggested to me that this was made by a health professional concerned about Gabori's welfare in the face of local demand) the Public Trustee was brought in to manage Gabori's money from afar. But not only did this arrangement make it far more difficult for her family to access the income from her practice, it also raised the spectre of a significant unpaid tax bill. In lieu of an adequate paper trail, Evans took to roaming the community, photographing vehicles in an attempt to show the Trustee where much of the money had gone.

There's also another well-documented risk to art windfalls like Gabori's in Aboriginal communities, one that Evans judiciously avoided mentioning during my visit: mercenary whites. In trying to show where the money had gone, he was simultaneously aiming to cover his own tracks. By 2010, painting sales had climbed close to $900,000 a year. It was around the same time that Evans had begun placing his own hand in the till.

It would take more than a decade for his crimes to come to light, but after the Office of the Registrar of Indigenous Corporations stepped in to investigate, they would finally be made public in 2022. Before leaving Mirndiyan Gununa under a cloud of suspicion in 2016, Evans had pocketed the proceeds of 176 paintings, 169 of which were Gabori's. He did this by forging art centre documentation for buyers and then directing them to pay money into his personal account. He'd denied his crimes, arguing that the paintings were his to sell because Gabori had gifted them to him, and going as far as producing letters to that effect stamped with a thumbprint he claimed was hers. But it didn't hold up in court: Evans would be sentenced to four and a half years in jail, and ordered to pay Gabori's estate, the art centre and the small number of other artists whose money he had also stolen, close to half a million dollars in restitution.

On hearing news of Evans's sentencing, I reached out by phone to Gabori's son-in-law Bobby Thompson, who I'd met during my visit to Gununa in 2014. Back then, Thompson had been an enthusiastic intermediary for Gabori; now he was the executor of her estate, which was being overseen by an independent art consultancy operated by Alcaston Gallery's Beverly Knight, who, through the gallery, also doubled as the primary representative of Gabori's remaining paintings.

Evans's marriage into a Lardil family had placed him in a kinship relationship with Gabori, who'd called him son-in-law, a link that only made his betrayal all the more egregious. What was it like, I asked Thompson, for the family to find out they had fallen victim to such malfeasance? 'They were really, really angry,' he said. 'Brett used his knowledge about English and things like that to really pull the wool over the old people's eyes.'

—

Once he was found guilty, Evans was established as the obvious villain of the Gabori saga. But to me it also made clear how difficult it is to cleanly discern the broader ethics of the Aboriginal art world. It's no longer an unregulated industry by any means, but much of it still operates within a series of overlapping grey zones. There are individual actors who are truly nefarious, but to take a hard look at how so much Aboriginal art reaches its market is to understand just how difficult it is, in a colonial country like Australia, to make more nuanced ethical distinctions.

After I worked on the Tiwi Islands, I spent a year in the East Kimberley region of Western Australia, and often return to a conversation I had with an elderly artist there. He explained the Aboriginal art world to me in terms of the local pastoral industry, in which he'd once worked for rations. The art centre manager, he told me, was akin to the white boss of the stock camps, while the artists were the 'workers' (his word) and the far-off city galleries the station owners. It is an imprecise analogy – it doesn't account for the fact that the Aboriginal art world, despite its flaws, ideally exists to direct money and recognition back to community-based artists – but I still find its central image of Aboriginal labour feeding far-off markets compelling. Sure, many of the art centres across Central Australia and the Top End, not to mention the artists themselves, kick firmly against exactly these kinds of colonially inscribed relations, but such relations are nonetheless there. Anyone who's worked in an art centre like Mirndiyan Gununa, as I have, would be lying if they said they hadn't felt them. From this view, a story like Gabori's cannot simply be taken as proof of some kind of hard-won postcolonial enlightenment. Rather, it shows how deeply colonialism's extractive urge still runs.

Yet, wilfully or not, many of us often reach for the simpler narratives, drawn by their promise to ameliorate hardwired colonial guilt. In Gabori's case, this narrative is now well established: painting provided her the means to return to her beloved Bentinck Island. Simon Turner, who as well as mediating Gabori's first sessions in the studio wrote a catalogue essay for her first exhibition, put forward what is likely the earliest version: 'Sally's story is the beginning of a language and the start of a dialogue,' he wrote. 'It's a story of a senior Kaiadilt woman who picked up a paintbrush and created a vehicle, a medium to return home, on canvas and by plane.' Almost a decade later, the curator John McPhee was among those who'd enthusiastically taken up the narrative thread and run with it. He argued that Gabori's paintings embody no less than 'all of the sorrow experienced at having been exiled from her homeland, and, when able to return, her delight in the land of her youth'.

It's a compelling story arc, but in Gabori's case the picture is far more complicated. When I met with Nicholas Evans in Canberra, he explained that he had begun visiting Bentinck Island in the 1980s, by which time it was already providing the Kaiadilt with a quiet alternative to Mornington. By the late 1990s there were often as many as thirty people there for the dry season, a mix of Elders joined intermittently by work-for-welfare participants and young mothers seeking assistance with their babies. As we spoke, he was careful to distance himself from claims that the proceeds of Gabori's paintings were what enabled her return to Country. There was some truth to this perspective, but he suggested diplomatically that such accounts had been 'overstated'.

'I think that there were certainly things people wanted to do,' he said. 'The Bentinck ladies were saying they would like to have a clinic there, for example. You know, setting out the things that they would really need to get an outstation going: a school, a kindergarten ... One can imagine a world where the money from the painting could partly be put into supporting that. That's not the world that came to pass.'

For Evans, it was visibility rather than money that ultimately provided the marker of Gabori's success: even though she'd grown up on the other side of the colonial frontier, and had lived the first eight decades of her life without ever picking up a paintbrush, her paintings had somehow made her world visible to outside eyes. As Brett Evans was being sentenced in 2022, this visibility reached all the way to Paris, where a major exhibition of Gabori's work opened at the Cartier Foundation for Contemporary Art: a glittering event attended, alongside numerous cultural and political figures, by Gabori's daughter Amanda and her great-granddaughters Narelle Gabori and Tori Juwarnda Wilson Gabori. In the accompanying catalogue, Nicholas Evans took the opportunity to write what will surely stand as one of the enduring essays on Gabori and her practice. In it, he avoided the vexed questions of money and market altogether, and instead linked Gabori's paintings to what he described as the nearly unparalleled intricacies of the Kayardilt language. 'One of the remarkable things about the Kayardilt vocabulary,' he wrote, 'is the rich and pervasive system it has for dividing space into topological blocks, reflecting the visible topography of Kaiadilt Country.'

Gabori's work often appears bracingly simple, but for Evans that's beside the point. Instead, he sees in it something of how the complexity of Kayardilt grows from the landscape itself, linking the people who speak it so indelibly to place: an accounting of their island world that takes in the myriad of its character, from the macro to the micro. From this perspective, it's possible to link the abstraction of her paintings – the patchwork of fields that abut one another in rough mosaics of quickly brushed colour – to the abstraction of language itself: the way that language grants order and meaning to what would in its absence remain entirely inchoate.

But let's not rush to claim this as anything but a brief triumph against the odds. Given how few of Gabori's audience come even close to speaking her language, let alone seeing the Kaiadilt world as she did, it's hard not to see her visibility as precluding anything like true understanding.

—

I've never loved Gabori's work, but the many contradictions of it have kept me thinking about it far longer than I otherwise might have. I can't quite dismiss it as the outcome of an overheated market – it's too distinctively hers for that – but nor can I embrace it on the terms her many champions seem to demand. As with so much Aboriginal art in Australia, the conditions in which it is made, not to mention the market interests that underscore it, are too often hidden from view; it obscures far more than it purports to illuminate. But perhaps this, too, explains something of its allure.

In 2014, just before I left Mornington Island, I met a local non-Indigenous woman who had worked for the art centre during the later years of Gabori's rise. She recounted Gabori's response to seeing a group of her paintings hung in the National Gallery of Australia's second National Indigenous Art Triennial in 2012. The woman, who wished to remain anonymous, had accompanied Gabori at the event and had filmed it. The evening after we spoke, she came to the unit where I was staying and we watched the footage on my laptop.

It shows Gabori sitting in a wheelchair in a large gallery space, at the rear of a group gathered to hear another artist talk. The space around her is dominated by a sequence of her own large works: discordant swathes of red, pink, orange and black, depicting the coral shoals and tidal eddies of Bentinck. With no fanfare, she rises wordlessly and begins to dance in front of one of her paintings. Although her act seems entirely spontaneous, its effect is almost immediate: the group turns to catch the spectacle and Gabori is caught in a flurry of camera flashes, her figure outlined against the gallery's white walls.

By then she was already frail, and within the next year would near cease painting, even as the market for her work continued to grow, and one exhibition after another was held in her name. In the moment, however, none of this seems to matter. She simply continues to shakily stamp her feet as her handclaps echo in the cavernous space around her.

The image returned to me the following morning. I sat cramped in my seat as the tiny aircraft laboured upwards, struggling to reach its brief cruising altitude. I looked out the window at the Wellesley Islands below. They spread out towards the shallow horizon, most of them so low they barely appeared to break the ocean's surface. Then, as the plane began to carve its way towards the mainland, I realised I was looking down at the very centre of Gabori's world: Bentinck Island – a flat mass, indistinct among a haze of rising heat, small enough to be framed by the window.

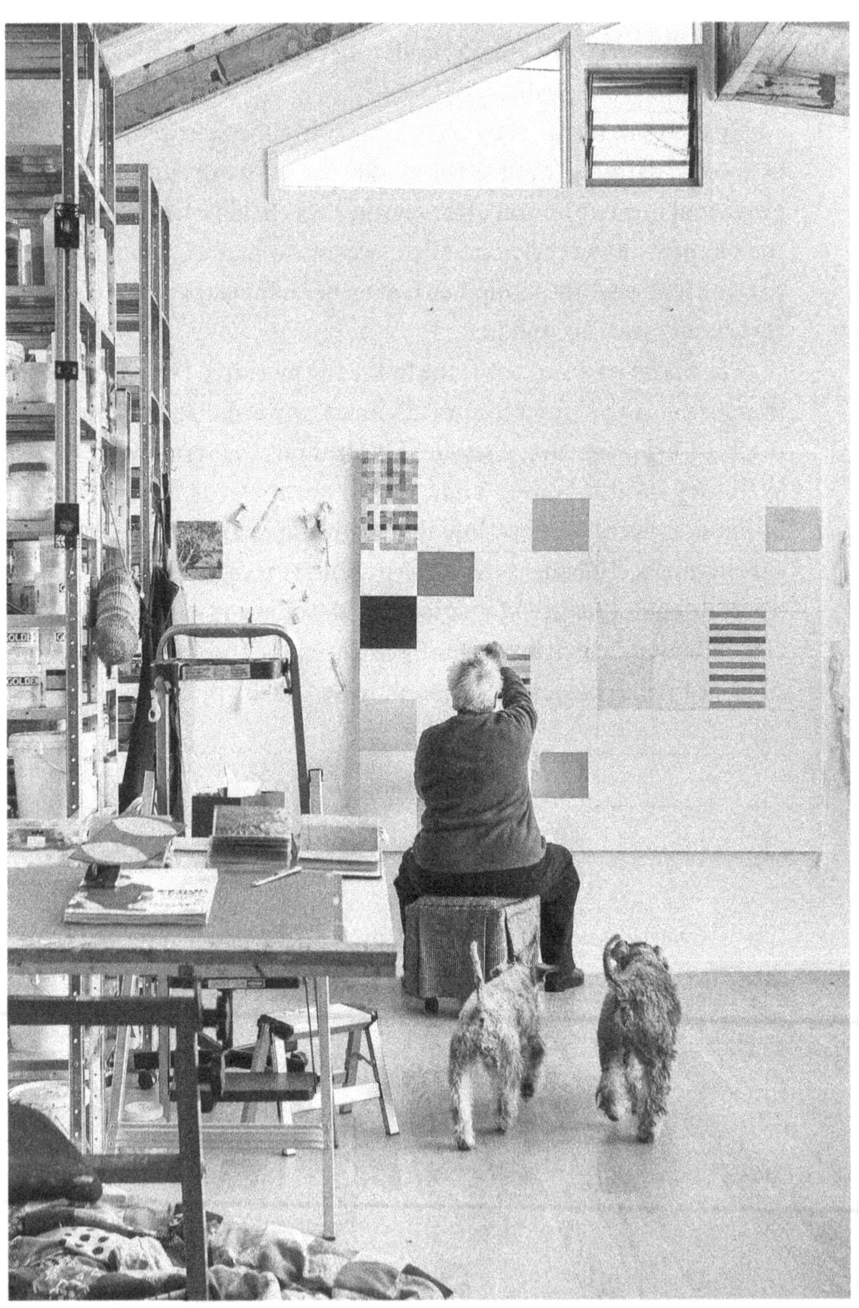

Vivienne Binns in her Canberra studio with Harriet (l) and Bosco (r) 2011

6

The World Is Made of Layers

We had been talking for about an hour when Vivienne Binns gestured from her unassuming sitting-room window at the view outside (low-hanging tree and native garden framing a bright Canberra street) and attempted to explain how she saw the world as a series of layers. 'It happens in the windows all the time,' she said. 'I'm so aware of it, even now. I can't look through a window without seeing about six or seven different layers.'

We were surrounded by well-stuffed bookshelves and, on the walls, the kind of art that an artist accrues, rather than acquires, over a lifetime: small things, for the most part swapped or gifted. Binns, who was a famously formidable but highly regarded painting teacher of mine in my first years of art school, had been systematically going over her career for me. There was her near-legendary flurry of post-art-school activity – paintings, assemblages, loose collections of detritus – that saw her burst onto the Sydney art scene in 1967 and would later help secure her reputation as an early icon of Australian feminist art. Afterwards came a period of unruly performances, and the groundbreaking community work in hardscrabble rural towns that in the early 1980s had set her in near-ceaseless motion throughout central-west New South Wales, holding art workshops in public buildings, church halls and, at times, drought-stricken paddocks. Now, ahead of a major career survey at the Museum of Contemporary Art Australia, in Sydney, she was attempting to describe for me one of those points that come only rarely for artists, if ever, kindling the energy needed to break new ground.

It was 1991 when it first came to her, she said. She was adrift in both life and art, and in an attempt to find her way back to her practice had begun to photograph another view, one far more spectacular than could be found in the Canberra suburb that has now been her home for more than three decades. It was the ever-changing estuarine waters of the northern New South Wales inlet of Brisbane Water, as seen from her uncle's house in the town of Saratoga, where she was living as a caretaker while it was on the market. The home stood at the edge of the tidal zone, looking out into the deep water beyond.

Binns would end up staying there for almost two years. She took in the view every day on waking, and soon came to understand the estuary as a vast unbroken body, alive with tidal energy, redolent with light and air. It flowed outwards from the mouth of Brisbane Water to Broken Bay, and beyond that into the South Pacific Ocean.

At first, she wasn't entirely sure what it was about the view that captured her imagination. Her first photos of it conveyed something of this uncertainty: they were granular, focused on glimpses and details, rather than the expansive whole. It was almost as if she was easing her way in, purposefully ignoring what might be overwhelming if she tried to capture it too soon. The images had an obsessive quality, in the way that an artist's work sometimes does when they are trying to understand what it is about a new subject that is drawing their attention. This likely explains the photographs' sense of endearing simplicity. They read as if Binns's intent was little more than a visual audit of the waterscape's most ephemeral characteristics: here is the flicker of sunlight across ripples; there, the fragile ridges left in the sand by the receding tide. When shells began to creep in, it almost became too much for her: she was an art-school-educated artist and had not so long ago been a leading light of Sydney's late 1960s avant-garde, and here she was producing images that veered dangerously close to coastal kitsch. But she knew enough to trust her impulse. She kept going.

She soon began to make sense of her new works. Layers: that was the key to what her camera lens was capturing. These separate visual layers bled together into an ever-changing whole. Light, water, air, sand: this is what looking at the estuary day in and day out had taught her to see. These were the layers which together made that world, and by photographing it she was pulling it apart, separating one layer from the next and holding it up for examination.

Until this point, Binns's practice had often been both emotionally and physically draining. Some of her earliest work had drawn on an intense process of psychological self-scrutiny, she told me, in which she'd been driven by a compulsion to 'discover what it meant for me to be an artist'. Her work from the period shows how fertile the moment was: after studying at the National Art School in Sydney in the early 1960s, she had pushed the old orthodoxies governing sculpture and painting hard against the freewheeling strategies afforded by the counterculture. Photos of her first solo exhibition, held in 1967 at Sydney's famed Watters Gallery, give a vivid impression. It was as if the contents of her head had been shaken willy-nilly across the space: angular assemblages of unpainted wood crashed into corners, toy-like sculptures that viewers were encouraged to play with rested upon makeshift plinths, rough-hewn mobiles – one adorned with burnt books – dangled from above.

Her now-iconic paintings *Phallic monument* (1966) and *Vag dens* (1967), which embed frank depictions of genitalia within psychedelic landscapes that evoke The Beatles' 'Yellow Submarine', provided her an early answer to her question of what it meant to be an artist. 'By the time I got to them ... I just had this physical sensation of *that's it: there I am*,' she said. At a superficial glance they appear wrenched from drug-fuelled depths, but looks can be deceiving. Although Binns had been in a formative two-year relationship with Mike Brown, a fellow artist and avant-garde figurehead for whom LSD provided a pivotal influence, she had for the most part not partaken. 'I didn't like the feeling of that sudden loss of control,' she told me. 'Whereas this process I went through, step by step, was really like learning to swim ... I actually felt that if I took drugs it would push me over the edge.'

Yet even though it was *Phallic monument* and *Vag dens* that provided her a breakthrough, it was the earlier work *Suggon* (1966) that prompted the biggest outcry among the art establishment. It took the hard-edge modernist abstraction that a generation of mostly male Australian painters had imported wholesale from America and turned it towards uncompromisingly feminist ends. Against a background of geometric forms, Binns painted two black apertures, one of them a neat circle, the other a long diagonal gash. Their softly feathered edges suggested orifices erupting from the work's otherwise pristine surface, but it was what Binns affixed to the centre of her composition that really spelt it out: a vulva-shaped form made from a repurposed metallic hair net that was hooked up to an electric motor, allowing it to rhythmically open and close.

One male critic decried the 'monumental repulsion' *Suggon* prompted in him; another argued presumptuously that it not only 'affronts masculinity' but 'makes females feel inadequate'. Yet if their intent was to sink the work without a trace, they failed: in 1977 the painting was acquired by the National Gallery of Australia. It was there where I first encountered it some twenty years later, hanging like the best kind of joke among the sort of abstraction it had so deftly dispatched with decades earlier. I still recall the insistent sound of the vulvic form quietly grinding open and closed in the otherwise silent gallery: you couldn't look at another painting and not hear it.

—

'I wasn't very comfortable to be around at times, I think,' Binns said of the years immediately after she'd brought works like *Suggon* into the world. 'I was starting to look at people when I was with them in much the same way I was looking at myself. When you're in that state, you start to sense more strongly the emotional and psychological makeup of people you're with – that's not a very comfortable thing to be around.'

After the attention garnered by her first exhibited paintings, she did something counterintuitive: stopped painting altogether. She moved into a group house in the Sydney suburb of Mosman with Yve Repin and Peter Kennedy, both psychology graduates from the University of Sydney, and with Repin embarked upon her first lesbian relationship. The period was, Binns told me, part of a difficult but ultimately productive process of 're-socialisation', during which she kept the psychographic revelations of her early work intact, but learnt to be in the world again.

In step, the question of what it meant for her to be an artist shifted outward. In a series of collaborative performances and 'happenings' – events like *WOOM* (1971), in which viewers were invited to wander through an immersive light environment that snaked through the two levels of Watters Gallery – she seemed to be asking how she could break the division between artist and viewer. When she taught herself the craft of vitreous enamelling – a process in which powdered glass is heat-bonded to sheets of metal – she was soon undertaking commissions from architects for decorative plaques and foyer panels, driven not just by a pragmatic need to generate an income, but also by a desire to liberate creativity from art's more rarefied air. The closest she would get to showing paintings for eighteen years would be *Funky Enamel Ashtrays* at Watters in 1971, an exhibition of oversized, brightly enamelled clam-shell-shaped metal ashtrays that looked like maquettes for the kind of mid-century modernist sculpture that by the 1970s adorned city plazas the world over. In the same year, she appeared on Channel 10 hosting an art and craft show called *Things to Make and Do with Vivienne Binns*. 'The central tenet of my practice is not a material or a style,' she would later tell the art historian Helen Hughes. 'It's process and relationship.'

When Binns became involved in community art initiatives through a part-time role with the newly formed Australia Council for the Arts, it led to her far-reaching work with rural and regional communities in the early 1980s. The question shifted again: *how can my practice as an artist uplift and inflect the creativity of others?* One of her best-known projects from the period, *Full Flight: views of life in the Central Western region of NSW through the creative expression of those who live there* (1982–83), saw her range over 62,000 square kilometres, settling for weeks at a time in places as distant as Orange, Lithgow and West Wyalong. She connected with existing art and craft groups, and taught enamelling and screen printing at local venues; she distributed newsletters that featured poems, stories and artwork by those she encountered, and collected oral histories on a portable tape recorder. The idea was to cede as much space as possible to the everyday creativity of the so-called non-artists that the project took in, particularly women and other demographics whose political and social visibility was limited. She didn't see herself so much as 'helping' them as creating the means for them to learn from one another, and for her to learn from them in turn.

Although she wasn't focused on what was happening in the broader art world, it caught up with her nonetheless. In 1982 she was visited in Lake Cargelligo by the American curator and author Lucy Lippard, a famously catalysing figure in the feminist art movement. Lippard, who had met Binns during an initial visit to Australia seven years earlier, was impressed, and later described Binns and her work in an essay on Australian art for New York's *Village Voice*:

> Binns is a charismatic character, whether bursting into music-hall ditties at the drop of a hat, driving hundreds of miles through the wilderness in her red diesel truck, or enthusiastically sharing a cup of tea with elderly ladies at a 'day care' home ... Watching her in action is in fact watching her in integration. Not too much seems to be going on, since she prefers to work through existing social forms – afternoon teas, sports events, fetes, and other 'understood gatherings'. This in addition to her art classes, mural project, craft work on an Aboriginal reserve and float-making for a parade with an Aboriginal youth group.

By the project's completion in 1983, Binns was understandably exhausted. Back in Sydney, she returned to the studio, and soon began to split her time between it and a sparse room in the Depression-era home of a friend in the Blue Mountains town of Lawson. She eventually began to paint again, but the working process she'd set early had endured: each new body of work she undertook tended to unfold over a period of intense activity that could still push her close to the edge. Exhaustion would usually flag an endpoint, after which a demand for renewal would almost immediately begin to pull at her until another body of work began to form.

By the time she relocated to the house at Saratoga, the question that guided her was as simple as they come: *Where to now?*

—

The gentle revelation that struck Binns at the edge of Brisbane Water – the idea of layering – was one that she soon understood as full of possibilities. In one way or another it would come to underpin everything. And if looking towards the ocean provided her a method, it also eventually provided her a subject. 'I was always aware of the seepage of culture that comes from the Pacific, and that we take for granted,' she told me. Over the two years she spent on Brisbane Water, that awareness was only underscored.

In April 1992, for instance, she attended the Artists Regional Exchange in Perth, an initiative aimed at bringing artists from different cultural backgrounds together for shared residencies. There she met fellow artists from Australia, South-East Asia, New Zealand and New Caledonia who were beginning to think in similar ways about the region in which they were working. Later that same year she travelled to the Polynesian island of Rarotonga to attend the Festival of Pacific Arts and Culture, an event held every four years in celebration of the region's enduring cultural forms: dance, music, art and food. She toured the island on a motor-scooter, visiting the various stages and tents that Pacific nations had erected for the festival. She watched performances and participated in cultural workshops. The whole thing prompted further revelation. Binns had never been overly compelled to reach for European precedent in her art, but if she needed further convincing, here was the proof, writ large, that Australia, at least in a geographic sense, was far closer to these kinds of cultural activities than it was to those of America or Europe. The contrast was cast in bright light: 'The Pacific, in my mind, was this sphere of sunshine and blue,' she said. 'Europe was all mellow browns and grey and history.'

In Rarotonga she was invited to observe a contingent of Tongan women making tapa, a ceremonial bark cloth, called *ngatu* in Tonga, that is adorned with geometric patterning, and forms a trade currency between various Pacific Islander peoples. The experience would prove particularly consequential. Those familiar with tapa cloth will know its seductive aesthetic qualities. Its preparation – in which an inner layer of bark, most often mulberry or fig, is soaked until supple before being layered and beaten thin over a hard wooden surface – results in a silken transparency whereby the structural sinew of the bark fibre remains clear. The imperfect geometries of the patterning then applied to this ground only add to its allure: it is stencilled, painted and stamped in naturally sourced pigment and vegetable dye that dries into an array of colours, prominent among them russet browns and satiny near-blacks. Binns responded to tapa cloth in aesthetic terms – she would go on to collect both painted and unpainted lengths of the material – but she soon came to understand it in formal and conceptual terms too: a frame within which her thinking about the complexities of the region (not to mention the complexities of being an artist in this region) might find fuller expression.

For a contemporary reader, the spectre of cultural appropriation might at this point loom large. But Binns was careful in her approach: her intent was not to exploit tapa cloth, nor to appropriate it wholesale as a cultural form, but to use it to question her own position as an Australian artist. Drawing on the method of layering that traced directly to her photographs of the waters at Saratoga, Binns began to ease an abbreviated tapa patterning into her work. She would later come to understand that it allowed her to quietly reframe dominant regional assertions about power and culture. Evidence of this came early, and simply: her 1993 work on paper *Tapa over a Republican Governor-General*, for instance, lays an unmistakeably tapa-like grid in coloured acrylic over a newspaper clipping about the anti-monarchist leanings of Bill Hayden, the twenty-first governor-general of Australia. Hayden's black-and-white portrait peers from beneath Binns's rhythmic lines: one set of cultural beliefs intersect, quite literally, with another. With the image so bluntly recast from the perspective of the Pacific, the viewer can't help but see the debate about whether or not the governor-general of Australia supports the British monarch as absurd: this place, one thinks, is already twined by the kinds of connective threads – social, political, cultural – that unavoidably negate those imposed from elsewhere.

The following year Binns returned to the photographs from Saratoga. She applied the same approach as she'd taken to *Tapa over a Republican Governor-General*: painting thin, tapa-esque lines in acrylic paint over the images in a fashion that both obscured and elaborated them. The resulting works are among the most restrained in her oeuvre, but in others from the period she reached for something more complicated. She began to seek what she would later refer to as 'helpful confusions' between disparate images and forms.

Her 1993 painting *Surfacing in the Pacific* presents a marquee example. It appropriates as its ground William Hodges's oil-on-canvas work from 1776, *A View taken in the bay of Oaite Peha [Vaitepiha] Otaheite [Tahiti]*, which is more commonly referred to as *Tahiti Revisited*. Hodges – the only son of an English blacksmith, who was tutored by the Royal Academy of Arts member Richard Wilson, and who eventually rose to that rank himself – made his name as an artist on Captain James Cook's second voyage to the Pacific (1772–75). Hodges's work epitomises the colonial relations of the day. His images of sun-drenched scenes were displayed back in the heart of the British Empire, where they promoted near-mythological notions of 'untouched' and 'savage' lands – verdant, seductive, bewildering in the strange mysteries they presented to

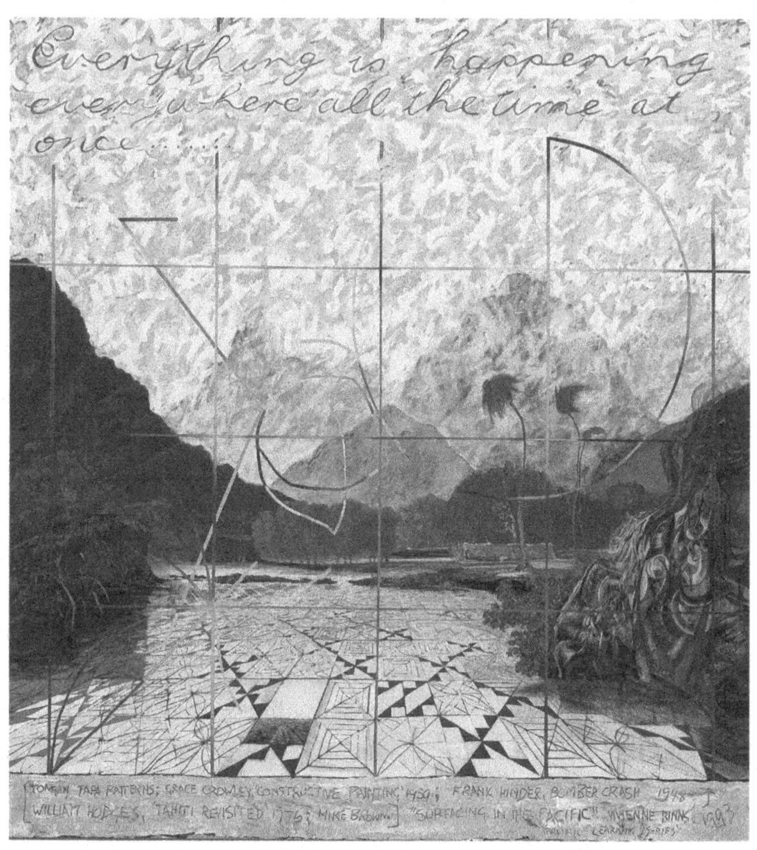

Vivienne Binns *Surfacing in the Pacific* 1993

European eyes. In *Tahiti Revisited* distant mountains reach into a gold-tinged sky; palms bend in supplication to an unseen wind; pale-skinned bathers in the foreground lounge before crystal waters.

In Binns's painting, those waters are replaced by a black-and-white tapa pattern, a square of which opens onto a generic Australian desert scene: red ground beneath a bleached-blue sky. The lounging figures disappear beneath an approximation of a 1949 painting by the Australian modernist Frank Hinder titled *Bomber Crash*, an angular abstraction that depicts an aeroplane crash Hinder survived in New Guinea during World War II, and in turn riffs upon the cascading geometry of Marcel Duchamp's canonical *Nude Descending a Staircase (No. 2)* (1912). Binns gleefully crashes Hinder's bomber into Hodges's imagined idyll. It's tempting to align this scene with the sudden destructive arrival of colonialism that Cook's voyage announced, but this is too simple a reading given that the painting's remaining 'layers' carefully direct the viewer elsewhere. The receding grid of the tapa is echoed by lines that cluster and sweep across the painting's face, which are based partly on a painting by Hinder's co-voyager in Australian modernism, Grace Crowley; the sky is in turn overtaken by interlocking shapes drawn directly from the work of Mike Brown, underscoring once again how his charismatic vision of art and life was for Binns a foundational influence. Above it all is the phrase, written in a cursive script reminiscent of Brown's work, 'Everything is happening everywhere all the time at once': as close as the painting gets to a unifying statement.

In the 1990s, much art was trafficking in postcolonial theory, and it is tempting to see Binns's practice in this light. She recalls diligently attending conferences and seeking out books on the topic, several of which still hold a place on her Canberra bookshelf; but hers was not an academic's approach, it was an artist's. In 1994 she wrote a letter to an imagined viewer of this body of work, which she presented as an artist's statement alongside her exhibition *Pacific Parts* at Melbourne's Sutton Gallery. In it, she explained that her process was less an 'investigation' – a term that evokes the bloodless undertakings of the scholar – and more a 'musing'. Research and travel were offset by 'more passive contemplation [that] inevitably ends in fragments washed up on a beach, surfacing in the water or on and through the picture plane'.

It's a description of her practice that once again evokes her revelation at Saratoga, but she was now articulating its possibilities more fully. Ideas of layering echoed the ebb and flow of tidal waters, which in turn conjured other things entirely: the interlocking pieces of memory and experience that make up an individual; the patchwork of history that constitutes a place. At one level the nation of Australia was undergoing a similar reckoning with the region – then prime minister Paul Keating was in the midst of his visionary yet ultimately hamstrung policy 'pivot' towards the Asia-Pacific, and the Australian republican movement was in full swing – but true to form, Binns's approach was always going to lead back to the personal.

—

Since her first exhibition in 1967, Binns had consistently used her practice as a means to learn about herself. In the 1970s and 1980s, this had prompted her towards her family, and over different times throughout this period she had drawn on the experiences of her mother and grandmother, partly through reworking family photographs. Now, thinking into the Pacific, she recognised an opportunity to turn towards her father.

Norman Alfred Ruben Binns – known by the nickname 'Binna' by Binns's mother, and as 'Alf' by his brothers – had served in World

War II, and while posted overseas he had taken photographs with the kind of simple folding Kodak camera that first popularised amateur photography. Binns dug out the small stack of tiny prints that had remained in the family, trying to glean what information she could.

She was trying to get a sense not just of his experiences, but of her own feelings towards a man who had been absent in the first years of her life, yet nonetheless loomed large. The youngest of five children by a good margin, Binns had been conceived just before her father was deployed to the Middle East, and born as he passed back through Australia, en route to Papua New Guinea, where he would serve in an artillery unit based in Port Moresby for more than two years. So although he was able to see the infant Binns in the hospital, the two would not begin to build a relationship until his eventual return to Australia.

By then, the family were living in a rented cottage on the outskirts of Young, in southwest New South Wales. Family lore would combine with Binns's own uncertain memories of the moment she first met him. The story would unfold as follows: the children playing by the creek, urgent calls to return to the house, Binns innocently enquiring, 'Who is this strange man?' Her father was later discharged with malaria, and another early memory would be of him bedridden with fever, her mother caring for him.

It took time for the father–daughter bond to grow, but by her adolescence she was infatuated: whenever she could, she'd hang close by him and listen carefully. Later, she would realise that even then she was driven by a need to understand their early estrangement. He passed away in 1972, but it wasn't until her focus on the Pacific that she found a means to do so.

This came in a series of works for which Binns used her father's photographs as sources. *Pacific strands and result of raid on Seven Mile*, from 1995, draws upon his photo of bomb smoke pluming over a non-descript Pacific landscape; *The Vibrant Canvas*, from 1997, scales up his portrait of a fellow serviceman standing dishevelled in a field of grass, his rifle slung at his side and his slouch hat tipped back to create a dark halo around his head. Binns chose such images for a number of reasons, some relatively clear to her, others harder to articulate. At times, her father's photographs recalled the kind she'd become privy to during her *Full Flight* project in the early 1980s. Many of the local women who'd participated in her art workshops during that period had been 'housewives', a term that carried a certain stigma, but which, the more she came to understand the minutiae of individual character and experience that each woman carried with her, Binns would see in far more nuanced terms. Many shared family photo albums with her, and she recognised in them the same framing that had obviously guided her father's forays into the photographic art: the frontality of the compositions, the way that figures were centrally placed but weighted towards the top – lessons, she realised, that had been drawn from the how-to manuals circulated with the early Kodak cameras.

Such self-consciously classical framing – which treated the figure with near-heroic reverence – seemed to add a touch of pathos to her father's images, a familiar echo of family photo albums laid over scenes of war. This was particularly true for the forlorn-seeming figure in *The Vibrant Canvas*. Take away his gun and uniform and he could be someone's great-grandfather, standing before a new plot of farming land or a hard-won crop. She would later wonder about this man in particular – *who is he? Where is he from?* – and think that if her father were alive, he might fill in the details. But she would also realise that it was the mystery of an image like that which drew her, the way it suggested how finely grained details of individual lives are lost to history, and how the shifting relationship between memory and time might act to compound and expand one's perception of each.

In 1997, Binns also embarked on another major work of her Pacific period – a painting titled *Mrs Cook's Waistcoat*. It depicts the partially finished tapa-cloth waistcoat sewn by Captain Cook's wife, Elizabeth, as she futilely awaited his return from his ill-fated third voyage. Binns first encountered the garment at the invitation of a friend who worked in the Mitchell Library in Sydney, where it is held, and readily understood that it encapsulated a number of her most enduring concerns: the thread a family's narrative traces through time, the tangle of intersecting histories that define the Pacific region, the layering that brings it all together. One looks at the resulting painting and senses these fragments of thinking poised beneath its surface.

That's not to suggest that *Mrs Cook's Waistcoat* is a simple painted rendition of the waistcoat. But nor is its translation into paint as deliberate as other major works of the period, such as *Surfacing in the Pacific*. Sure, four years of studio practice separates the two paintings, but time alone fails to explain the difference. In *Mrs Cook's Waistcoat,* gone are the snippets of text overtly teasing out this reading or that; gone too are the painted grids and the ghost-like images that merge into patterned backgrounds. Text – for the most part handwritten in pencil – bleeds through the painted white ground in places, but it doesn't dominate or direct. Nor does the flurry of careful incisions that Binns has made through the canvas support, from which thrust small plumes of crumpled tapa cloth – the material counterpoint to its painted depiction. Instead, she lets the waistcoat itself do the heavy lifting. The silken needlework, the slightly harsh geometric edges of the cut tapa cloth, the unexplained stains that leached in from each edge (in her painting Binns has added one to those already there – a transparent pink at the top right corner – but it fits perfectly):

together these elements already constitute a series of layers that together speak volumes of the colonial encounter. It is an object that captures both the individual and the collective.

The waistcoat also allowed Binns to do something else: layer a feminist frame upon the myth – even less challenged at the time of her painting's creation than it is now – of Cook's voyages as journeys of heroic discovery. We look at it and can't help but see the touch of Elizabeth Cook herself, clearly rendered by the incremental passage of her needle, waiting at home in London. We may think of the six children the pair had together, and the vast ocean that separated them from their father, which would soon be replaced by the far more insurmountable distance of death. But lest the waistcoat seem only a gently introspective object, a thread of violence is recorded there too. It's not just apparent in the knowledge of Cook's brutal dispatch at Hawaii's Kealakekua Bay, or of the generations of dispossession set in motion by his three passages through the Pacific and along Australia's eastern and northern coastlines, but in the arrested progress of the waistcoat itself; in the way the stains (how can they not be read as blood?) overcome the embroidered design and, perhaps most of all, in the failure of such an object to achieve anything more than a brief unity between cultural worlds.

—

For many years in Canberra, Binns worked either in an offsite studio or in a humble conversion of her garage. But when she retired from teaching in 2012, at seventy-two, she had saved enough money to commission something a touch more elaborate.

She took me outside to see it, and as we made our way through her garden, she pointed out the remnants of an apple tree. It was, she told me, 'majestic' when she first moved into the house in 1998, but it had recently split in two and fallen. Along with an established pear tree, it had helped dictate the design of her studio: a long L-shape that made its way down one side of the block, past the then-thriving apple tree, and cut in behind the pear. Inside, the foot of the L provided her a generous painting wall, while the trunk of it granted a long space for storage drawers, shelves and a sink. The walls around the sink were adorned with tiny works purchased over the years from her painting students, each carefully labelled below with name and date of graduation – a kind of memory wall for the many artists whose practice she has helped shape.

She opened a set of plan drawers and gently riffled through the contents. Eventually she pulled out several of the over-painted photographs of Brisbane Water that she made when she revisited the images in 1994. It was the first time I had seen them, and I paused to take in the way that Binns's tapa-like lines delicately responded to whatever faint geometry each image offered up: the intersecting highlights of sun-caught ripples, or the dark dashes of mangrove shoots silhouetted against tidal sand.

'There they are again,' she said. 'Layers.'

One can interpret Binns's other works in far more detail than these unassuming images. Across the bottom of *Surfacing in the Pacific,* for instance, she scratched a series of names into a thin skein of white oil-paint brushed over the dark ground. It's a list of the direct sources that underlie the painting – Tongan tapa patterns, Grace Crowley's *Constructive painting,* William Hodges's *Tahiti Revisited* – but it's also possible to see such a list as a self-portrait at one remove; the disparate-seeming pieces of a self, arranged in fleeting formation. What strikes me about the overpainted photographs is that they manage the same without any explicit effort at all.

As I look at them, I think: *The world provides the ground upon which the artist projects their vision.* It's a simple idea, but this is where its power lies. Maybe the ideal is for these overlaid parts to move in concert, but I suspect not, at least not for Binns. These images she has pulled out for me – seemingly so fleeting in conception – show that such a process is just as likely to create points of misregistration as harmony. It's the idea that one's self might be glimpsed in the spaces between things – in those points of misregistration – that has ultimately endured.

'My life is pretty simple these days,' she wrote in an artist's statement in 2016, which I read not long after my visit. 'I work in the studio in my backyard in Canberra with whatever thoughts, feelings, ideas and memories come to me.'

She had at the time just finished a major painting – a nearly three-metre-long canvas titled *Minding Clouds* that would soon hold pride of place in her retrospective. It's a beautiful work, dominated by a palette of high-toned blues, and passages of soft, textured paintwork. Arranged across its length are a sequence of twenty or so clouds, some of them brushed directly onto the canvas, others cut from composition board and affixed as collaged elements. On the latter, Binns has painted snippets of scenes taken from newspapers, postcards and friends' photographs, among other sources – figures on a beach, a house at the edge of the ocean, a colourful stack of apartments: everyday things, but each of them, in their own way, oddly affecting.

As she'd finished the work, she'd felt something change. She found herself letting go of her career-long compulsion to return to the studio whether she felt ready or not, and instead settled into a looser, quieter rhythm. Her statement continued:

> I'm not politically active now and I don't travel much. So the world comes to me, mostly through television, newspapers, magazines, books, movies, friends ... All this stuff is the fuel for my continuing quest of making sense of existence:

> the world, living, society and humanity, art and relationship, understanding and love, hatred and intolerance, killing and death, pain and dying, acceptance and peace – the universe and everything!

It would seem that by then her simple revelation that the world is made of layers – and that the artist, if they are alert to this fact, is there to examine these layers one by one, and then fit then back together in ways that encourage us to see anew – had opened her mind just about as far as it could possibly go.

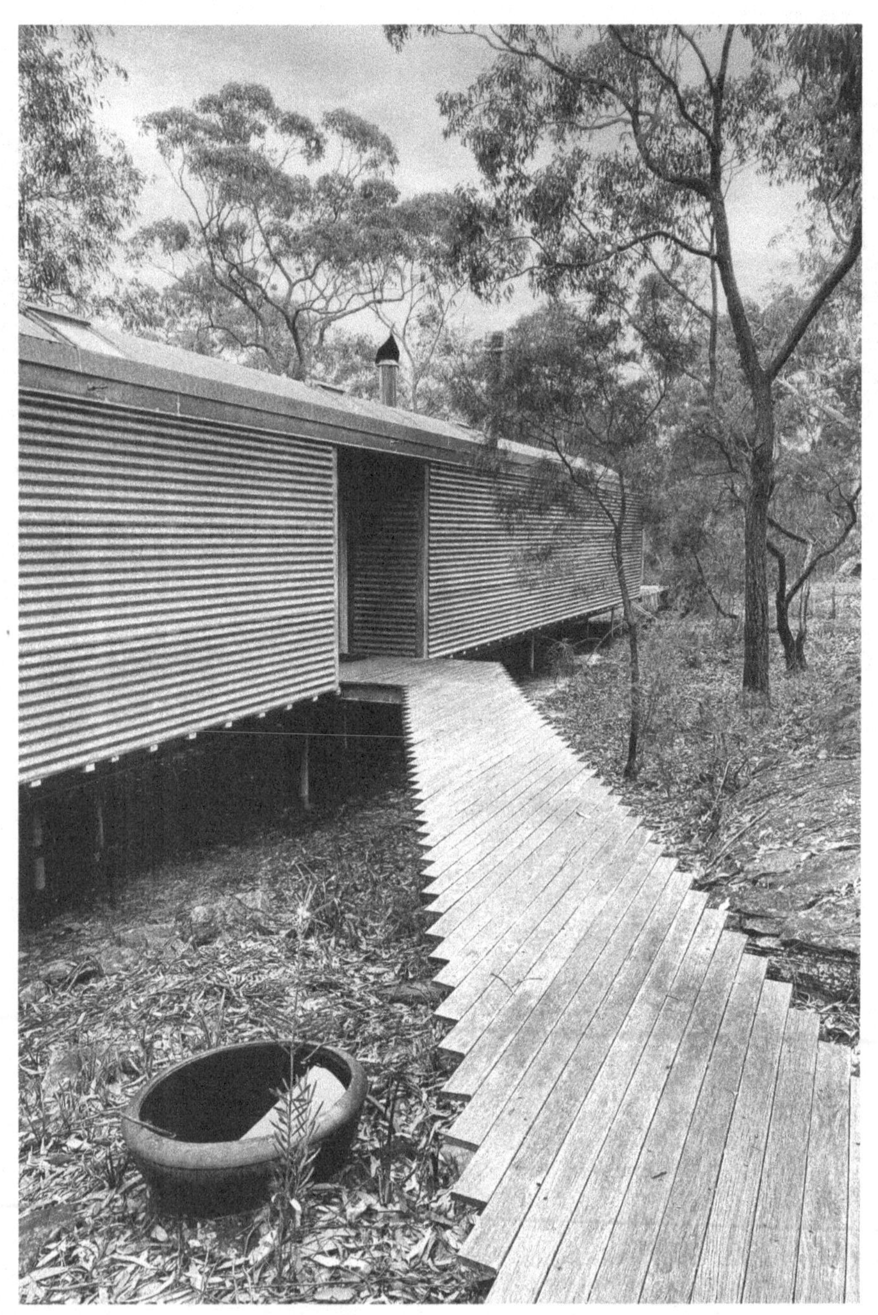

Ball-Eastaway House, Glenorie 2023

7

The House at Glenorie

The Ball–Eastaway House at Glenorie lies tucked into bushland about an hour northwest of Sydney. Designed by Glenn Murcutt, it reveals itself slowly: a long, hunched shape prone along the edge of a gently descending rock shelf. And although it's famous in architectural terms, it's about as far from ostentatious as one might imagine. The only way I can think to describe its presence is that it feathers gently into its environment, its edges seeming to dissipate into the surrounding bush.

It's not that it's disguised in any way: it doesn't seek to mimic its surrounds, either through material (predominately corrugated tin) or form (a deceptively simple curve, open at both ends). It's just that it somehow manages to seem as if it's been there for as long as the yellow and red bloodwoods, with their flaking, hide-like bark, the reaching forms of the angophoras, the tangle of low banksias and the soft leaf litter.

This bush – a dry sclerophyll forest – is most likely to strike a first-time visitor with an overwhelming impression of greyness, which the tin house at first reinforces. Not grey as in leached of light, but warm and enveloping: the grey of oiled steel, perhaps, or of felted wool. Look closer, however, and an entire spectrum is revealed. Grey becomes olive becomes green; blue, pink and purple are there too. If the light is right, the leaf litter flashes silver in the undergrowth and, if the season so desires it, flowering shrubs – narrow-leaved geebung, broom heath, prickly shaggy-pea, sunshine wattle – enliven the visual field with tiny bursts of colour.

The painter Sydney Ball knew this spectrum well. Along with his one-time partner and fellow painter Lynne Eastaway, he commissioned the house from Murcutt in 1976, and lived there from its completion in 1983 until his death in 2017. Working near-daily in one of two studios on the ten-hectare site (repurposed horticultural sheds, both studios are curved like the house and abut the same huge shelf of sandstone upon which it gently rests), Ball never appeared driven to capture the nuanced colour variations outside his window. Instead, he worked in counterpoint. As with Murcutt's design, his paintings, which were for the most part uncompromisingly abstract, were not concerned with mimicry. They were not of the bush, but found the means to somehow sit alongside it, profoundly different yet deeply complementary.

Ball's final series, *Infinex*, which he worked on in the seven years leading up to his death at eighty-three, consisted of shard-like geometric supports, either canvas or aluminium, painted in bright, monochromatic hues and hung in modular arrangement. Sunflower yellow, bright green, purple, fuchsia, orange and turquoise dominate.

How do we look at abstraction, the uninitiated viewer might rightly wonder when presented with one of these works. The answer is simple: the same way one looks at the bush. By being in its presence, its character is revealed. It happens at first incrementally. And then, it floods you all at once.

—

Ball and Eastaway enjoyed a quietly unconventional partnership for which the house, in its own way, became a binding symbol. They separated in 1984, just over a year after construction was completed, but it was never absolute: they remained tethered to each other for the rest of Ball's life. Now Eastaway lives there again, but Ball remains present. She works in the second of the two studios – always hers in name, but quickly overtaken as a storage space for Ball's work during his lifetime. His studio remains almost as he left it: works-in-progress are arranged on one wall, studies for a group of his *Infinex* works on another; the entry wall still bristles with his handwritten notes, postcards, reference images and photographs.

For the decades of their ostensible separation, Eastaway would come and go between Sydney and the Glenorie block, across the Harbour Bridge and up through a sprawl of suburbs that eventually gives way to rich agricultural land scattered with greenhouses and fields.

'Syd used to treat me like I was still part of him,' she tells me. I had driven up that morning and joined Eastaway for a simple lunch on one of the house's two verandahs before the two of us had picked our way slowly over the sandstone shelf to her studio. The domed interior is lit by regular bands of translucent roofing, with glass doors at one end. A large window on the left wall takes in a concentrated view of the surrounding bush.

'He never seemed to understand that I'd left,' she continues. 'He'd say, "Well, it's just like you're down there and I'm up here: we're still partners."'

Eastaway is also an abstract painter. Yet although she engages with similar ground as Ball – she also works with hard-edged fields of colour – the results are a touch more searching in character.

The two met in the early 1970s when, after a brief stint in advertising, she enrolled at the National Art School in Sydney, where Ball was teaching. According to Eastaway, she was at the time achingly shy. Ball struck her as worldly, and at one level he was. Already in his forties, he had established himself in the 1960s as a local proponent of American abstraction. Born in Adelaide, he'd twice lived in New York, first studying at the Art Students League in the early 1960s, and then returning to the city seven years later with his first wife, Australian painter Margaret Worth.

He'd rubbed shoulders with twentieth-century American art royalty: his painting teacher at the League had been Theodoros Stamos, a one-time member of the group dubbed the Irascible 18 for their commitment to the uncompromisingly modern work that became abstract expressionism, and which included Jackson Pollock, Willem de Kooning and Mark Rothko. Through Stamos, Ball had met the group's reigning theorist, Clement Greenberg, and had been trusted enough that when Rothko died by suicide in his Manhattan studio in 1970, Ball helped make an inventory of works he'd left behind.

When Eastaway began art school, the longest shadow cast on painting students was the French impressionism of Cézanne. But when Ball – rangy, bald, charismatic – appeared on the scene, the emphasis shifted across the Atlantic. Although abstract expressionism had by then largely run its course in the United States, in Australia the movement still seemed vital. And Ball had not only met some of the key players, he'd seen many first-wave American museum surveys of their work. He was also a natural raconteur, not at all averse to fleshing out the associated art theory with well-told stories that sketched in human texture. By the end of Eastaway's studies the two were a couple, and working alongside each other in a shared city studio.

The experience gave Eastaway an education of a different order to the one she'd received at art school. Ball was then working on his large-scale 'stain' paintings, made by pouring thin washes of colour directly onto a stretched canvas laid on the studio floor. The paintings were huge – sometimes nearly four metres across – and Eastaway would often help at the critical moment, assisting Ball to lift the canvas strategically so the colours ran together and pooled upon the surface in particular ways. Although the results directly recall their American precedents, they nonetheless flicker with their own intensity, due largely to Ball's celebrated talent for colour:

high-key primaries are offset by swathes of magisterial purple, deep green, orange and plum. Perhaps unavoidably, Eastaway's own work, which under Ball's influence had already become similarly abstract, grew in scale. But as much as she valued her proximity to such an accomplished partner, she found it stifling too: like so many artists, Ball was anxious, prone to fits of doubt. He required constant reassurance. 'Lynn-ee,' he would say, 'come and look at this.'

Ball was also well along his career trajectory, whereas Eastaway had barely begun. His practice always came first, and anything he thought might help it – whether a pink that Eastaway had mixed for her own work, or a composition drawn directly from one of the handmade Christmas cards she gave him each year – was fair game. He took as he saw fit.

Such appropriations were at one level flattering to Eastaway, but they could also be infuriating. In one particularly galling incident she threw away a group of drawings she'd deemed too derivate, only for Ball, unbeknown to her, to salvage and rework them as his own. She would always recall the shock of attending an exhibition of his in Melbourne not long afterwards and recognising her own work, still visible beneath the surface of his.

Whether or not they knew it at the time, the idea of building the house at Glenorie came at a hinge point for them both. Ball had by then been teaching for almost a decade and, although he enjoyed interacting with students, he was growing increasingly frustrated with the institutional demands of the university. He was exhibiting regularly and wanted to paint full-time. Eastaway had begun teaching too – both at the National Art School and at Western Sydney University – but found the role far more fulfilling than Ball did: it gave her the means to push beyond her shyness. She recalls saying next to nothing around Ball's artist friends, many of whom were not afraid to show off their knowledge. She was by contrast deeply unsure of herself, hypervigilant, afraid that she might get something wrong. The art-school studios had given her a forum in which her knowledge mattered, and she slowly established an independent voice. She would go on to teach until her retirement in 2018.

Then, in 1976, Ball had been evicted at short notice from his Sydney studio, which prompted him to search for somewhere distant enough from the vagaries of the city that he couldn't ever be moved on. He and Eastaway got into his white Kombi van and drove to Glenorie for the first time. The block had once been partially cleared, but its shallow soil made for poor agriculture and by now it was covered in established regrowth. A dirt access track led a couple of hundred metres in, stopping at the southern edge of the rock shelf upon which the house would eventually stand. Beyond that, the land dropped towards a far-off creek bed, invisible behind its veil of bush. Excited by the prospects, they soon purchased it and almost immediately started camping there. Eastaway still recalls how they slowly became attuned to the environment, sitting and looking, noticing small things. They found shallow limestone overhangs above the creek, and observed that, on certain nights, the bush was lit by silvery light. Eastaway discovered bioluminescent fungi, glowing a faint green in the night, and would later note with pleasure that the gentle mauve of their spores fanned out against the daytime grey of the leaf litter.

Commissioning a house was a natural idea for Ball, who had long been interested in architecture. In the 1950s he had undertaken preliminary studies in the discipline and had begun his working life as an architectural draughtsman, an experience that still echoed in the carefully plotted sketches he often produced for his paintings. He wanted to build something significant and, aware of Glenn Murcutt's work, sought an introduction through a mutual friend, architect Bill Ashton.

It was a well-judged choice. Murcutt, then in his mid-forties, had only completed a handful of projects, but he was already recognised for a distinctive vision that synthesised European and American modernist architecture, such as that of Alvar Aalto and Ludwig Mies van der Rohe, with a feel for distinctly Australian conditions: the bush, the light, the flooding rain, the threat of intense fire. Murcutt's second realised house design, a glass- and steel-enveloped pavilion in the northern Sydney suburb of Terrey Hills, had been completed in 1974 and later received the Wilkinson Award, presented by the New South Wales chapter of the Australian Institute of Architects. It had sparked a growing flurry of interest in his work. Soon-to-be-iconic houses in Kempsey and Mount Irvine followed, each finely tuned to their surroundings. As with his eventual design for Ball and Eastaway, these houses sought without imposition to elaborate the landscapes they inhabited. Their forms accorded to the views they took in: they turned away here, opened there, the sweep of them lifting and falling with softly unassuming drama.

But the bush at Glenorie pushed in at all sides. Everything was close, a mess of exquisite detail, of light and shadow. It demanded its own solution.

—

Not long after I visited Eastaway at Glenorie, I organised an interview with Murcutt. Now in his late eighties, he is still working, which he does – largely alone – from the unassuming duplex in a North Shore Sydney suburb that he shares with his second wife, fellow architect Wendy Lewin.

Murcutt now enjoys a significant international reputation. In 2002 he received the Pritzker Architecture Prize, the most significant in the field, and to date remains the only Australian to do so – leading some to dub him 'Australia's most famous architect'. His other awards are numerous, and still coming: days after he and I met, he was flying to Japan to mark his receipt of the Praemium Imperiale (an annual prize awarded across five creative disciplines, Murcutt was joining recent laureates as significant as the American land artist James Turrell, the cellist Yo-Yo Ma, the photographer Sebastião Salgado and the dissident Chinese artist Ai Weiwei). Although he has long had the opportunity to do so, Murcutt has never scaled his practice up in the manner that so many successful architects do, choosing to eschew larger financial returns in favour of a high degree of selectivity over which projects he undertakes. I already knew why from an earlier phone conversation: Murcutt firmly believes that the thing at the centre of a practice – the act of making – is the most important aspect of any creative endeavour. The larger one scales a practice, architectural or otherwise, the further one risks getting from this simple fact. In 1980, when he first met with Ball and Eastaway over lunch in the Sydney suburb of Leichhardt, this concern for the integrity of his work was already prominent in his mind.

'The thing is this,' he begins, seated across from me in the centre of his open-plan living space, which has undergone a simple yet deeply effective Murcutt–Lewin redesign, 'you've got to sort out the people who are genuine – who absolutely want to do it – from those who want a status symbol.'

This may make Murcutt sound formidable but, although he speaks of his work with a certain concentrated intensity, his character is open and curious. And his commitment to holding the centre of his practice close has clearly paid off: he remains acutely alive to its mysteries, and even after some seven decades is often still surprised by the way a landscape can activate his designs. 'I make my buildings work hard,' he'd told me on the phone. 'So if it is raining you hear the rain trickling into the tanks – that beautiful, life-affirming sound of water. So if you open vents, you can bring the perfume of the landscape inside.' He had always been interested in the passage of sunlight – how it reaches into a building at different times of day; how it changes with the seasons, and can be bounced off interior walls to diffuse softly through space. After a client alerted him to an unexpected spill of moonlight in the house he'd designed for her, he had become increasingly alert to its lunar equivalent. A building, he explained, is best conceived of as an instrument, something that the surrounding landscape plays.

Murcutt recalls readily accepting the commission from Ball and Eastaway. 'Working with artists is a great pleasure for me,' he says, as his ancient black chihuahua jumps shakily onto the chair next to him, where it curls up and falls instantly asleep. 'It's such a wonderful thing because there's such overlap in what we do: we're talking about light and whether their own work is going to be displayed, or whether the work of other artists is going to be displayed.' The only firm design note came from Ball: he wanted an unusually long interior wall somewhere in the house so he could hang a vast, multi-panel painting he'd made in New York.

'It was a very nice problem to have,' Murcutt recalls, before gently correcting himself. 'I don't really think it was a problem; it was an issue. I call them issues.'

Another was the view. 'Almost all clients, when they have a beautiful view, they want the whole lot, all the time. And it's a huge error. A great view has to be limited – you've got to find different parts of it, and then frame each of those as a painting.'

The resulting design is a masterclass in the power of withholding and the power of revelation, with Ball's long central wall acting as a hinge between the two. The entrance is reached by a long walkway of planks that run at an oblique angle to the house's longest side, their edges not trimmed flush but left as a perfectly staggered zigzag. The house sits at the edge of the sandstone shelf, which falls away in a series of gentle intervals. On approach, one readily senses the drop-off to the view beyond, but open the door and it's the long wall – a kind of backbone that runs down the interior – that a visitor is confronted with: it conceals the landscape, redirecting the focus to Ball's painting. Any view to the bush outside comes in concentrated glimpses until finally, on each of the house's two verandahs, it is seen, heard and felt in something close to entirety. 'You see your landscape more clearly by not having it all the time,' Murcutt tells me.

Eastaway still remembers Murcutt's first visit to the block. He walked off alone into the bush, spending time sitting and thinking, just as she and Ball once had. She would come to understand the northwest facing verandah, which is recessed flush behind the painting wall, as a carefully framed expression of the central view Murcutt had taken in on that first day. It's where Eastaway and I had lunch during my visit, the sun-warmed wall radiant behind us and the bush right before us – close enough, it seemed, to reach out and touch. This is the fullest view to be had from the house, but to access it, one must pass through an unassuming door that, when closed behind, seals the verandah off from the domestic interior completely. In the early 1980s Eastaway had taken up meditation, and Murcutt had originally conceived the space with this in mind, but Eastaway has since come to associate it with something else: the experience of sitting under one of the larger of the rock overhangs that lie down the gully from the house, by the creek. The connection resonates. Like a shallow cave, the verandah is all muted comfort and bright aperture.

The sandstone shelf provided an obvious site for the house: a ready-made platform elevated above the sloping bush and naturally devoid of trees and shrubs. To run the house level with the shelf meant that at its far edge it was raised almost a metre and a half above the ground. Part of this was about ventilation – the height allowed air to flow beneath the house and cool it in summer – but there was more to it. Murcutt knew that even the relatively minor elevation would make the dappled light of the bush more apparent: sunlight filtered through the eucalypts, bringing out the varied colour of their leaves and lending the tree cover an intense sense of transparency, which his early travels in Europe had convinced him was specifically Australian in character. With similar sensitivity, he designed a system of steel-pipe columns – fourteen in total – that sunk directly into the sandstone. As holes for these footings were carefully drilled, he directed the builders to set aside the resulting stone dust to mix back into the cement that would hold each column in place.

As Murcutt tells it, it's easy to trace the origins of his architectural practice to his childhood, particularly the influence of his self-reliant polymath father, Arthur.

The first of five siblings, Murcutt was born in London in 1936, during a journey that his parents had taken to see the Summer Olympics in Berlin. The couple was living in Papua New Guinea, where Arthur had relocated from Australia in 1919, finding work as a carpenter in Port Moresby before establishing a small alluvial goldmine in the remote upper Watut Valley, where Murcutt's mother, Daphne, had joined him in 1934. The family returned there from Europe and stayed until the Japanese advance during World War II forced their return to Australia. Murcutt was just shy of his sixth birthday, but the experience of living in a simple corrugated-iron, steel and fibro house raised off the ground on stilts, surrounded by the dramatic highland landscape, had already proven deeply formative.

After serving in the air force, Arthur opened a joinery business in Manly. During his time in Papua New Guinea, he had purchased a staggering ninety-six blocks of uncleared bushland in the then new Middle Harbour suburbs of Seaforth and Clontarf, where he initially chose to settle. The surrounding bush was still largely pristine, and the roads only half-sealed. The first house they lived in was commissioned, but the second, which was completed in 1950, was designed and built by Arthur himself. It was three storeys, and, along with the family, eventually housed seven pianos. The block was adjacent to the foreshore reserve and looked directly over a low cliff and a strip of beach that would vanish at high tide. Murcutt recalls family dinners on the rocky outcrop that marked the edge of their garden, the sun sinking low. 'That was the reality,' he tells me. 'We were brought up at a time in this country that was, in landscape terms, what I regard as paradise.'

Vivid memories underscore the shaping influence of his father's committed environmentalism, a good part of it dedicated to the quixotic task of holding back encroaching suburbia. Murcutt and his siblings were enlisted to collect and propagate the seeds of the area's endemic tree species, which were being felled to make way for new houses: majestic angophora costatas, black wattles, melaleucas. They learnt to quicken germination by baking the seeds in the oven, and then to nurture them in nutrient-rich soil taken from their neighbours' septic tank outlets, before planting the resulting seedlings on covert missions over the area's newly cleared slopes. Some of them, Murcutt tells me proudly, are still growing there today. If Arthur heard trees being chopped in the surrounding bush, he was known to take to the verandah with a loudspeaker to warn the perpetrators off in no uncertain terms; schoolfriends of Murcutt's, who might have been gathering wood for a bonfire and been subjected to one of the amplified tirades, would tell him, 'You ought to be careful, there's a madman living out your way!'

Once, when Glenn and his younger brother Douglas returned from a day's fishing with a bumper catch of leatherjackets – far more than the family could consume – Arthur calmly directed them to freeze the excess. As punishment for overfishing, he made sure that no matter what the family were eating, the two boys were only served fish, until, almost a month later, the supply was exhausted. *Don't take more than you need to eat*, he told them at the end of the ordeal. 'My father came very close to fanatical,' Murcutt says.

Arthur also encouraged his children to engage with art, music, architecture and books. He read and re-read cherished first editions of Freud, Jung and Thoreau, among others, and emphatically passed on what he learnt to his children.

By age twelve Murcutt was working in the joinery, and at seventeen was applying the descriptive geometry and drawing he'd been learning at school to the task of producing technical plans for a third family home – also Arthur-designed – in Seaforth. Thanks to his father's subscription to international architectural journals, Murcutt by then had a nascent working knowledge of some of the modernist greats: not just Aalto and van der Rohe, but Frank Lloyd Wright, Gordon Drake, and Charles and Ray Eames. He and Douglas both laboured on the project, digging trenches for footings, mixing and pouring concrete, and helping produce timber-glazed walls at the joinery. Soon afterwards, the two built a small racing-class skiff together, a project that partly explains why Murcutt sometimes likens his buildings to boats: simple machines that can perform a series of actions in response to surrounding conditions. Vents open and close to capitalise on the movement of air, metal louvres can be shut to offer protection against bushfire, sliding screens provide modular shade. With these basic actions in mind, it's easy to picture the young Murcutt brothers in their hand-built skiff, adjusting its windward course. Murcutt's houses don't move, but he does all he can to ensure that the outside world flows in and around them like the currents of a river, or the ocean.

By the time he designed the Ball–Eastaway House, Murcutt had long sublimated the lessons of childhood. They were felt most fully in his overarching concern for the integrity of each site, particularly in his sensitivity to native flora and fauna. In the 1980s, the term 'touch the earth lightly' began to be commonly appended to his buildings – a phrase first applied to them by the Western Australian architect Brian Klopper, who was in turn paraphrasing an Indigenous concept of living respectfully on Country – but Murcutt carefully adds nuance to any oversimplification that may result.

'I didn't start out with that in mind,' he says. 'But I have always been conscious, through my background and my father's background, of the economics of all things.'

He means this in broader terms than a concern for money. 'It's about the use of material: the limitation of how much you use. You're conscious of the longevity of materials, and how they can be replaced. And you put a building together so that its components can be retrieved as many parts and reused, or used in new places.'

For this reason, nails and glue were kept to a bare minimum in the construction of the Ball–Eastaway House. Murcutt's preference is for screws and bolts, fasteners that can be removed with little or no damage to the materials they connect. 'You think about a building's afterlife while you're conceiving its present,' he says. The tin and hardwood, the glass and aluminium, the downpipes and benches: if needed, all these can be replaced in the simplest fashion. But, bit by bit, they could also be disassembled as a discrete collection of functional parts. Not a demolition, but a deconstruction towards a future configuration. All that would be left would be the fourteen small contact points where the footings sunk into their sandstone base. After a season of rain and leaf-fall, these too would likely disappear from view.

—

On the evidence of Ball's paintings, moving to Glenorie and into the Murcutt-designed house was not without its challenges. Ball initially struggled to reconcile his commitment to American abstraction with the Australian bush, and to address this he slowly began to introduce shadowy figures, renderings of tribal sculpture and elements of landscape into his paintings. The shift was not without precedent – several noted American and Australian abstract painters underwent a similar turn towards figuration in the late 1970s and early 1980s – but Ball's new paintings were not always met with enthusiasm. When he travelled in Korea, Tibet and China in the mid-1980s, themes of symbolism and shamanic religion began to manifest in his work as well, as did ideas loosely drawn from his personal reading of Buddhism. When his representative gallery in Sydney closed, he wouldn't secure another for more than a decade.

Eastaway was similarly searching. By the time the house was being built, her interest in meditation had steered her towards a group called Self-Transformations, which focused on demanding sessions of transcendental meditation. She recalls the experience as 'intense'. It called for punishing hours of introspection that opened her sense of self wide. She would return from weekend-long retreats near euphoric, but still scattered. 'It was almost like I was high,' she says. She remembers Ball being fascinated by the changes the meditation wrought in her, but although he almost attended the sessions alongside her, he eventually demurred. 'You do it for both of us,' he said. When she met another man through the meditation group, existing tensions in her relationship with

Ball became unavoidable, and Eastaway was soon living in Sydney again.

The informal arrangement that would define much of the remainder of Ball's life then began: he in the Glenorie house and studio, Eastaway coming and going. They remained close, settling into a deep sense of camaraderie. Their conversations were studded with private jokes, and Ball often attended Christmas celebrations with Eastaway's extended family. They continually found their eyes independently drawn to the same phenomena in the Glenorie bush. 'Did you see that?' one of them would excitedly ask the other, perhaps in reference to an early-blooming wildflower or the almost impossibly pink trunk of a particular angophora. Invariably the answer would be 'Yes!'

Back in Sydney, Eastaway's own career continued to take shape. She taught; she began to exhibit regularly. And although Ball often still called on her to look at new work in the studio, his influence on her receded. Over the coming decades she would develop paintings that were complementary to his, yet entirely her own; quiet, cerebral-seeming abstractions in which blocks of colour met one another on otherwise clear grounds. When I visited, part of a series from 2016 lay on one of her studio tables: unstretched canvasses painted crisply in muted colours. They were folded snugly into flat, purpose-built boxes. Eastaway pulled one out and demonstrated how she intended it to be unfolded and re-folded like a complex, oversized table napkin.

When Ball suffered a stroke in 2017, Eastaway was in Sydney. The 1990s had been difficult for him but, after securing a new gallery in the early 2000s, he had experienced a late-career reawakening to his work. He had received an honorary doctorate from the University of South Australia, and had been the subject of a large touring survey exhibition and an elegant three-part publication. By then he had long turned back to abstraction

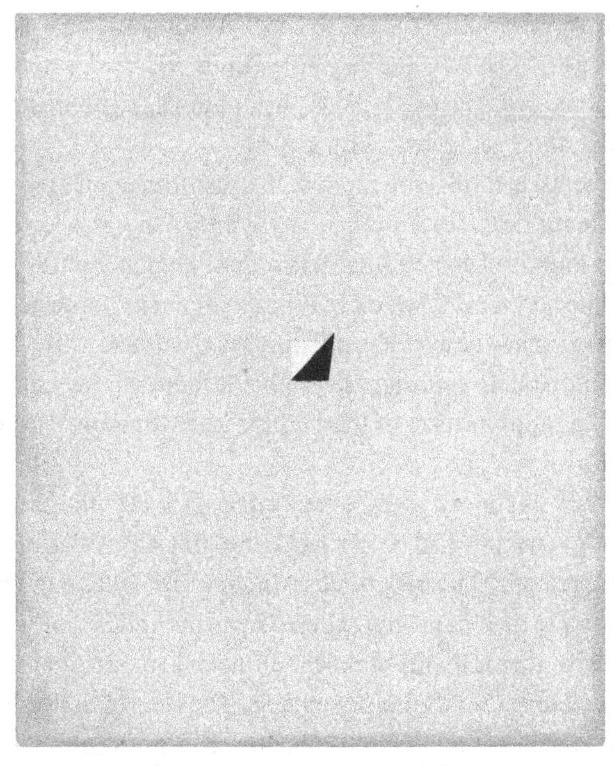

Lynne Eastaway *Blue* 2021

– alongside the modular *Infinex* paintings, he'd undertaken a striking, richly coloured series later grouped under the title *Structures*, in which geometric shapes were treated like the insignia of tiny bush republics. He had, in a sense, come full circle.

When he couldn't be reached by phone at the Glenorie house, Eastaway called a neighbour to check on him, and he was rushed to Hornsby hospital. She sat with him in his final days. He was conscious, but confused: 'What have I done, Lynn-ee, to get so sick like this?' she recalls him asking.

'Syd, it's just life,' she replied. 'It's just life happening.'

After he died, she drove back to Sydney at night, accompanied by the sounds of some of Ball's favourite chamber music playing by chance on ABC Classic FM – in the moment, it seemed like it was every piece he ever loved, one after the other. At the funeral, she couldn't help smiling. 'He kind of left me this joy,' she recalls now. 'His appreciation of life and his love of nature: that's what sticks with me.'

It took Eastaway two years to settle back into the house. The decision to return had been a hard one, and she initially doubted her judgement. The task of cleaning out her studio and setting her mind to new paintings seemed insurmountable, so when she did begin, it was by the simplest of means: making unassuming watercolours at her dining-room table. The view of the bush before her was densely modulated by Murcutt's aluminium louvres, sectioned windows and screens.

Murcutt would later tell me what he needed to begin a design such as the one he'd done for the house at Glenorie. 'Reverie,' he would say. 'A state between sleeping and waking.' He had already told me about the Finnish architect Juhani Pallasmaa's 2009 book *The Thinking Hand*, in which Pallasmaa, a close friend of Murcutt's, argues for the innate intelligence not of the mind that guides the creative act, but of the act itself. As Eastaway embarked upon her new watercolours, she would surely have recognised the idea: it's one that echoes strongly throughout the history of twentieth-century art and is perhaps most famously expressed in pioneering abstract artist Paul Klee's belief that 'the eye travels along the paths cut out for it in the work'. It's a belief in the agency of the artwork itself; whether a drawing, a painting, a building, a piece of music or a passage of prose, it contains a form that its author discovers, rather than designs. Whatever the process, it might initially feel elusive, but then something takes hold. Murcutt begins with sketches – little more than doodles – and slowly works them towards something tangible. 'All of a sudden it breaks,' he tells me. 'And you just know that you've landed on something. There's a lovely feeling of resolution: you've found a solution. Not *the* solution, but *a* solution.'

As Eastaway worked, she realised – much like Ball had before her – that she couldn't simply paint the bush. But it was equally clear that something in her work had to shift. 'I began by looking for another colour palette,' she says. 'I'd come up to the block, and things were so different, and I just thought, *I've got to find another palette.*' Her mind turned to an American First Nations mask she'd recently seen in a museum in Paris, coloured beautifully with dusty pink, red, purple, grey and white. She started there, adjusting the colours ever so slightly as she gradually made her way through a block of watercolour paper. All the while, the light outside the window shifted incrementally, and the colours she saw there – initially too subtle to apprehend – started to ring clear.

Her new palette expanded: she added greens, yellows, blues and ochre reds. Whereas Ball had settled on colours that contrasted sharply with the surrounding environment, she found herself meeting it on its own terms. 'I realised it was colour and light that I was responding to. I couldn't deal with all the little fiddly bits of the view – that was too much. But the colour and the light – that was just spectacular.'

In her studio, three recent paintings hang on the wall. They are small. Each is a muted yellow, green or red, with tiny geometric forms painted at their centres: black squares, abutted triangles, standing rectangles. They aren't pictures of anything but themselves, yet they are redolent of the world just outside the adjacent window; in the same way that salt-burnished sea glass takes on something of the ocean, they have distilled the bush into abstract form. They exude warmth. I want to take them from the wall and hold them.

'The more you're out here, the more you see,' Eastaway says. She smiles at the memory of herself sitting at the table with the first of her watercolours, the view that Murcutt framed ever-changing before her. '*Oh, thank god,* I thought. *The decision to return was right.*'

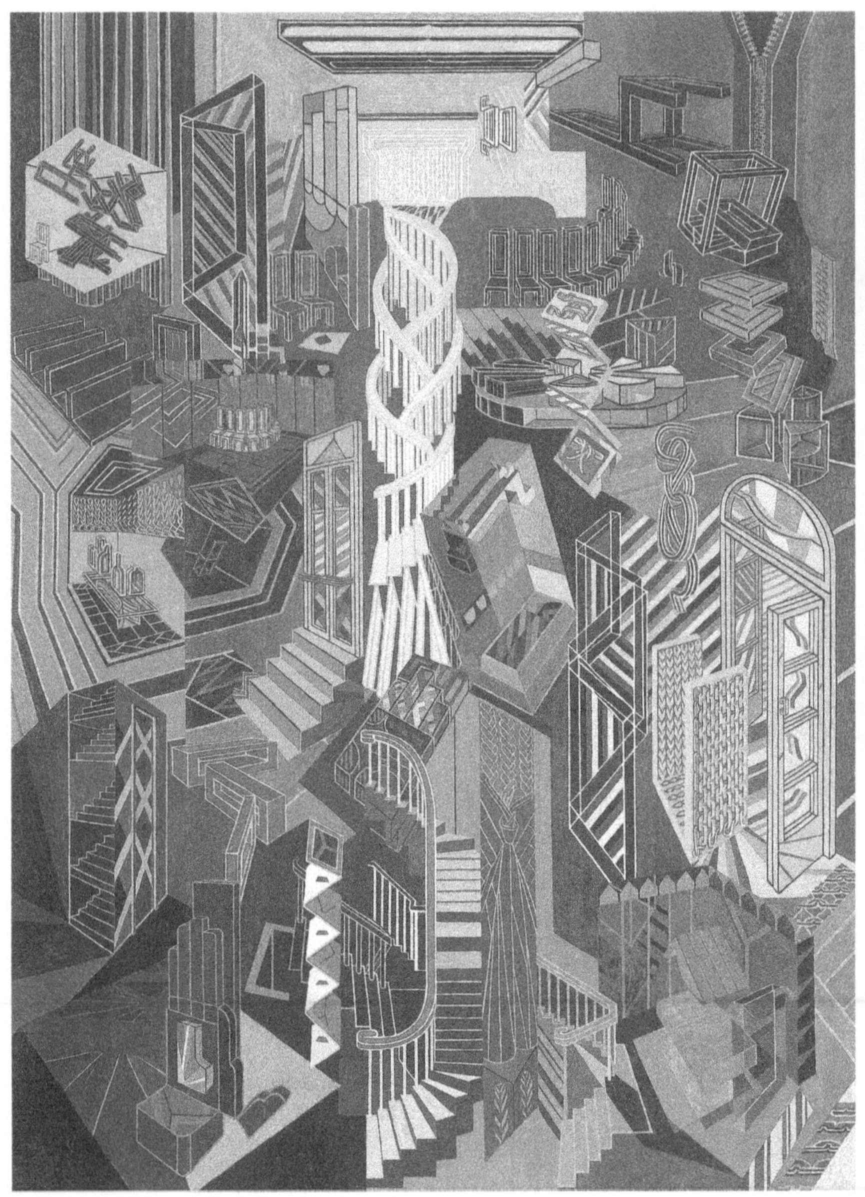

Helen Maudsley *Renewal, to find permission* 1989

8

A City in the Distance

I don't recall the first time I saw a painting by Helen Maudsley, but I certainly recall the feeling it left me with: a kind of niggling bemusement that threatened, ever so slightly, to tip into something outright unsettling.

The work would have been one like *Renewal, to find permission* (1989), which is held in the collection of the National Gallery of Victoria, and which many would argue comes at a high point of the artist's career: a period in which she consolidated the long promise of her practice into relatively large-scale and often highly intricate compositions.

That painting, like many Maudsley paintings before or since, is difficult to put into words. It's complex, constructed shallowly on the picture plane from sectional forms that have been either folded or unfurled into highly mannered geometric arrangements that recall the architectural follies of a partially completed cityscape. From there, the visual associations keep coming, even as the imagery, such as it is, remains stubbornly obscure. One senses a bustling future world precisely imagined from the mid-century past. Or a blueprint for a vast ribbon factory. Or an early gene-splicing experiment rendered in all its microcosmic glory. Or – and I'd hazard that this lands somewhere close to what Maudsley's strange pictures do indeed capture – a sequence of feelings rendered as forms, each prompting the next towards some far distant revelation that, although anticipated step by carefully weighed step, is destined to remain unknowable.

I've chosen *Renewal, to find permission* at relative random. Many works from this period – the 1980s to the early 2010s, which is roughly from when Maudsley was between sixty and eighty years old – loosely embody the above description. For Maudsley is among those artists for whom a practice is something like an unbroken thread along which individual works are strung. Each is different, yes, but only in subtle ways; there are few sudden breaks or stylistic shifts. Such consistency can be evidence of an artist having been captured by market expectations – by the demand for a certain kind of work. But for an artist like Maudsley, it is evidence of something else entirely: a particularly rich creative enquiry where even the smallest of variations from one work to the next sustain a driving fascination. She returns to similar visual conundrums again and again, as if worrying at a knot. When she succeeds in untying it, she ties it again, often more elaborately, setting the challenge anew.

Consider her palette, for instance. It has always been characterised by an unusual emphasis upon emerald greens, greenish greys, and purples, but at times she adds patches of warmer colour – a rich orange, perhaps, or a golden yellow – that serve to illuminate discrete sections of her compositions like beams of evening sun falling among a stand of trees. Variation might also appear at a more formal level: in the way certain of her elongated geometric forms, which are often rendered as open, box-like structures, slot together on the picture plane. Or at the point where these forms begin to describe actual things, among them a chair fallen on its side, or an angular light globe, its filament sending forth jagged lines of electricity. All this adds to a striking density of vision. After spending time with Maudsley's stubborn yet generous images, one is left with the feeling of being granted access to a deeply interior world, fully formed and completely original.

—

Maudsley, who is now nearing ninety-eight, has been described for decades with such words as 'tenacious' and 'underrated'. One would think she'd lived her life in obscurity, but that isn't strictly true. Although her work remains little known outside the art world, her tenacity is less remarkable for that fact than for the way in which she maintained her studiously obtuse practice in relation to that of her late husband, one of Australia's most famous painters, John Brack.

In contrast to Maudsley, who exhibits under her maiden name, Brack is as close to a household name as an Australian artist might hope to become. A number of his works, particularly those from the mid-twentieth century, have become icons of Australian art, akin to Sidney Nolan's celebrated paintings of Ned Kelly. Whereas Maudsley has only begun to receive significant institutional attention over the last decade or so, the National Gallery of Victoria purchased Brack's painting *The barber's shop* (1952) before he'd even held a solo exhibition, and went on to present his first major retrospective in 1987. By then he was already securely in the canon, a position only reinforced in the time since his death in 1999: to date, significant exhibitions of his work have been held at the National Gallery of Australia, the Art Gallery of South Australia, the Heide Museum of Modern Art, the National Portrait Gallery, and at the National Gallery of Victoria once again (this time in 2009). But his visibility extends much further: a handful of his most famous paintings – *Collins St, 5p.m.* (1955), for instance, which offers a simple visual indictment of the rat-race – has become the kind that high-schoolers are asked to write essays about.

I had thought I might arrange to visit Maudsley at her studio to talk over works in progress, or at the very least speak to her over several phone conversations. I'd read the few profiles of her that had appeared in art magazines and newspapers and knew that, although she was staunchly committed to sustaining the mystery of her work – offering little by way of direct interpretation – she was also apt to couch her practice in terms that seemed tailored to writerly interlocutors. At some stage in her long career she had taken to referring to her paintings as 'visual essays'. 'When you notice something, you think about it, and then you do your essay about it,' she explained to the journalist Gabriella Coslovich in 2007, as if this was the most obvious, and indeed only, way to describe her paintings. I cautiously anticipated a fruitful conversation. But then the doubt set in. The more I'd looked at Maudsley's work, the more its apparent obscurity had grown on me. In case it's not already clear, she shares nothing of her late husband's preference for a clearly definable subject, which she has characterised as his desire to speak directly to 'the common man in the street'. It's almost as if at some early stage of being designated the wife of a more famous husband, she'd decided to make no concessions to potential viewers at all and instead doubled down.

I pulled up an image of *Renewal, to find permission* on my computer screen and looked again. I began to wonder if I really wanted to know more about a work like this than what I could take from the work itself. Wasn't that the point – that a certain kind of painting required labour to see fully, and that somewhere in this labour the artist's intention becomes clear? Perhaps it was a lesson for me to simply look at the practice, and piece together what I could.

Ultimately, the decision was made for me. When I reached out to Maudsley's long-term gallerist, William Nuttall, he suggested that she 'might not be up' to speaking. He put me in touch with one of her four daughters, Freda, an architect in her seventies who, like her mother, lives in suburban Melbourne. She concurred. Although Maudsley was still painting, Freda explained that she had recently been struggling to put her thoughts into language, and that at times this struggle could result in frustration, even distress.

When I heard this, I couldn't help but think of a painting of Maudsley's I had seen at an exhibition six months earlier: a near-to-square canvas of floating forms on an almost garish purple ground. These forms were mostly letters, as if words had been caught in the process of assembling or disassembling. I couldn't help but feel that, deliberately or not, the painting attempted to catch the thing that had increasingly pressed in at the edges of each of Maudsley's recent exhibitions of new work: the unavoidable fact of her advancing age. She'd created large-scale works like *Renewal, to find permission* on and off until the early 2000s, but over the past decade or so her paintings had grown smaller and smaller. The lines in them had begun to gently shake, and the overall compositions appeared ever so slightly gauzy, as if viewed through water. To borrow her own literary analogy, they now functioned more like visual aphorisms than longform essays.

I asked Freda if these qualities, no matter how effective, could simply be understood as a faltering of capacity. She paused briefly to consider, then put it another way. She described it to me as an 'emptying out', but not so much in terms of a loss as a concentration, a stripping back to something essential before death.

She described another recent work, yet to be titled, and afterwards sent me an image: a tiny canvas on which her mother had painted a clamshell, the two parts of which were floating one above the other. A ribboning black line ran through the top half of the shell, while the half below seemed to emanate faint lines of energy. Otherwise, the shell was empty, its inner whiteness stark against a background of soft green, mauve and purple. People who'd seen this painting had remarked to Freda how beautiful and quiet the image was, restful even. But to her it appeared different: a picture of the last, or near to last, energy escaping from the earthly container that once held it.

Like many of Maudsley's paintings, the work showed no discernible evidence of reworking or erasure, and thus appeared to have been conjured fully formed. Although I found it immediately affecting, it was also marked by a characteristic emotional restraint. I looked at it and imagined the mantra that might guide Maudsley's studio labours: hold the world at bay, examine it in fine detail, try to capture the complexities of its inner workings. But, whatever you do, only divulge your findings in the most coded manner.

This coding is as evident in her works' titles as it is in their content. *Renewal, to find permission,* is something of an exception. It doesn't obviously match with the image it names, but it's stunningly simple when considered alongside others, which are not only more verbose but draw on spacing and punctuation that tip towards poetry.

Some examples:

A 2023 painting of floating forms (old-fashioned nappy pins, shells, dry leaves, a mannequin hand, abstract shapes) on a grey ground: *The Ear, The Leaves, and The Swan. / The Hanging Lights. / And 8 is For Ever.*

A 2018 painting of geometric objects and open apertures crowding together in fractured space:

> *Our Souls, our Minds, our Thoughts, all cased in our Heads.*
> *Our Consciousness/Awareness; Our Unconsciousness/ Unawareness.*
> *Our Stupidity.*
>
> *Male; Female.*
>
> *Our Ignorance; Our Cultural Permission;*

Rules and Regulations; Rejection if you don't Conform.

I make the Rules; You will Obey or I will Kill You.

However Hard we Try, We never Get it Right.

A 1975 painting in pink and green and purple that, even though created more than two decades earlier than those above, is only different by degrees (and, for the record, does not obviously contain either a nude or a portrait): *Nude. Survival; they say I'm not what I am. / Nude. Portrait. Trying to survive.*

In 2021, Maudsley explained the genesis of her titles to the curator Kelly Gellatly. Early in her career, she tended towards the short and evocative: *The Encounter*, for instance, or *The evening creature*. But then she'd been prompted by a child-psychologist friend of Brack's to be more descriptive. 'Couldn't you give the titles as a hint to something more?' she recalled him saying. So, in her own idiosyncratic fashion she did, aiming to give the viewer 'a leg into it', which is to say, a point of orientation. 'And I still do this,' she told Gellatly. 'I still give titles that I think are going to orient people.'

I assume she said this with a straight face, even though it's surely clear to anyone, except perhaps Maudsley, that orienting the viewer is exactly what her titles do not do. Yes, they provide something like an emotional architecture for her images, but it is an architecture that appears built by hands reaching in the dark. They read as if she were attempting a detailed, street-level description of a city she can only see from a distance.

—

Maudsley was born in 1927 and identified as an artist early. She began to draw seriously in her early teens as respite from a bout of osteomyelitis (a bone infection) that confined her to bed for an entire year and, according to some accounts, probably should have killed her.

On her recovery, her parents encouraged her to pursue higher studies in music – she had also taken up the flute during her long illness – but she ultimately decided otherwise: she didn't want to be beholden to other performers, nor to a set repertoire. By her late teens she was enrolled at the National Gallery Art School, a studio-based school at the National Gallery of Victoria that drilled into students the tenets of European tradition. It was there she met Brack, a returned serviceman seven years her senior and so apparently joyless that, for a joke, Maudsley's friend bet her she wouldn't be able to get him to invite her to dinner. Maudsley persisted and eventually won; the two were soon an item.

Her parents' disapproval was immediate. She had been born into the upper echelons of Melbourne society – her grandfather was a London-trained physician who was knighted for his service in World War I, and her father was a well-known psychiatrist. Brack, whose father was employed in a brewery, and firmly pro-union, was working class through and through. When the two married and Maudsley fell pregnant, her parents essentially disowned her, and it was only when her daughter, Clara, arrived prematurely that they reconciled. Clara came suddenly in the pre-dawn hours and, after rushing Maudsley and their newborn to hospital, Brack jumped back in the taxi and hightailed it to his in-laws'. Arriving unannounced, he still clutched the bloodied bedsheet they had swaddled Clara in: 'Helen's had her baby,' he said. Three more girls – Vicki, Freda and Charlotte – came in quick succession, none of them planned. By just twenty-seven Maudsley was a mother of four.

Money was scarce. According to Freda, the growing family lived frugally, constrained by limited means. Both parents remained committed to their practices; a difficult choice, but not one taken alone. The Melbourne art world of the day was so small that most serious artists knew one another, and the Bracks were part of a milieu that included other art families, most of them similarly destitute – the Boyds, the Williamses, the Percevals and the Blackmans. Yet Maudsley stood a touch apart: none of the others came from a background like hers. Class loomed large in social relations, even in the bohemian art world. She had been educated at the exclusive St Catherine's, a school for girls located in Toorak, and, consciously or not, carried herself with what could seem a whiff of superiority. 'The others were, I think, a bit intimidated by her,' Freda told me.

Maudsley fitted her practice around a strict baby-feeding timetable dictated by the now infamous Truby King, which emphasised rigorous schedules and limited parental interaction. She worked on watercolours in the living room (she only turned to oil when her children began school and she had longer hours at her disposal) while Brack laboured in a spare room that the children were discouraged from entering.

Freda recalled a complex dynamic between her parents. Both were firm believers in the solitary demands of creativity, but with family came compromise: it was decided early on that Maudsley would do the lion's share of child-rearing, while Brack worked three days a week as the art master at Melbourne Grammar School (he later took up a position as head of his alma mater, the Gallery School) and poured his energy into his nascent career. She provided feedback on his work, but it wasn't necessarily reciprocated – as far as Freda remembered, although Brack would have seen Maudsley's work in constant progress, he never attended even one of her exhibitions. Blunt evidence of the patriarchy in action? Yes and no. There were likely more personal reasons too. Freda recalls her parents as stubbornly intelligent, elusive characters, hard for even their children to know. 'To tell you the truth, I think that arrangement suited both of them well,' she said. As for his lack of feedback, Maudsley would later surmise it was because her work was 'too foreign to him'. 'He became cross I wasn't following in his footsteps,' she told Kelly Gellatly. 'So in the end, it was just two separate identities.'

During the first decade or so of the marriage, Brack created some of his most famous works. Many of them feature nameless Willie Lomax types stoically enduring the drudgery of mid-twentieth-century life. They are shown glumly drinking in a public bar (*The Bar*, 1954), moving stony-faced through peak-hour crowds (*Collins St, 5p.m.*), grimly selling suits in a department store (*Men's Wear*, 1953) or hunched despairingly at the wheel of the family station wagon (*The Car*, 1955). One rare couple appear content amid the modern accoutrements of their new home (*The New House*, 1953), but Brack is satirising them. The apparently joyless serviceman had become an apparently joyless painter. Even *The Old Time* (1969), which depicts a cluster of competitive ballroom dancers mid-swing, is not nearly as exuberant as its subject suggests it should be: the couples are stilted and angular, their faces frozen in rictus grins.

Early on, Maudsley did appear to follow in Brack's footsteps, painting figurative work with a critical eye not unlike his. She similarly tended to render even the most everyday social niceties strange, poking at the frigid core of convention. The young woman she once was is clearly sensed in these images. She's adrift among Melbourne's mannered classes, looking in from the outside: a group of young mothers stand and talk in their Sunday best; a wealthy, gauchely dressed man ogles a woman, his eyes bulging. But then, in the mid-1950s – which is to say, just as Brack turned towards his idealised man-in-the-street viewer – the obscurity that defines her work for the rest of her long career began to creep in. Against the backdrop of his work, it could almost seem wilful.

As he painted *The Bar* and *Collins St, 5p.m.*, for instance, she was experimenting with pieces such as *The listening lady* (c. 1955–56), in which a string of folded forms extend spine-like between open volumes that may or may not describe a ribcage and pelvis – a lovechild between Georges Braque and H.R. Giger. An early moment of public recognition, which was the only such moment for decades to come, almost arrived in 1960 when the curator Ursula Hoff purchased Maudsley's *Plant Landscape* (1958) for the National Gallery of Victoria, but it was not hung. Although not nearly as openly weird as *The listening lady* and other works like it, *Plant Landscape* nonetheless shivers with oddness, its clinically observed floral forms suggesting that the roots of Maudsley's later visual language were always, at least in part, natural rather than synthetic in origin.

For the next two decades her work oscillated between the clearly figurative and the apparently abstract, often uncomfortably, but by the late 1970s she had settled into what constituted her mature style: her 1978 watercolour *Portrait of Elizabeth* is firmly abstract, only a portrait in the most indirect fashion. It's all tightly interlocking forms and spiralling geometry, thinly painted in that now familiar palette of bruise-like purples and slightly sickly emerald greens.

All the while, Maudsley watched Brack's star rise. His early success led to a strong market for his work, and in 1968 he was able to retire from his role at the Gallery School to focus on painting full-time. (Maudsley would later bring in extra income through work as a tutor in painting and drawing at the Centre for Adult Education.) By the late 1970s, he was seen among a select few – including his friend Fred Williams – as a key figure of his generation. When he died in 1999, it was just a few weeks shy of the opening of his major exhibition at the National Gallery of Australia. Declining health had led him to stop painting five years earlier, and Maudsley had nursed him towards death. 'I'm not religious or anything like that, but I find it extraordinary, this "going out",' she would later recall of the experience.

Afterwards, with museum and art auction houses circling, Maudsley was suddenly in demand for her unique insights into her husband's work. Freda sent me a good number of the short essays and catalogue entries on Brack's work that Maudsley would go on to publish, and I read through them one after another, marvelling at the near-forensic fashion in which she interprets her husband's images. She does this to a level of detail that can't help but seem a very deliberate staging of artistic intimacy. They read like a kind of intellectual claim on his work: *I know these pictures better than anyone else ever could*, she seems to be saying. Maybe, the reader thinks, even better than Brack himself.

One of her longest essays is reserved for *The Bar*, which the National Gallery of Victoria purchased for a record $3.2 million in 2009. The painting is a reimagining of Édouard Manet's *A Bar at the Folies-Bergère* (1882), a famously sumptuous image of bourgeoise French life that Brack retools into dour kitchen-sink realism for the mid-century antipodes. But Maudsley urges us to look deeper. She claims the image, with its barmaid overseer rising in front of a sea of male drinkers, as one of overlapping symbols. Even the smallest detail is, in her mind, ripe for interpretation: 'The beer-tap in the lower right is a sinister shape with many overtones,' she writes. 'It has a helmet-like shape of an inquisitor, and calls by shape to the rows of ghostly drinking glasses, an army of innocents, waiting in vulnerability.' She continues:

> *The Bar* was an essay on men whose labor provides existence, but also on women whose task is the species' survival. In the figure of the Barmaid he was looking beyond the stereotypes of Motherhood or of seduction into the hardness of women, into the practical necessities that women take on and do, people of action with or without credit, sustainers of Life, of our survival.

The gender archetypes are outmoded, sure, and perhaps reveal more about Maudsley's own relationship (or lack thereof) to second-wave feminism than they do about Brack's painting, but I'd argue this misses the point. I return to this passage for what seemingly lies just beneath its surface. At the risk of an overly biographical interpretation of Maudsley's essay, it is hard to read it and not wonder how much its carefully generalised language may apply to something very specific. What of the domestic and creative dynamic between Brack and Maudsley – he reaching for posterity as the great chronicler of twentieth-century urban malaise, she not only supporting her husband but corralling four daughters and running a household while fitting her own work into whatever gaps she could?

In recent years, Maudsley has been asked in ways both direct and indirect about this dynamic, and she always demurs to say much beyond inferring that she and Brack were, in the truest sense, both travelling the path their respective practices laid out for them.

In this sense, one might think her a prime candidate for reappraisal. The narrative of a long-suffering female artist labouring away in the shadow of a more famous husband has understandably found wide traction in recent years. Maudsley was recently included in a large-scale project at the National Gallery of Australia, *Know My Name*, which was aimed at balancing the well-documented gender bias of the Australian art world.

But revisionist feminist history doesn't claim her easily. A story she has told a number of interviewers over the years illustrates this well. In 1975 the firebrand American feminist curator Lucy Lippard visited Australia and gave a public lecture at the University of Melbourne about the structural challenges faced by female artists in a male-dominated art world. Maudsley was in attendance, and was incensed enough to stand up at the end and offer her own take. 'I made myself terribly unpopular,' she told Kelly Gellatly in 2021. 'I said, "It's not easy for John to sell his pictures. It's not even easy for him to get them seen. And it's not easy for me either; it's equal."'

Yet the titles she chooses for her paintings return to a set of similar, circuitously expressed ideas that seem to illuminate a concern for prevailing gender dynamics in a way her public comments do not. Repeat viewers recognise patterns of thought: opposites attract and repel, nurture and threaten; undertones of psychic, and sometimes physical, violence are coupled with a bracing sense of dependency. One thing is soft, the other hard; one thing yields while the other holds. The struggle for individuation is posed against the threat of other subjectivities pressing inward. A state of equilibrium or balance appears the goal, but it is only ever fleeting. As attested by a 2014 work, Maudsley's titles – as with her compositions – remain in constant flux: *The Not Knowing. / Each One There; Difference. / Your experience of Me, is not Me. / My experience of You, is not You.*

But if such concerns do touch upon gender, they reach further. Nothing, for Maudsley, is absolute. Indeed, if she's grappling with anything in her art, it's the very nature of selfhood. *Is it at all possible to really know another person*, she asks. And, on the flip side: *is it at all possible for another person to know me?*

—

After speaking with Freda, I reached out to the curator Elspeth Pitt at the National Gallery of Australia and arranged to view a group of Maudsley's works on paper.

Pitt – who had recently published an elegant essay on Maudsley and her work for the gallery's magazine, *Annual* – guided me down a long, rubber-floored ramp, past a display of collection works and through a nondescript door. Inside, on a low table that ran the generous length of the room, the works I'd selected lay waiting beneath sheets of conservation-grade glassine.

Most came from a group that entered the collection in 2013, gifted by Maudsley alongside a selection of Brack's sketches and studies for paintings that she had held since his death. I wanted to see them because they were odder than the usual collection fare, mostly provisional-seeming pencil drawings and watercolours that together mapped something like the genesis of her practice.

One by one I made my way through them. An untitled gouache-and-ink work from 1951 showed a group of ladies dressed in their Sunday best and a wide-eyed child standing so awkwardly that, if not for the garishly coloured print on one woman's dress, it could well be a funeral reception. At the time Clara would have been no more than two; Vicki, only a year or so – the work would have been painted in the gaps between motherhood's demands. As she does in similar images from the period, she places herself, and thus the viewer, on the outside: the foreground is dominated by one woman's back as she raises her hand in greeting to the others, effectively shutting us out. A small pencil drawing dated February 1955 is far more open. It depicts an unnamed newborn in such specific detail that it could only be one of her own (most likely Charlotte, Freda later tells me). Her limbs are neatly folded, her prematurely wizened eyes closed serenely.

A group of exquisitely observed ink-on-paper plant studies from 1958 lead into several later works. In *The morning creatures,* loosely dated as circa 1950 to 1970, Maudsley renders similar plant forms in a far more formalised, abstract manner, which, in concert with the work's title, makes them into tall, spindly personages. A beautifully precise image titled *The comic* seems to complete this shift from an observational to purely imaginative mode: it depicts an abstracted face, its eyes erupting into petals and its mouth bordered by long, jagged shapes – talons, I think, or some force of personality made manifest.

We like to believe that good artists show us everything, that their work functions as some kind of window onto themselves that they offer to their viewers. But it's not strictly true. A good artist enacts fine control over what they divulge and what they don't – Maudsley makes this more than clear. As I look from one work to the next I see how much she asks of her viewers. She withholds as much as she shows. She lays out clues but provides no obvious answers. This is not to suggest her work is an exercise in calculation. Far from it: she is clearly asking of herself at least as much as of her viewers.

Finally, my eye settles on a much later work – a pen-and-ink drawing from 2003 titled *The heads, the divinity of being, the pain of becoming*. The image is dense with architectural forms and blocky, decorative-seeming flourishes: a perfect example of her late style. It's finely rendered in short, feathering pen strokes. Maudsley has drawn her image within a border neatly ruled five or so centimetres in from the paper's edge, and around the outside margin has scribbled and scratched with the nib of her pen, testing its line, and perhaps the resolve of her hand, as she goes. Inside this ruled border everything is rendered with precision; outside lies uncertainty and doubt.

This margin would of course usually be covered by a framing mount, but unframed, the one bleeds directly into the other. Spidery cursive runs along the bottom margin, which only relates obliquely to the work's title. It reads as if Maudsley is thinking in real time about what the work is revealing to her: *How do we manage the ancient, primal forces within us all, including jealousy, envy etc., need for dominance; to be 'civilised'?*

She draws a line up and across, allowing the thought further room to expand: *'Civilised' meaning control of the feral.*

And then: *How do we live with the feral? How do we use the feral? How do we manage the feral?*

It's a bracing sentiment given that this image, like so many of her images, almost vibrates with emotional control – not exactly calm, but certainly not 'feral'.

Finally, at the far edge she writes '*WHAT IS THE TASK*', omitting the question mark and instead circling the first and last words as if emphasising a long-sought revelation.

For the viewer, though, the precise nature of this revelation remains obscure: as ever, Maudsley leaves its mysteries intact.

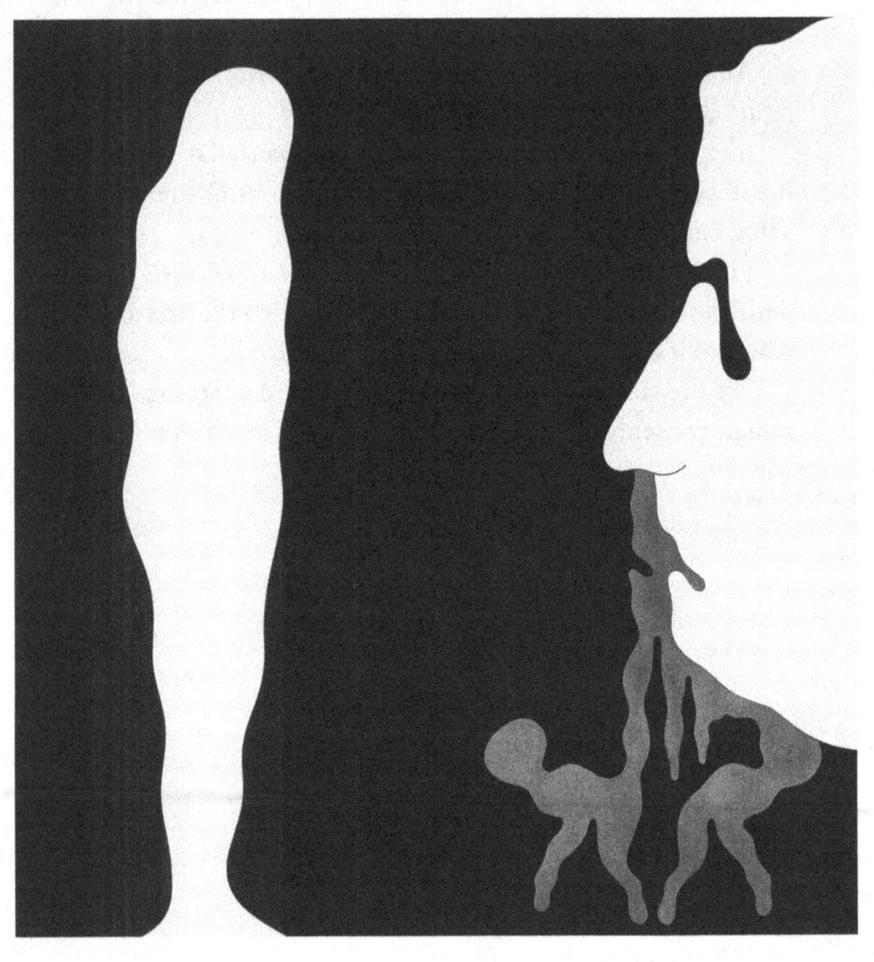

Brent Harris *Grotesquerie (le regarder)* 2002

9

Surrender and Catch

Brent Harris still recalls the moment when his father first told him of his plan to murder his wife and children. He'd shoot them at night, he said, as they slept in their beds, before turning the gun on himself.

It was the mid-1960s and although the event that Harris senior claimed would force his hand – the dropping of a nuclear bomb on their home country of New Zealand – was unlikely to occur, ten-year-old Brent wasn't to know. After all, it was the height of the Cold War, and the West's very real fear of the bomb was fanning all sorts of media hysteria, some of it valid, some not. The deadly fallout would cause horrible illness and drawn-out death, his father told him; if the bomb was dropped, he'd make sure that his family's suffering was only brief.

One unfamiliar with the dynamic of Harris's childhood might be tempted to write this off as some kind of twisted joke, but as a child Harris didn't see it that way. He'd been conditioned not to. His father ruled their small suburban house in Te Papaioea (Palmerston North) through a well-established pattern of intimidation and bullying; Harris took him at his word. He'd recently been given his first proper gun – a .22 rifle that he kept in his room, along with ammunition – and he hatched a grim counterplan. Harris promised himself that, should he ever be woken by gunshots working their way methodically through the house, he'd be up and ready in an instant. He'd push his bed against his door, load his weapon and wait with his finger on the trigger, ready to shoot the moment his father broke his way in.

Harris, now in his late sixties and among Australia's most acclaimed painters, possesses a measured yet open demeanour and wears his dark hair in a neat, boyish cut. He tells me this story during one of several visits I took to his Melbourne studio. It's the kind he can't avoid. Throughout his practice, and especially since the mid- to late 1990s, his remarkable paintings, prints and drawings have hinged to differing degrees upon confronting aspects of his difficult childhood. As content, it's rarely obvious: his work has long operated in a register of quasi-abstract figuration that purposefully complicates simple interpretation. It is free-associative and organic, as if the soft, bodily forms that he often depicts have been caught in the process of becoming. They fold in and around each other, coalescing here into drooping figures and there into mountain ranges that appear poised to melt under vast, velvet skies.

Although he works intuitively, beginning to grasp the meaning of a new image only once it manifests before him, Harris can nonetheless talk about his work with precision. It begins as small drawings, mere notations of thoughts, feelings and dreams. Some of these arrive at night, others during moments of daytime reverie. He records them as abbreviated scrawls. At times there are only a handful, but he has also been known to produce hundreds. Compositions strive to take shape, and he selects those that 'work' and scales them up: first come larger, more studied drawings in charcoal and pencil, and then his supremely controlled paintings, in which the colour is usually applied in thin washes that accrue into densely hued surfaces and perfectly flat, graphic forms. He has spent long years in therapy and believes that the images he produces, no matter how apparently obscure, grant him an opportunity to take hold of thoughts, feelings and emotions as they rise, and then to make some kind of sense of them. He once took particularly compelling examples from a series of prints to his therapist for analysis.

Not long before I began visiting Harris's studio, he'd been the subject of a career-spanning survey exhibition – by far his largest to date – that had opened at the TarraWarra Museum of Art, east of Melbourne, before travelling in slightly expanded form to the Art Gallery of South Australia. I had seen its first iteration and recognised immediately how well it laid out key aspects of his process: the incremental push and pull between various psychologically laden subject matter, the use of printmaking as a means to subtly recast his defining motifs, the tendency to work in discrete series in which certain recurring preoccupations could be held up to prolonged scrutiny. The underwriting impetus was spelt out in the exhibition title, *Surrender & Catch*, a phrase borrowed from the German-American sociologist Kurt H. Wolff, who coined it in the late 1970s for his influential theory of self-knowledge. 'To surrender means to take as fully, to meet as immediately as possible whatever the occasion may be,' Wolff wrote. 'It means *not* to select, *not* to believe that one can know quickly what one's experience means.' 'Catch' refers to what Wolff terms 'the cognitive or existential result, yield, harvest'. Harris's practice can thus be seen as a process of uncritical self-scrutiny, that opens, at least ideally, onto moments of aesthetic and psychological revelation.

It's not a complex idea, but that doesn't mean the process isn't difficult. 'You've got to put yourself in this position where you're waiting for stuff,' Harris tells me. 'You've got to surrender yourself to what might come to the surface, and then you've got to be ready to catch it.'

His recent work illustrates just how effectively he now wields this method, but the tendency was always there. Take one of the earliest paintings included in *Surrender & Catch*. It's from 1987 and is titled *Weeping Woman*, which is not a reference, as one might assume, to Picasso's 1937 painting of the same title in the collection of the National Gallery of Victoria, famously stolen in 1986 and returned under mysterious circumstances. Although he didn't set out with this in mind, Harris's painting reflects the indelible memory of his mother's tears. They came so often – prompted either in anticipation or in response to his father's incessant bullying – that her crying provided a kind of soundtrack to his formative memories, a soft keening that reached all corners of his childhood home. Such animating darkness spreads its way through his practice like an inkdrop in water. And although one doesn't need to understand its origins to understand his work, it certainly helps.

In his studio, I point to a recent drawing. Over subsequent visits I will see it worked up into a small, elegantly resolved painting in yellow, grey, white and burgundy. In it, an apparently innocuous electrical cord dangles into the picture from above; it supports a drooping lightshade that evokes a limp, dishevelled hat – a perfect example of the kind of visual bait-and-switch that Harris so often deploys to great effect. I tell him it recalls the light cords that the late American artist Philip Guston used to paint. It's an obvious reference: Guston's name has already come up in our discussions, and more than once Harris has riffled through one of the many stacks of art books in his studio to pull out a monograph on the artist's work for reference. Guston's cords similarly hang alone from the top edge of a picture, but they end in a naked bulb. They function as visual shorthand. Painted late in Guston's life, they refer partly to the long hours in which he locked himself away as a child to read and draw in a closet illuminated by a single hanging bulb, an attempt to build a world apart from the difficulties of his childhood.

I wonder if Harris's cord similarly functions as shorthand for something far more complex. Of course it does: he explains that to get into trouble in the Harris household was to be lashed about the bare legs with the cord from the electric kettle. As he speaks, he mimes the length and heft of the cord in question: 'You fold it in half, so you've got the two plugs up here,' he says, gesturing to the end his father would grip. 'And down here' – the folded middle – 'is what you thrash them with.' At times his father would place it carefully over the back of a vacant chair during family dinners – the bluntest of warnings to behave, or else.

The memory of such beatings does not remain vivid, but Harris tells me that he does dream of his father. 'He's often this incredible force that you can't fight off. And he's often laughing at me.'

He falters, searching for the right words. 'You just can't fight off this force that's coming at you, you know? You just can't.'

—

I don't want to convey that everything in Harris's painted world is grim. Far from it. It's true that his work has tended over the years towards sepulchral gloom, but this has always been offset by sustained tracts of beauty and poise, joy and humour.

Recent exhibitions, such as *Monkey Business*, which he held in 2022 at Tolarno Galleries in Melbourne, have seen him set cartoonish characters and objects at play across twilit grounds – the titular monkey, a moustachioed broomstick scarecrow, an anthropomorphic polka-dotted dress borrowed from Sidney Nolan's paintings of the cross-dressing Kelly Gang member Steve Hart. The results are not exactly light-hearted, but they undoubtedly convey a certain analytical absurdity, as if Sigmund Freud had penned *The Magic Pudding*.

A large painting that was in progress during our discussions, which Harris later titled *The Visit*, is surely among his most uplifting. In it, a pair of legs dangle loosely from above. They appear boneless, as if liquified by feeling; one foot is tucked behind the other, while the outline of the one visible big toe is curled in apparent ecstasy. The legs are painted in a warm white that is echoed in a dollop-capped mountain below; larger, colder-looking peaks recede behind. On my first visit, only small adjustments remained to come: a heightening of the olive green at the base of the foremost mountain and the possible addition of a solitary white cloud. Harris clearly revels in these seemingly tiny decisions, spending hours tuning his images until their tone and balance are just right.

When his father died in 2016, it closed a period of twenty-five years in which they hadn't spoken or seen each other. In the years since, New Zealand-esque landscapes have increasingly appeared in his work, as if marking a symbolic return to the country he grew up in. The mountains that populate *The Visit*, not to mention many other recent paintings, recall those he could see as a child from the roof of the family home. Harris's father was a builder, so there was always a ladder at hand. Harris would climb up and look out beyond his suburban surrounds to the mountains that rose on the horizon, among them Ngāuruhoe and Ruapehu to the north and snow-crowned Taranaki to the northwest, all recognised by Māori communities as living persons. 'To me, as a kid, seeing that distance was a form of escape,' he says. 'There was something out there, something other.'

Harris's inclusion of landscapes has also allowed him to negotiate the career-long influence of iconic New Zealand painter Colin McCahon. He shows me two images in a recent McCahon monograph also at hand among his stacks of art books: the paintings *Dear Wee June* and *Triple Takaka,* both from 1948. The echoes are clear: the flat olive greens, the folded forms of hills and mountains; the horizon lines that smoothly direct the viewer's gaze beyond the picture's edge.

Harris first saw McCahon's work as a child, but it was a small survey of the artist's religious paintings from the late 1940s and early 1950s that he encountered in Palmerston North's Manuwatu Art Gallery in 1975, at age nineteen, that truly stuck with him. For many, including myself, it's McCahon's late text-based paintings that resonate most strongly. Most often large, these imposing, sombre canvasses draw almost exclusively on Biblical passages, which for McCahon provided means to wrestle with questions of doubt and faith. By the time he produced these works, he was approaching the end of a long, difficult career, gripped tightly by the alcoholism that would eventually kill him; the sense that the undeniable beauty and vulnerability of his paintings was hard-won rings clear, adding a grace note to their darkness. Harris, though, has always held McCahon's early work – including what he first saw as a nineteen-year-old – most dearly.

'I still lament him ditching the figurative work,' he says while leafing further through the McCahon monograph until he finds a reproduction of the painting that would prove among the most influential for him: *The Family* (1947). It's an awkward scene of the holy family painted, like the landscapes, in oil on a bolt of unstretched canvas. St Joseph is depicted in the extreme foreground, his back to the viewer. The Virgin Mary stares blanky in the midground, her face drooping downward, the baby Jesus thrust to her naked breast. The painting possesses a deliberate naivety at odds with Harris's work, but again the resonances are there to see: the mute profile of the father, the mother's haunted presence, the palpable misery that creates an all-but-visible bond between them. Harris points out the obvious: 'It's not a happy family.'

When he first saw them, he readily recognised himself in McCahon's glum, doubt-riven figures. His difficult early years were at risk of calcifying into a life he didn't want. After a failed stint as a bank teller, his father had pressured him into working alongside him as a builder, and he was in the final stages of a carpenter's apprenticeship. Then there was the question of his sexuality. Although Harris knew he was gay, he had recently married. He shows me a photograph of his wedding day to emphasise the bind he was in. The bride smiles widely for the camera, whereas Harris appears impossibly grim.

Combined with the dark atmosphere of his childhood, it soon became too much; after three years he came out to his family, got divorced and moved to Auckland. It was there that he began painting, using a spare room in his shared house as his first studio. He fell in with a group of older gay men who introduced him to a world of concerts and exhibitions, and at twenty-five moved even further from his unhappy origins, relocating to Melbourne in 1981, where he was accepted into the Victorian College of the Arts for the following year. Upon graduation, he set to work in a series of shared inner-city studios, supporting himself through shiftwork in hospitality. His initial flush of success came relatively early, in 1988, when his work caught the eye of James Mollison, then approaching the end of his founding directorship of the National Gallery of Australia. The gallery acquired a group of early works, including *Weeping Woman*, and in the years since has collected many more.

Their subsequent friendship would prove key to Harris's career. When the two met, Mollison already possessed a long history of handpicking and supporting artists, among them sculptor Rosalie Gascoigne, whom he enthusiastically championed during the early years of her success. Harris was among two subsequent generations of interlinked Melbourne artists who would similarly benefit from Mollison's attention, especially once Mollison relocated to Melbourne in 1989 to become the director of the National Gallery of Victoria. Most were young men at the outset of their careers, a list that would go on to include Bradd Westmoreland, David Noonan, Ricky Swallow and Benjamin Armstrong. 'He just loved surrounding himself with young artists,' Harris says, adding that it was the chance to watch the 'forming of an artist' that appeared to drive him.

Mollison had once been a schoolteacher, and he retained a clear passion for guiding young minds. He would take Harris to galleries and have him stand for ages in front of particular paintings. 'He'd really get me to look,' Harris says. At times they travelled together, or met up overseas. Later, in London, Mollison took Harris and his partner, fellow painter Andrew Browne, to the collection rooms at the British Museum several times, where they were shown, among other treasures, drawings by Michelangelo and prints by Gauguin. Implicit was a lesson – one typical of Mollison – to not only see one's self in light of history's greats, but to embrace the ambition that such recognition encourages.

Mollison was also adept at engineering introductions. In late 1989, for instance, he and Harris met up in New York, where Mollison invited Harris to visit Louise Bourgeois, whose pivotal sculpture, *C.O.Y.O.T.E.* (*Call Off Your Old Tired Ethics*, 1941–48) he'd acquired for the National Gallery of Australia in 1981. The meeting would prove deeply formative for Harris, who at the time was striving for a more emotional register in his work, a quality that Bourgeois's had in spades. She lived in a brownstone in the West Village, and after he and Mollison were ushered into the darkened, book-lined interior by Bourgeois's long-time assistant, Jerry Gorovoy, Harris found himself overcome by the company. He sat mutely on a bench seat as Bourgeois held court before a shared bottle of Beaujolais. Beyond small scraps of paper pinned to a board, there was no artwork in sight; from his vantage, he could glimpse little beyond a tiny kitchen, and windows that looked down to a wintry, detritus-filled courtyard. He listened, fascinated as Bourgeois brought up a few of her famous contemporaries only to energetically dispatch them one at a time, accusing them of such unforgiveable indiscretions as stealing her ideas or sucking up to the art establishment. Only later did Harris suspect it was a kind of performance; that when people visited, she turned it on or off as she saw fit.

But he also came to understand that the sense of insecurity and frustration underlying Bourgeois's demeanour was very real. 'Getting to know her work more and more, I've realised she sort of generated a lot of her energy from this kind of internal anger,' he says. Ever since, Bourgeois has occupied space for Harris alongside figures such as Guston and McCahon. In differing ways, he's recognised a similar quality in all of them: a certain steely vulnerability that enabled each to take hold of a feeling and interrogate it for all to see. 'The thing that her work opened for me was being able to make images of psychological states,' he says. He and Browne now own five of her prints, which they purchased on later visits to New York.

In the years after Mollison relocated to Melbourne, he and his partner, Vincent Langford, made the cavernous front section of their home – a converted hall in North Melbourne – available as a studio for their favoured artists, one at a time. Harris worked there for eighteen months between 1995 and 1997. It was part of an important period for him, one that would ultimately lead him to face the realities of his childhood ever more directly. To date, his work had largely been abstract – his well-known 1989 series *The Stations*, for instance, had responded to the horrors of the HIV crisis with stark, black-and-white geometric forms – but in a new series of paintings that he eventually titled *Appalling Moment*, this changed. As he worked in the North Melbourne studio, recognisable images took shape from one work to the next: the reaching trunk of a baby elephant; free-floating cartoon eyeballs, the pupils wildly dilated. His palette shifted to baby blue, lilac and cream, all of it outlined crisply in black.

Harris had recently undertaken a residency at the Cité Internationale des Arts in Paris, and en route had returned to New Zealand and confronted his father about his abusive treatment of the family. It was to be their last meeting. It was partly in this light that Harris recognised the 'appalling moment' of his new series as a kind of key to his own psychology, one that had now ruptured the coolness of his previous abstraction with increasingly absurd-seeming figuration. Soon, the elephant's trunk became a thin tubular phallus that dangled and thrust from scrotal blobs. He replaced baby blue and lilac with bubble-gum pink, and completed another series, *Just a feeling*. The title was a perfect evocation of the way he was reaching blindly into his subconscious and striving to give form to what he found there.

He would invite Mollison, and often Langford, into the studio near daily. Working in such proximity to a mentor could be claustrophobic, but he found Mollison's presence fortifying. 'It was just encouragement on the purest level,' he says. This was particularly important in relation to the new paintings, which seemed to be taking his practice into ever more bizarre territory. 'I'd ask "Is this too stupid?"' Harris continues. 'And James would say, "Well, you've done stupid before."'

Inevitably, Harris came to see Mollison's presence in his life as a counter to the long shadow of his own father. 'For me, he occupied the role of the good dad,' he says, only half-jokingly. Aside from a brief period of partial estrangement in the years before Mollison's death in 2020, their closeness extended long after Harris moved to another studio. At some points Mollison would call him at 8.30 each morning and the two would talk for half an hour before Harris set off to work. The substantial catalogue accompanying *Surrender & Catch* is dedicated to Mollison's memory.

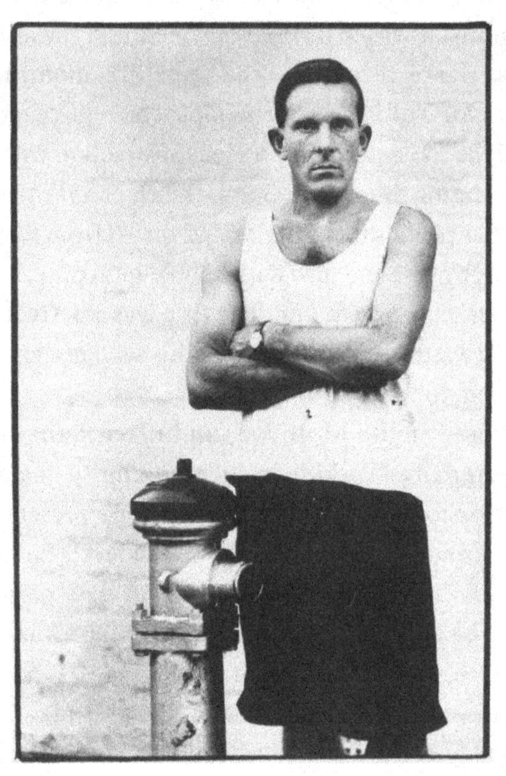

Martin Kantor *Portrait of Brent Harris* 1989

—

Harris's partner, Andrew Browne – whose own darkly magisterial figurative paintings are held in high regard – became a similar ballast in his life.

The two first met while studio residents at Melbourne's 200 Gertrude Street in 1987, but Browne was yet to come out and they simply became friends. That changed in 2000, and the two have been together ever since. Their generously scaled studios are now one above the other in a two-level section of a converted warehouse they own in Collingwood. A small sign at the otherwise unadorned entrance simply reads *Harris & Browne*, as though they are partners in a bespoke consultancy rather than two of the best Australian painters of their generation.

In 2001, they undertook a residency together at Bundanon, the property near Nowra, New South Wales, that Arthur and Yvonne Boyd gifted to the Australian people in 1993. It's a stunning setting: backed against the bush, the studios look over wombat-filled paddocks, and past the Boyd family's imposing sandstone homestead towards the river beyond. Pulpit Rock, the subject of some of Arthur Boyd's best paintings, rises on the far bank.

Browne was at the time of their residency working on paintings of night-time landscapes, usually silhouetted details illuminated by flares of blinding light. For him, Bundanon presented an opportunity to respond to the natural beauty of the bush setting, but for Harris it was different. 'He was kind of hunched over his desk in his room for that period,' Browne recalls during one of my visits to his and Harris's studios. Harris had recently begun a new group of drawings in Melbourne, from which archetypal characters had emerged: he called them, somewhat ominously, 'The Mother' and 'The Father'. In Bundanon, he laboured each day to shape these drawings into ever-more-precise studies for a new series of paintings – a focused process offset by evening drinks and sessions of canasta with Browne and fellow artist resident Peter Churcher. Browne already knew some of Harris's troubled history, but as he watched the drawings emerge, he learnt more. 'The family aspect of it was very disturbing and very sad,' he tells me. But he also recognised a sense of imminent breakthrough: it was clear to him that Harris was uncovering a new symbolism. It would prove to be particularly effective. Back in Melbourne, Harris began the paintings that would soon be grouped under the title *Grotesquerie*, a series that would arguably become his most pivotal.

I first saw the results a year later, in 2002, when Harris showed half of the initial series at Kaliman Gallery in Sydney. I was a recent art-school graduate, and a painter myself. My own work – similarly flat – also took loose, bodily forms into apparently abstract territory. But that's where the similarities ended. My paintings, as with so many like them, were all about surface effect; real content – yet to be identified, let alone articulated – was elusive. Harris's cut clear to the hard core that lay beneath. Encountering his work in that moment was like encountering the effect of a full orchestra after fumbling to play the recorder. I've been a fan ever since.

The first of the *Grotesquerie* paintings is an imposing vertical work almost three metres tall. The figure of the father looms above the mother, establishing the dynamic that plays through the series. Silhouetted white on a black ground, he appears as a kind of beast, his head crowned with blunt, deer-like horns; she cowers beneath, her face only visible as an undulating, McCahon-esque profile, her hair a flat, lemon-yellow field. In several subsequent paintings, the father's mouth is stoppered with a red jellybean-like form that, as Harris explains to me when we view images of the series on his studio computer, is a dummy he put there 'to shut him up'. Elsewhere, though, the dummy is gone, and bodily forms spill forth from the father's mouth like monstrous speech bubbles, or floods of gravity-defying bile. In the particularly striking *Grotesquerie (no. 9)*, blood cascades from a slit in the father's neck – Harris's painted act of patricide. It gathers into crawling figures that appear set to flee the scene: 'They're the children,' Harris says. The last painting in the series, *Grotesquerie (no. 20)*, was completed in 2009. It's the smallest, as if the previous terrors are now diminished. It depicts the father in profile as he regards a round, glowing aperture to the painting's right – a mirror, Harris explains. Its surface is blank. Whereas the father appears elsewhere in the series as a literal monster, he is now reduced to human form. His downcast features suggest that the horror he has enacted upon others is now his alone: Harris even denies him the company of his own reflection.

Since *Grotesquerie*, Harris has inhabited his painted world as fully and as freely as possible. *Surrender & Catch* unfurled in slow and steady chronological order. It showed his practice as one of poise and restraint increasingly inflected by the risk and vulnerability of his subject matter: a rare example of work running both hot and cool at once. Compositions flow and sweep, surfaces appear to soak up light, even noise. The results are almost stupidly easy to look at, but this doesn't mean they don't linger in one's mind. Together they amount to an entire psychology. 'It's hard to see thirty years of your life laid out in imagery like that,' Harris says. But he hastens to add that the experience has only emboldened him further. 'I'm just going to paint whatever comes to the surface now. I just want to be in the studio all the time, that's all.'

In the weeks after I saw the exhibition, my mind often returned to one large painting in particular: *Abraham*, from 2007. Harris was not raised in any church, and remains non-religious, but the painting comes from a small group of portraits of religious deities, including Jesus and Ganesha. From one perspective, they sit oddly in his oeuvre, but they actually make perfect sense.

Harris tells me that they are images of faith, but he doesn't have to. It's more than clear. I can still picture *Abraham* now: the saint's serene face is enveloped in flowing yellow, his simple, stylised features picked out in warm grey against alabaster skin. All the darkness is gone, and whether it threatens to return or not seems, in the moment at least, of little consequence. To look at this image is to close one's eyes and turn to face the sun.

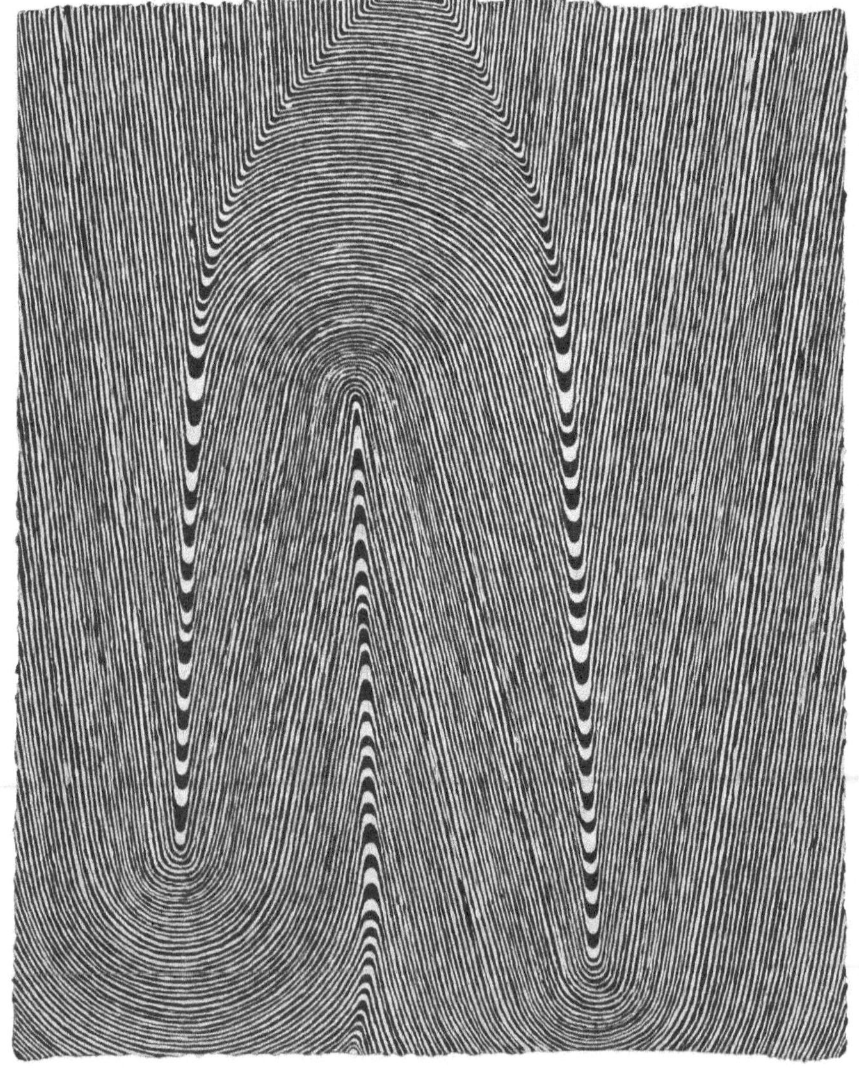

Karl Wiebke *Buildings B/11* 2004–2008

10

The Atmospheric Conditions on Any Given Day

By the time I decide to try to write about the painter Karl Wiebke for the second time, almost six years have passed since my first attempt, which had arrived on the page without the life and feeling that Wiebke and his work demands. Although I wasn't sure exactly what it was, there was a sense that I'd missed something central, and this sense had, from time to time, returned to me like a puzzle for which a solution was almost but not quite within reach.

The reason for this, at least, was clear: Wiebke is one of the most intriguing yet intractable artists I know. His work encourages one's attention, yet it deftly belies easy categorisation. It's abstract, sure. But it's more than that, too. He somehow embeds something close to real life in the surfaces he paints.

After attending art school in Germany in the early 1970s, Wiebke migrated to Australia on a whim a decade later. Initially based in Fremantle in Western Australia, he achieved something subtle yet significant: somehow synthesising the rigour of conceptual European abstraction with the light and atmospheric conditions of his adopted home. Since then, he's had his successes – his work is held in the National Gallery of Australia, along with several state galleries, and he has been the subject of two survey exhibitions at respected university art galleries – but beyond this he has just quietly painted, day in and day out, following the path that each new work set for him. I knew there was an important lesson in Wiebke's practice, but I wasn't yet certain what it was.

When I next visited Wiebke's studio, which lies in a complex of artist studios in an industrial-zoned quarter of Melbourne's Thornbury, I was determined to find a different way to approach writing about him. Wiebke, who is in his late seventies, greeted me at the studio entrance. He has a creased, open face framed by closely cropped silver hair, and a soft yet tonally resonant voice that remains heavily accented.

On my drive into the city I'd wondered why I had struggled to write about him, and decided that regardless of the writerly shortcomings I might bring to the equation, it was at least partly because Wiebke is a famously exacting character: one second-guesses any firm conclusion that might be reached about either his paintings or Wiebke himself out of concern that it might not be *exactly* correct. He possesses a softly judgemental mien. Some struggle with this, but I find it refreshing. Wiebke says what he thinks, especially when it comes to art and artists. He'll candidly share his opinion of someone's work, good or bad. Because of this, I tend to trust his judgement: with Karl, you know where you stand.

Take this, for instance, which he said to me as we made our way down the plywood-walled corridor to his studio: 'I can't understand artists who listen to the radio when they're working – if your mind is elsewhere, you're not really painting. And if you're not really painting, you should stop.' This sounded reasonable until I thought of how in the fifteen or so studios that surround his there were surely a handful of other artists at work at that very moment, and that most of them likely had their ears plugged with music, or one of any number of podcasts doing the rounds. I know some of the artists who work there, and all of them are in the midst of decent exhibition careers, but one could be forgiven for mistaking that, for Wiebke, they are yet to discover what it is they spend long hours each day doing; that this is why they drown out the quiet of making. His thinking might be summarised like this: if you fear that quiet, you're lost.

It's a hardline position, but it illuminates something about Wiebke: he demands both everything and nothing from art.

After looking at his practice off and on for more than a decade, I now realise that this is another part of what draws me to his work. His paintings balance qualities of lightness and weight; they are both complex and simple. They seem at first glance to achieve these qualities effortlessly, but this is a sleight of hand. His work is invariably underwritten by sustained daily labour undertaken either in his studio, or at his kitchen table, where he draws rather than paints. He goes deep into the quiet of his work, and stays there for extended periods. It's this labour that keeps his practice moving.

Back in 2014, not long after we first met, I'd made a visit to his home. It was a mid-morning in early spring. Karl and his wife Frederike live in a relatively new apartment tower that looks out across once-industrial land reclaimed as commons, and sunlight was flowing in through the sliding glass doors that open onto their balcony. The small figures of dogwalkers and runners were visible on the green expanse below. Karl caught me by surprise by gifting me a painting of his that I'd admired – a brightly coloured abstract of loosely interlocking forms – and when I suggested the work might be too much to accept, he gently dismissed my concern. He insisted the gift was no big deal, that it was a pleasure for him to give away the things around him. He explained that he wanted to avoid the trap many older artists find themselves in: as keepers of their own archives, they risk becoming overwhelmed by their past practices, unable to move forward. If in this case the painting simply established a connection with someone interested in his work, it was more than enough. 'Don't even think about the value of it,' he said.

There was undoubtedly a lightness to the gesture, but I also sensed in it something unsettled. He spoke that morning about wanting to do something entirely different, of beginning a new series of works that no one would recognise as his. It seemed important, he said, to try to learn an entirely different way to make a painting, and to do this again and again. For him, this was the secret to a meaningful practice: the unlearning, followed by the relearning. Each new body of work would stand apart from that which had preceded it. Each would set a new challenge that he could turn his lifelong practice towards solving.

Perhaps his desire for a reset simply came down to the fact that he had an exhibition looming, and he was spending long, laborious hours in the studio, but it seemed more than that. I don't want to suggest it was a crisis of meaning, because it wasn't, but he was thinking carefully about where the value of painting lay; searching, as he had done for years, for the point where the act of it became indivisible from the myriad of other daily acts – mundane or not – that constitute a life.

Later, when I hung my new painting at home, I began to think about this idea more closely. The work was called *Sans Titre* – 'untitled' or 'without title' – and proved to be generous. It was not large, but it held the wall with quiet confidence; in the first weeks I lived with it, it seemed to offer up minor revelations almost daily. At that stage the paintings of Wiebke's I was most familiar with came from a series titled *Buildings*, which comprised small works that had been 'built' up by palette knife in incremental layers of contrasting colour. Beginning with an overall composition – which consisted, say, of three circles – each layer would shrink inwards millimetre by millimetre. As it did, the eye would register the gap between that layer and the last as a line. The results of this process were optically vibrant: when viewed from a distance, the works appeared to consist of telescoping spirals. It was only on moving closer that this quality revealed itself to be topographic, as well as linear: the centre of each shape, where the layers were much greater in number than the outer edges, rose higher. Once I'd noticed this, the works began to resemble dense stacks of cut, coloured paper, each of which climbed inward towards a rough peak. All this seemed to operate just at the edge of perception, each painting's internal logic revealing itself even as the eye struggled for purchase.

But *Sans Titre* looked different. Its ragged complex of interlocking shapes appeared to me not like carefully arranged pieces of paper but like a pane of artfully shattered multicoloured glass. Although I realised it had been painted in the same manner as the *Buildings* series, by the above logic, work on it had ceased halfway through. As a result, the painting's surface topography was far less pronounced, the effect more one of small, open fields of colour framed by ragged, layered edges descending into a network of crevasses: not entirely dissimilar, but nonetheless different. If work on it had continued towards the logical conclusion flagged in the *Buildings* series, it would essentially be the same.

It all seemed so deliberate that when I had first seen *Sans Titre* in Wiebke's apartment, I couldn't help drawing attention to this quality. I asked why he had stopped working on it when he did.

'Well,' he said, clearly relishing his response, 'I just stopped!'

It was the simplest of reasons, but his tone betrayed that this moment – the abandonment of an otherwise carefully plotted process – was the decisive one. The rigorous method that underwrites his paintings might suggest otherwise, but no matter how deliberate each step can appear, Wiebke knew that it was in fact the quicksilver possibilities offered by chance that mattered the most. This is what I mean when I say his works are both complex and simple.

—

In the years since, I've often seen Weibke's philosophy in action, visiting his studio every so often and staying abreast of his exhibitions. I've learned that new bodies of work, each marked by subtle and not-so-subtle differences, came for him at a steady-seeming clip. Each was separate, but nonetheless closely related.

There were, for instance, a relatively brief series of vertically striped paintings. They sound dry on paper, but in real life they are anything but. Wiebke describes them in pragmatic terms that belie their beauty. 'The concept behind these works is making vertical lines with horizontal brushstrokes,' he once told me.

Those paintings, which he began in 2015, do indeed consist of brightly coloured bands that run from top to bottom that have been painted by dragging the brush from right to left, rather than up and down. But then there's the way in which each of these 'stripes' meet: softly feathered edges where colours overlay to create new hues, and with them unexpected rushes of feeling. This is the quality that elevates the works beyond what they objectively appear to be – the thing that makes them more than the sum of their simple parts.

Soon after, he exhibited a large series of small paintings that drew upon more than 800 tiny studies (these studies would later grow to 2000) he'd made with coloured ink on paper at his kitchen table. Each depicted two houses separated by steep-sided valleys and abstracted landscapes. By the time he began making these into paintings, the houses were often barely discernible among their surrounding planes and fields of colour, but they were nonetheless there, a kind of armature upon which each composition could unfold.

But why houses? I distinctly recall him once telling me that the houses represented Frederike and he, that while he sat of an evening at their shared table, working on the initial studies, she had often been seated across from him, bent over the intricate needlepoints that she creates. But he seemed to move away from this reading, later writing in a short artist statement that he didn't recall why the two houses had emerged as a subject at all. Either way, there they were – tiny and desolate-seeming among fields of colour, the one always looking across at the other.

So it went for six or so years: Wiebke working away, looking for the chance moment that would open each body of work onto the next, his paintings changing – whether drastically or incrementally – as he went. When I thought about his work, I would invariably begin to think about the quality that seemed to trace much of what he did: on the one hand, an absolute belief in the poetry of painting, and on the other, a reticence to put this belief directly into words.

Once, sitting in his studio in front of a small group of new works, the gap between the way Wiebke described them and their unalloyed beauty opened between us. It was another day, another visit, and Wiebke and I had been talking about the simple materiality of his work, but our conversation had faltered, and a silence descended.

Wiebke gathered his thoughts. When he continued, it was in a reflective register. 'I remember when I was young, when I was in India for the first time, in Mumbai, I met an American traveller at the airport and it turned out he was a painter as well,' he said. 'And we chatted for a long time waiting for a plane, talking about our work. And he asked me, "Why do you paint? What is your ambition?" And I said, "I want to set painting free."'

Until then, Wiebke explained, he had always needed a clear reason for each step he made in his paintings. Once he had this reason, he would continue working whether he liked what he was doing or not, which is to say that the immutability of the concept provided him a guiding principle. But in the airport he'd felt a shift. Afterwards, his approach began to change. 'I realised I was more interested in *choosing* what to do, instead of *deciding* what to do,' he told me.

The conversation moved on, and the distinction between choosing and deciding was left hanging – a couple of days later Wiebke would even call me to wonder if he should have in fact reversed their order when he spoke, and we would have a slightly confusing conversation about the difference – but in the moment I felt I'd understood.

He meant to say he wanted his work to be more intuitive; that regardless of the rigour of his approach, he knew there had to be a sense of lightness. He wanted to know that he could stop whenever he wanted.

—

Wiebke's encounter at the airport in Mumbai occurred in 1973, during the first of two extended trips he took to India at either end of that decade: the first three months, the second six.

He was twenty-eight at the time and reaching for a resolution that extended far beyond questions of painting. For most of his life he'd experienced the unnerving sense that he had been in the wrong place. Part of this was due to the pervasive anxieties of Germany's post-war condition: Wiebke was born in the city of Detmold in 1944, one year before the Allied victory, and had grown up under the heavy cloud of recent history. Evidence of conflict lay everywhere: as a child Wiebke recalls collecting bullet shells and playing in the burnt-out tanks that were still scattered in the surrounding countryside.

When Wiebke was six, his father was promoted within the German Railways, and the family moved to the northern city of Bremerhaven, at the mouth of the Weser River. As a key seaport for the German navy during the war, it had endured heavy bombing by Allied forces, and for the family's first years there parts of the city, including buildings on either side of his childhood home, still lay in a tangled mess. Wiebke and his friends learnt to scavenge metal debris from the ruins and sell it to the local scrapyard for pocket money.

The war's aftermath also had a deeply personal impact. His mother would take Wiebke and his two siblings – a younger sister and brother – on an annual pilgrimage to visit the graves of his maternal grandparents, who had been killed in a bomb attack while sheltering in their basement. It happened only a month before Wiebke was born, and his mother had never fully recovered from the shock. Each year on the day of the visit she would be inconsolable; Wiebke would spend the train journey, which could take as long as five hours each way, wondering in vain how he might make things better.

When a friend's father died, Wiebke, then around eleven years old, was gifted a cache of his painting materials, which he took to with enthusiasm. As he grew older art began to seem like a natural career, but even though his own father was a hobby painter and an accomplished violinist who had once dreamed of a life in music, his parents refused to entertain the idea. 'They were just obsessed with security after the war,' Wiebke said.

Goldsmithing, which he chose at random after seeing a film in which the protagonist practised the craft, seemed to present a tangible mid-ground between creativity and pragmatism. It was only later, once Wiebke had successfully completed a goldsmithing apprenticeship and narrowly avoided national service (he spent two years as a civil servant instead), that he felt he could defy his parent's wishes. In 1972 he enrolled in art school in Hamburg, where the post-war counterculture was just then gaining traction. In step, his world began to open; Wiebke found himself engulfed by new ideas.

For the first three months at the academy he cycled through different studios, each run by an artist who introduced their students to a range of conceptual and material approaches. Among them were the Austrian Gotthard Graubner, an autocratic figure who stretched his vibrant colour-field paintings over cushion foam so they appeared to push softly into the world around them, and Franz Erhard Walther, a conceptualist known for democratising the relationship between a viewer and a work through interactive 'painting-like' objects – standing forms against which viewers could press their weight, and bolts of fabric in which they could wrap themselves. Both Graubner and Walther became formative influences for Wiebke, but it was his immediate peers that had the most enduring impact. With ten other students he founded a commune in the centre of the city; Martin Kippenberger, the famously louche painter who would go on to become one of Germany's most significant post-war artists, was among those who lived there. Wiebke may not have recognised it at the time, but he had landed in the midst of the country's emerging avant-garde.

It was against this backdrop that he was first introduced to the 'Manifesto of Suprematism', a foundational document of modern art by the Russian painter Kazimir Malevich that had been published in German in 1927. It knocked Wiebke for six. Anyone who has read the manifesto knows its brooding intensity. Malevich decries objective representation with the force of dogma. 'The visual phenomena of the objective world are, in themselves, meaningless,' he writes at the outset. In their place he argues for a radical absence. Feeling is the only thing that matters; everything that forms the world of life and art must be 'cast aside' in its favour.

'After reading this manifesto I really just flipped out,' Wiebke said. 'I mean, I lost ground – it was something I couldn't handle; this emptiness, and nothingness.'

Malevich had already created one of the most conceptually radical artworks of the twentieth century: *Black Square* (1915), a literal rendering of its title, and a reduction of painting to its barest materiality. The work was everything and nothing all at once: a perfect vacuum of resonant meaning. Malevich saw it in quasi-spiritual terms as 'an icon for our time', and first exhibited it in a room of similarly reductive paintings, where, to great controversy, he granted it a space traditionally reserved for the luminous religious icons of Russian orthodoxy: the point where the walls met the ceiling. A black hole where once hung the worldly face of God – from the perspective of post-war Germany the implications of Malevich's act, much like the implications of his manifesto, extended far beyond art's borders. It seemed to embody the anxiety of an entire generation.

On weekends Wiebke often left the city and travelled by train back to Bremerhaven and then onward to the village of Debstedt, where he shared another property with three friends. One of them introduced Wiebke to Buddhism, and in doing so offered a possible counterpoint to Malevich's position. Wiebke began to rise with the sun, teaching himself to meditate before settling in with a book of sutras. If his experiences at the academy in Hamburg had shown that the possibilities of painting were unfolding at a rate that mirrored the surrounding social change, through reading Buddhist philosophy he sensed how that idea of change might be internalised. He began to understand that under the shock of the Suprematist doctrine ran something similar: a desire to remove artistic practice from the material prompt of the world, and to instead reach inward. Malevich's embrace of nothingness, Wiebke realised, might not be so dire after all. It might hold a kind of freedom.

'For me it was really about how the Buddhists analysed the mind,' he told me. 'I basically tried to replace the mind with painting and apply the same thinking.' *What does this insight mean to my painting practice?* he'd ask himself. Each time he read the sutras, he took careful notes. Soon he arrived at the question that remains central to his practice today: how can you make something that references nothing but itself?

Nearly every work that Weibke has since made might be seen to provide a different answer to this question. One early response came in the form of an untitled work he made over a month of sustained labour. It consisted of 10,000 sheets of paper, each hand-cut to the exact same dimensions – something close to the page of a standard book – and piled one atop the other. During the work's production all Wiebke did was eat, sleep and cut paper. Each day's work became one pile – thirty-one in total. Today, they still sit in his studio. Wrapped in browning butcher's paper, each stack is sized according to the amount of activity expended to produce it: placed one beside the next, together they render tangible the otherwise transitory relationship between an artwork and the focused energy required to produce it.

Much like the discipline embodied in the sutras, the untitled paperwork, which remained un-exhibited until Wiebke had settled in Fremantle in 1983, demanded he enact radical control. It allowed him to draw an inner world to the surface. He found himself embodying each step with increasing awareness, counting pages in much the same way the sutras urged him to count his breaths. Soon his action was sublimated; it was as if he were observing himself at one remove.

His first one-person exhibition came in 1977. It was held at an alternative gallery in Bremerhaven called Kabinett für aktuelle Kunst, which during the same period held exhibitions by a range of now-canonical international artists including Gerhard Richter, Bas Jan Ader, Carl Andre and Sol LeWitt. Wiebke showed a series of hand-dyed paper 'flags' that he had made three years earlier, arranging them in an unbroken line across the wall, riffing upon similar ideas of focused labour and repetition as his earlier untitled work. The piece was well received, but even when an invitation followed to exhibit at a respected gallery in Antwerp, Wiebke remained unsettled. He was by then working as a goldsmith to support himself, and during the long hours he spent at his workbench he listened to the radio. The feeling that the country remained stifled by its history was strong. The public discourse seemed to be little more than political scare-mongering: the widely touted post-war notion of *Vergangenheitsbewältigung*, which translates as 'coming to terms with the past', struck him, at best, as a distant ideal.

He realised he had to go elsewhere.

—

By chance, it was Wiebke's birthday when he arrived in Perth. He was then married to his first wife, Marina, a kindergarten teacher, and after six months in India, the two had recently welcomed their first child, Mia. (A second daughter, Heidi, was born in 1983.)

For reasons Wiebke now struggles to fully explain, they were seeking to settle as far from Australia's populated eastern seaboard as possible. He still recalls the strangeness of their arrival; the feeling of walking through the unfamiliar city, the circuitous path they eventually traced towards the sprawling bushland of Kings Park. Culturally Perth seemed a void, almost shockingly so, and they were unsure enough of their decision to stop at a travel centre and search the window display for return flights to Europe. But the park changed things. The flora was unlike anything Wiebke had seen: what he later learnt were jacaranda trees were just coming into flower; banksias reached their yellow combs skyward. All of it was bathed in a light of a clarity he'd not before experienced.

Prior to leaving Germany he had seen himself in a dream at work in a studio complex surrounded by like-minded people, and he soon discovered in Fremantle a place that was strikingly similar to this vision. But even more surprising was what he learned next: a silversmith had just ended his studio lease and had left behind a metalworking bench. Wiebke didn't hesitate. He moved in, and with minimal alterations soon had a functioning workspace to recommence his work as a goldsmith. When two nuns arrived unannounced a month or two later, he accepted his first commission from them: a pair of simple candelabras for a local church. His letters home took on an enthusiastic tone. He wrote of the light, of the blue sky, of the silvery expanse of the Indian Ocean that lay a short walk from his studio. He even recounted how people would talk casually in the street: he hadn't realised until then that in public spaces in Germany a heavy silence prevailed.

Feeling one's way through the territory that Wiebke has since come to embrace in his work can be challenging, but one thing is clear. To make successful paintings, it is essential that he enjoy the process. This is the lesson he learnt early: if he stays present, he can be mindful of each step.

By the same measure, if his mind wanders, he risks losing the thread that binds each work and ultimately makes it whole. It's for this reason that he advocates painting in silence. As soon as his thoughts drift, he knows it's time to stop. He'll either start again, or not, but as clear as each choice is, it remains relatively random.

'You cannot begin a painting and finish it,' he once argued as we sat together in his studio. 'You can only start it and stop it.'

This is an idea Wiebke often returns to – that we are mistaken to think a painting can somehow be finished. What he's trying to convey is that a painting possesses a momentum of its own. He connects with each work for a different period of time; some hold his attention for longer than others. He's come to understand that whether he likes it or not, each cradles within it the possibility to continue indefinitely.

Sometimes it's just as easy not to stop, or to at least test the theory and delay stopping for a near-ridiculous length of time. Wiebke often works on a painting for multiple years, until the built-up density of material results in something that seems concentrated and plastic. At times this process has stretched into a decade, as with a number of individual paintings from an untitled series he worked on between 1991 and 2004. Painted on sealed wooden supports, Wiebke first set these works on easels in his Fremantle garden, where the wind that blew in from the ocean and drove drifts of sand up the main street could push wet skeins of enamel paint across each surface. He applied thin washes of colour, one after the other, which became ever more intricate as each lay over the last. Loose drops and raised dashes solidified as they dried, and over time created a pebbled, braille-like surface. If it rained, the paintings got wet; if the sun shone brightly, their surfaces grew hot. When he and Frederike – then a fellow goldsmith who had emigrated to Perth from Germany in 1983 to join Wiebke in his goldsmithing workshop – moved to Melbourne in 2002, the paintings came with them, and the process continued.

The results, which surely rate among the most singular abstract paintings ever created in this country, appear accrued in the way of cave formations, or coral. They are also deeply resonant of place – more so than many figurative landscapes I can think of in the Australian canon. It's as if the wide-open skies of the continent's western coastline are somehow distilled within them. One imagines excavating their surfaces to reveal the atmospheric conditions that surrounded them on any given day: here is the bleaching effect of the sun, and the embedded grit of sand; a little deeper, the residual dampness of a sea mist or a rainstorm.

It's for this poetically deft control of his chosen medium that John Kinsella, the Western Australian poet and writer, once

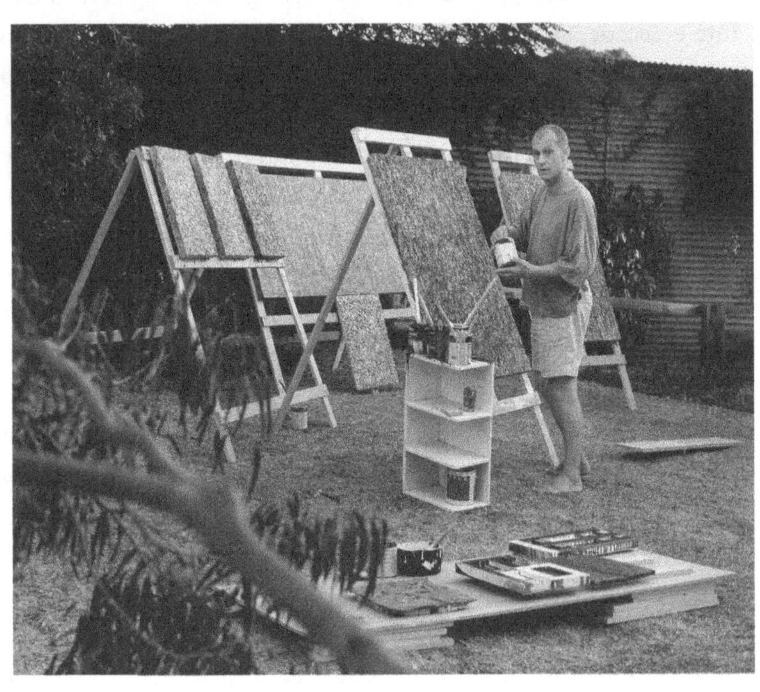

Karl Wiebke painting in his Fremantle garden 1995

called Wiebke a 'writerly painter'. When I first read this I realised immediately how apt a description it was. Not only does Wiebke often speak about painting as if its methodical play is part of the play of language itself, but his very approach to it lays bare the structural bond that painting and language share. As with the spoken or written word, works like his are made from simple and widely understood elements ('paint, surface and instrument', as Wiebke himself puts it), but they are nonetheless able to function in myriad ways. They can be adapted to the minute distinctions the world demands of us and bent to definitions that need to be *just so.* Kinsella's point is that Wiebke's paintings prompt a similar question to that which often attends language: how can such a blunt tool, wielded in a certain fashion, convey detailed description or complex emotion?

The question is a good one. It goes to a mystery at the core of so much creative practice, one expressed by the tension between the pragmatic task of making – the daily act of it – and the indefinable matter it seeks to capture.

I remember one visit in particular to Wiebke's studio, although when it was, exactly, I no longer recall. Our conversation, as always, had ranged widely, but it was drawing to a close, and I was hoping Wiebke might arrive at an overarching definition of his work – a faint hope, admittedly. A suite of recent paintings were hanging around us, one of which consisted of a faint network of transparent grey lines traced by random-seeming yellow highlights. True to form, Wiebke was carefully resisting absolute terms as he spoke of this work. Everything was about feeling, about thinking deliberately, but I still had no clear idea what the feeling was, or the thought.

At first I was disappointed, but with the passage of time now separating me from our conversation, I'm able to see what I was missing. For Wiebke, a successful practice was about the way in which questions, carefully posed and systematically broken down into their constituent parts, may draw one further from discernible answers. If we can simply say *this is about a feeling*, it is surely more than enough. It is, for him, less about finding something solid to which he might tether his work, and more about settling his mind into the flow of it and then allowing that flow to take him where it will. If I was after the 'lesson' of his work, this was surely it: don't expect a concrete revelation. Or, put another way, don't expect for the puzzle to be solved.

'I am really happy working now,' he told me, almost as if his greatest achievement lay in this simple fact. 'It's just a nice space of being, just *light*. And if you are good, you are aware of what you do – I like that.'

For years, the painting that Wiebke gifted me on my very first visit to his apartment, *Sans Titre*, hung in my family living room, where its colour enlivened the space around it. But after a recent move, I shifted it to my six-year-old daughter's room. It makes sense there, bright and playful among a perfectly discordant selection of her similarly bright and playful drawings and paintings on paper that otherwise adorn the walls. It fits right in.

I often look at it and think of one of the last things Wiebke told me that day in the studio: 'Someone once said paint for me was something mystical. It's not. But it is something that has its own life.'

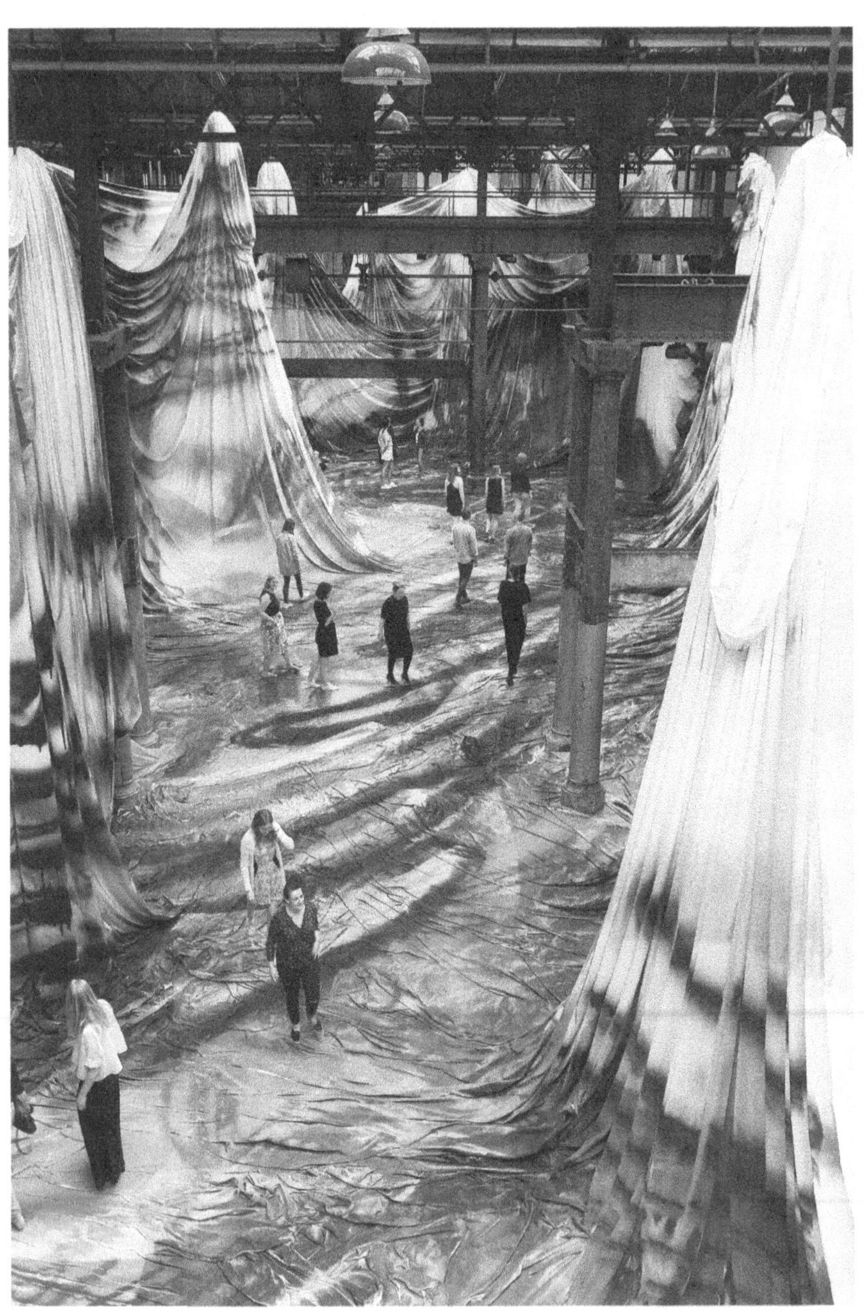

Katharina Grosse *The Horse Trotted Another Couple of Metres, Then It Stopped* 2017

11

The Horse Trotted Another Couple of Metres

'The smallest space we build for ourselves is our clothes,' the German artist Katharina Grosse says, pulling at her blouse for emphasis. 'Our clothes are an added-on space that give us a very interesting sense of where the body ends. They help define the distance to another person.'

It's 2016 and Grosse, a sternly elfin woman in her fifties whose own clothes are angular and precisely patterned, is sitting in the cavernous atrium of Sydney's Carriageworks. Her newly opened installation, *The Horse Trotted Another Couple of Metres, Then It Stopped*, hangs from the building's huge steel girders behind her and spills out across the worn concrete floor. It consists of sheets of raw canvas – large enough to dwarf a viewer – that cocoon the internal space of the former railyards in near entirety. It veils an unseen interior like the drapery of an oversized dress, or curtains closed hastily before a stage.

The work ushers forth a range of possible analogies. Alongside clothing, Grosse offers the human drive to construct a habitat or take shelter in enclosed spaces – tents, for instance, or cubbies – but regardless of her new work's evocative title, she hastens to clarify that *The Horse Trotted Another Couple of Metres, Then It Stopped* is not 'about' anything, at least not in a straightforward sense. 'It's the difference between when you have an object and you look at it, and when you're directly confronted with its being,' she says.

Initially this strikes me as a calculated obfuscation, but I soon realise it conveys a certain truth. Grosse is an internationally renowned proponent of what is often termed 'painting in the expanded field'. In similar fashion to fellow German Anselm

Reyle, or the Canadian-American Jessica Stockholder, both of whom adopt varied found and industrial materials to push open painting's possibilities, she works with her medium's core principles – colour, form, tone, ground – but draws them beyond the limits of its well-trodden conventions. Her work can still be classified as painting, but a canvas hanging discretely on a gallery wall most often provides for her not a destination but a departure. Like so many of her large-scale installations, Grosse's new work appears as if the history of abstract painting had been fed into a black hole, inverted, and then spewed out in its most archetypal configuration.

We meet on the first morning the installation has been open to the public, and small groups of visitors have been slowly trickling past the bench where Grosse and I sit. They are headed towards one of three carefully concealed entry points in the canvas drapery: vertical slits that are all but invisible until sought out. Just before meeting Grosse, I too had stepped through one of these, and as we speak, I picture the viewers inside her installation, phone cameras at hand as they take in her signature riot of acid-toned colour. Grosse had recently spent almost ten days wielding an industrial spray-gun across the interior canvas surface to roughly layer one hue over another in an apparently antic but actually finely controlled performance. Although the results were visually jarring, they were beautiful too: tones of yellow mixed against green and orange; fuchsia sketched through by signal blue; skeins of transparent black dusted over pink to create a brown fog drifting in the middle distance. All of it was heightened, slightly off; a discordant, punk-like take on comparatively restful art historical precedents, like the American colour field painting made famous by artists such as Mark Rothko and Helen Frankenthaler. As Grosse pointed out, her work might evoke any number of things, but for me it was Judy Garland's Dorothy, dropped into the technicolour land of Oz.

Although Grosse has always made paintings on canvas, she owes much of her significant international reputation to works like *The Horse Trotted Another Couple of Metres, Then It Stopped*. Early examples were far simpler, sprayed roughly onto museum walls. But the surfaces to which she applied her colour soon expanded to include non-architectural elements. These carried, for Grosse at least, a kind of elemental meaning. For *Picture Park*, displayed at Brisbane's Gallery of Modern Art in 2007, it was a jumble of oversize latex balloons, tilted canvasses and a mound of nondescript soil; *Sticks in a Shop*, a 2013 exhibition in Curitiba, Brazil, saw her signature spray applied to a fully grown uprooted tree that had been jammed horizontally between the gallery's internal pillars. Bolts of hanging material first appeared a year later when she was invited to cover the altar of a Berlin church during Lent. Whereas her previous installations had often wilfully invaded the spaces they occupied, her use of material eventually led her towards discrete interior worlds that drew viewers inside.

It's the resulting sense of immediacy that Grosse embraces in such works. 'Painting has a different time structure than music, or a book or a film,' she tells me. Those forms, she continues, are often driven by a 'causal structure', by which she means a narrative that unfolds piece by piece, a sequence of cause and effect. 'In painting, everything is there at the same time, even the things that happened first: you can see those at the end as well.'

Grosse attended art school in Düsseldorf in the early 1980s, where her teachers included famous international figures like Gerhard Richter and Nam June Paik. But when I press her for influences, she reaches back to her childhood. She grew up in the declining industrial city of Bochum, where at an early age she became visually attuned to the arbitrary beauty of a fading urban landscape. 'There were a lot of old factories, leftover places that weren't cared for anymore,' she recalls. 'I'd find maybe a concrete block with weeds growing around it, and the sun was shining on it in summer.'

Moments like that stuck with her, but she soon understood she could never capture them directly. Not that she didn't try: early on she attempted it on canvas – a detailed study of a tree, perhaps, or a drinking glass – but she struggled to isolate a subject and focus in on it in the way that figurative painting demanded. 'When I look at the world, I don't see isolated things,' she says. 'I see it all in a floppy mess.'

Her parents' passion for avant-garde dance also shaped her thinking. It helped spark a defining interest in movement through space that would later inflect her approach to painting. They would often take her to the neighbouring city of Wuppertal, where the renowned choreographer Pina Bausch was based: Grosse suspects that, until her early twenties, she may have seen everything the famously experimental Bausch produced. Even back then, the singular and urgent quality of Bausch's work grabbed her: she would find herself in the audience wondering about the negative spaces between bodies, about how the choreographer's invisible directions dictated the performer's every move, or the way in which something as seemingly simple as a shock of water thrown across a black stage managed to excite Grosse's own creative energies. Later, she would gesture to this formative influence in the purposefully oblique titles – many of which read like quasi stage directions – for her own ambitious installations. This tendency echoed in the clipped narrative suggested by *The Horse Trotted Another Couple of Metres, Then It Stopped*.

More recently, her mind has been turned towards soccer, which she watches with keen interest. She barracks for no team, but the game nonetheless fascinates her. She sees the ball as a mercurial element around which a coach must shape the movements of an entire side, attempting to predict endless variables that could each derail even the most carefully plotted strategy. As she tells me this, it's clear she's offering another analogy for her practice. Not only does she also corral a team of assistants to a common purpose, but she too must make intricate preparations within which the soaring possibilities of chance might best unfold. For the Carriageworks project, her team in Germany created three separate models of the proposed installation in ascending scale. Then came the challenge of sewing together the industrially scaled bolts of canvas, followed by the complex question of how to suspend the work from the building's internal girders. Finally, with the raw canvas installed in Sydney, the unpredictable act of painting played out as a process of finely sustained risk.

With all the preparations complete, this is the decisive moment: Grosse alone in the centre of the installation, her paint gun attached by hose to an air compressor outside. At her command, an assistant pours paint into the machine. She responds in the moment to what the work demands: 'Stop! No more yellow!' she might call out. Or 'I need red!' At times, the fine mists of colour mix mid-air, coming to rest like dust residue across the canvas surface before her; other times, it lands thickly, flowing together into unruly colour eddies.

'The actual painting is totally developed on site,' she explains to me. 'The light and the situation is so particular that it doesn't make sense to have a plan that restricts you.' Because of this, all the possibilities must be measured in real time: each decision – whether as straightforward as changing colours, or as nuanced as angling the paint gun away from the surface of the canvas so the pigment falls like mist – branches outwards until the painting is done.

Grosse often asks herself what painting might offer the world at large. She wonders what impact it might have, how it might take up different information, moods and emotions and play these back into the body of the viewer. When she began painting in the 1980s, the medium had been torn apart and reinvented numerous times: it was easy to think that its possibilities had been exhausted. Instead, she found herself treating it as if everything was hers for the taking: the various breakthroughs that had been made throughout its history provided her the richest of grounds.

'Paintings used to try to present the matrix for how the world works; they tried to describe how to act and behave,' she tells me. She offers the foundational Biblical narratives of the Sistine Chapel as an example: painting as divinely bestowed social doctrine. 'But now I think we've all come to understand we no longer have coherent structures. Everything is broken up.'

The resulting fissures open rifts in the everyday. This is what she intends *The Horse Trotted Another Couple of Metres, Then It Stopped* to convey: that art can do this too, but to different ends. It can open a space into which new possibilities, even new ways of understanding the world, can slip. Ideally that's what viewers get from walking through the results of her painted labours: the means to glimpse, however briefly, another vision, and to take that vision with them when they return to their everyday lives.

Grosse gestures behind her, where viewers are milling about the hidden entry points in the hanging canvas, awaiting their turn inside. 'If a gap opens for a split second, you can see something totally different,' she says.

I glimpse a figure ducking through an entrance, revealing a flash of bright colour.

'That's what I look for in my work,' she continues. 'As an artist I see myself as the one that has to bring that quality, a little bit, to society. To show perhaps where another vision is possible. I think that's what any artist does.'

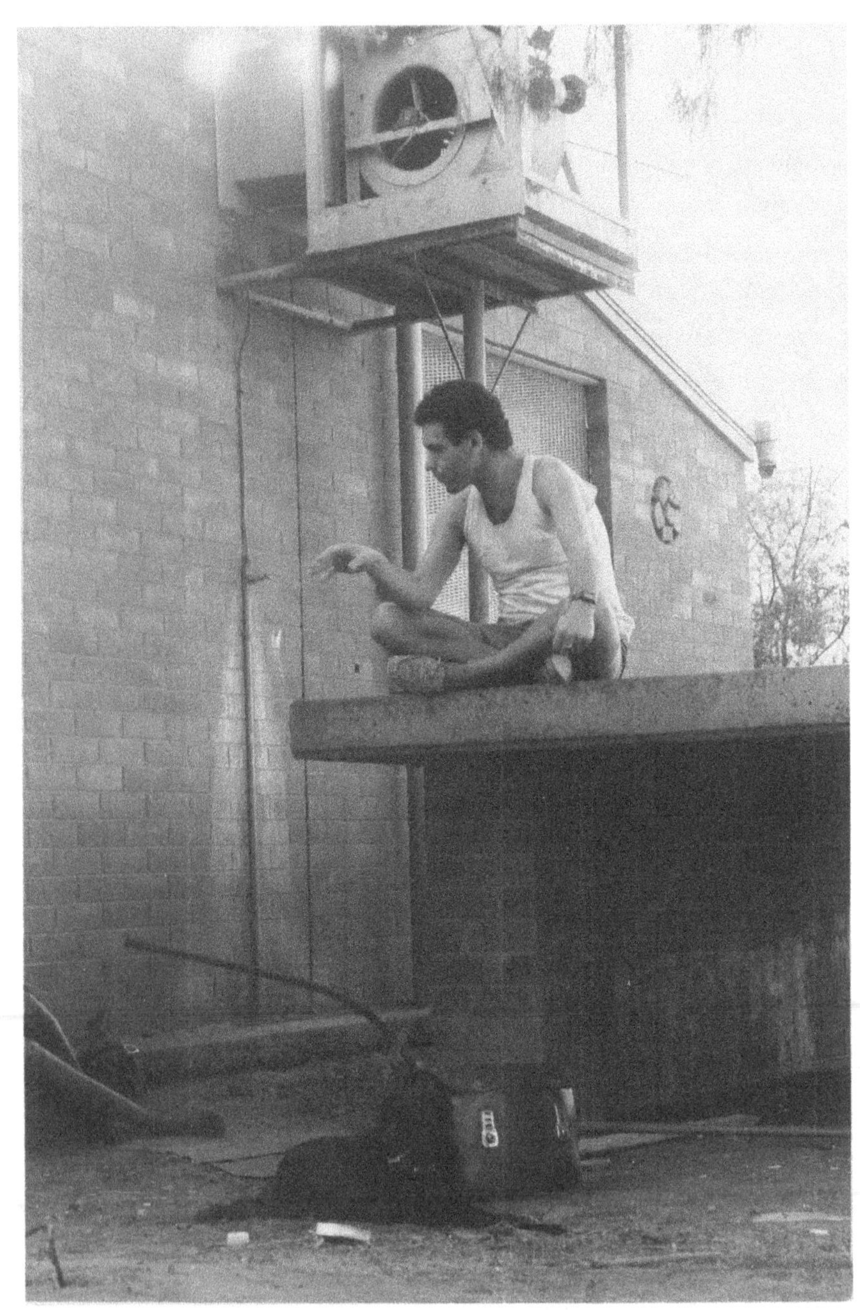

Eric Michaels, Yuendumu c. 1985

12

Eric, in the Desert and Elsewhere

> *August 10, 1988*
> Philip called from Alice. (...) Lots of good local and bushie gossip. Jim B. was there just back from the Hobart AIDS conference. He tells me about this Michael somebody from San Francisco who has been at terminal stage for three years and (...) treats it merely as a chronic illness and keeps on keeping on. I told Jim I don't know if that seems such an attractive prospect, staring yet again at the blank walls of Wattlebrae as I spoke. Then, after the phone call, I thought: Why not go to Alice Springs? Even if I die getting there, the project still has more style than simply lying here and being bored to death. (...) So I indulged a fantasy of Bucknall driving me out, lying in the back of the station wagon, watching the desert go by again, getting to Alice Springs and receiving in state for the few weeks left. Even if by doing this I cut off a few possible days or weeks extra, it seems worth it. I sure can't motivate any optimism for continuing like this here in Brisbane, but a few extra weeks might seem worth it in Alice.

In the months leading up to his death, the more acerbic qualities of Eric Michaels's personality calcified into something approaching art. Those who knew him had long recognised the abrasive facets of his character: Michaels had always been sharp-tongued; as a gimlet-eyed media theorist and anthropologist, he was known for this quality well before he relocated to Australia from his home in Philadelphia in late 1982. But with little left to lose, he leaned in. As his immune system grew ever weaker, marking his final days, he identified a spiralling cast of antagonists, big and small. In his diaries he included copies of the angry missives he directed their way. The activity at times threatened to overwhelm him. 'What I do mostly,' he wrote in one simple entry, 'is lie in bed and compose letters of complaint and revenge, intended to repay the shits who are trying to kill me.'

A photo taken at the time by his friend Penny Taylor captures much of Michaels's prevailing mood. It shows him sitting on a bed at the Wattlebrae Infectious Diseases Hospital at the Royal Brisbane Hospital, naked to the waist. The white wall behind him is bare, and the camera's flash throws a wash of light across the scene, flattening it out. His hair is unkempt, and although he was known to wear a carefully trimmed pencil moustache, he's here sporting a full beard, thick and black. He meets the camera's gaze with purpose, and his tongue extends energetically from his open mouth, Gene Simmons–style. The result lends the image a confrontational quality that at first obscures its underlying vulnerability. It takes a moment to register the dark lesions scattered across Michaels's flesh: the Kaposi's sarcoma skin cancers that flare along the blood vessels and lymph nodes of a late-stage AIDS patient, evidence of a fatally compromised immune system.

Although Michaels would die only weeks later, his mind was still working overtime. Words to him were purposeful: he believed they could alter the world around him; that if they were arranged in the right way they might enact radical change. It's this belief that charges much of the writing he left behind, linking his early publications on media and culture to the later essays on community video and art production in the remote Aboriginal community of Yuendumu. Much of his thinking in relation to these latter subjects would prove controversial to some, at least when revisited from the vantage of today, but it was never less than acrobatic. And if Michaels was known to be a particularly harsh critic of the work of others, one of his strengths was that he always turned his gaze towards himself too.

Now, after a dizzyingly productive five years, in which his work had taken shape amid a flurry of fieldwork and travel, he was confined to bed. He stared at the irregular patterns the cancers had traced across him, and in his diary attempted to make sense of the unimaginable.

'Perhaps the oddest thing about AIDS,' he wrote, 'is that it takes so very long; one is required to live through all its stages, at each point confronted with insane, probably pathological choices. This week it's who to tell, and how.'

—

One thing Taylor's photograph attests to, beyond the horror of late-stage AIDS, is the performative element of Michaels's personality. In full health he was known to be a withering interlocutor. Even more than three decades since his passing, friends still recall his combative flare for conversation – the way, if the moment took him, he would begin to pace as he spoke, his arms flailing energetically, chain-smoking the whole time. John von Sturmer, a fellow anthropologist and close friend, perhaps put it best. 'To be a loved one,' he wrote after Michaels's death, 'always involved the strange suspicion that what drew Eric to you was a sort of exultant detestation.' To this he added less diplomatically, 'Eric was a hazard to be around.'

In his writing – not just in the diaries, but in the dense academic essays he published throughout the 1980s – the same character is clear. It's what makes Michaels's prose hum with finely tuned intellectual menace. In these essays he doesn't so much address a research question as select a target – the growing mythology around so-called 'traditional' Aboriginal painting, for instance, or the newly published work of a fellow anthropologist – and set about destroying it. Even readers who aren't drawn to the cascading density of his ideas surely can't help but sense a certain singularity: it rings clear in even his most difficult tracts of writing.

It's there in Taylor's photograph too, grabbing the viewer's attention and holding it tight. Michaels knows exactly what he's doing in that moment. He was, after all, a sublimely fluent visual theorist, someone who understood the power of images far better than most. *Here it is,* he seems to be saying, *the unstoppable fact of the disease.* But also, *Here's an image, a form of power, that will outlive me.*

For most contemporary readers it's easy to forget that the broader moment is also central to the image's effect. This was the midst of the AIDS crisis, a time when the death toll was rising inexorably towards its mid-1990s peak. A contrarian to the end, Michaels wrote in his diary that he wanted to 'counter the sentimentalised narratives that San Francisco has been able to produce about this sequence', by which he meant the kinds of stories AIDS had already left in its wake in the United States. But his would nonetheless hit plot points familiar to many already touched by the virus. The photo was taken on 26 June 1988. Not long before, he had contacted his conservative-leaning father in the States with what could only have been an impossibly painful triple reveal: his sexuality (proudly homosexual); his health (HIV positive); and his prospects for survival (by that stage, non-existent).

In those final weeks, his mind wandered from his drab surrounds, seeking respite. He returned often in his diary to Yuendumu, a relatively large former mission community in the Western Desert that was home to a fluctuating population of between 500 and 1000 mainly Warlpiri residents. Along with Alice Springs, it was Yuendumu that had formed a touchstone in Michaels's professional and personal life. This was where he had undertaken his research into the Warlpiri's use of television and video media – groundbreaking work that would solidify his reputation for decades to come. It had also become a kind of second home. The thought that he might return there, or at least to Alice, to live out his last days tugged at him. He imagines the scene in his diary: the long journey from Brisbane, cramped in the station wagon, his friend Bucknall driving, Michaels mostly supine in the back seat, or hunched in the front. I picture the window cracked open beside him, his cigarette smoke billowing out like a contrail as the car cuts its way across the continent: west along the arterial path of the highway, through Longreach and Mount Isa, until finally, where the country is bare and dry, the Stuart Highway turns south towards Alice.

For Michaels, who quickly came to love the desert, things would have been more familiar the closer they got to their destination. If I had imagined a steady flow of conversation between he and Bucknall, I now picture an easy silence. It descends once they pass through Tennant Creek (battered fibro- and tin-clad houses, a thinly stocked store, rundown petrol station and bush pub) and holds for much of the 500-plus kilometres that follow. Soon it's the desert proper. They pass the concave passages of dry riverbeds, the clusters of spinifex and collapsed trunks of ancient mulga, the hard, dun-coloured earth that gives way eventually to red sand, stands of she-oak and clumps of paddy melon.

I imagine that Michaels has been anxious as their destination draws closer, but that as the Yipirinya (caterpillar) ancestor – known by whites as the East MacDonnell Ranges – appears on the horizon the feeling settles. It's late afternoon; dark foliage clusters around the dry bed of the Todd River. Streetlights stand forlorn on dusty corners. Here and there figures move about, as does a constant procession of air-conditioned vehicles, but for the most part the closest thing the desert has to a city seems sleepy. In my mind, they drive to a friend's house – Marcia and Philip's, perhaps, or Jim's – and the engine coughs into silence. The streets here are simple: fibro houses, low cyclone-wire fences, gums and saltbush half-heartedly fulfilling the role of civic vegetation. The vastness of the sky is everything.

But the diary entry in which Michaels sketched out his return – the long drive, then resting in bed in a darkened room, too weak to move around but 'receiving in state for the few weeks left' as his Alice Springs friends filed through, one after the other – would prove to be his last.

His spiralling health was only part of the reason he couldn't go. In a cruel twist, the Australian immigration authority had recently denied his application for residency status and were seeking to have him deported. The bureaucrats had somehow caught wind of his illness, and although a run of temporary entry visas had enabled him to stay in Australia for five years, now that AIDS was in the frame they were suddenly insisting there was no basis for extension, let alone residency. His protests – delivered mainly via a lawyer at the South Brisbane Community Legal Service – fell upon deaf ears.

Among his antagonists in his final days, the immigration department loomed the largest. They denied all requests in the most impersonal language: 'There are no grounds for consideration under Section 6A(1)(a), Section 6A(1)(b), Section 6A(1)(c)'. They even sought updates from his friends, trying to ascertain if he were able to travel, the plan obviously being to wheel him onto a flight to America as soon as possible.

Michaels knew any such return would be disastrous. He wouldn't be able to afford his treatment – his US health insurance had lapsed – and he expected to be 'totally alienated' there, left to live out his remaining time in a state of hysteria. He would have no friends around him, and his recent work would go unknown. It kept him awake, composing his angry missives in his head in the early hours, wasting precious energy that he might otherwise have poured into the various pieces of writing that still hounded him.

'That people are willing to do this staggers me,' he wrote in his final entry. 'That they can represent the official arms of the state depresses me more than I can say, or think.'

—

When he first arrived in central Australia, it appeared to some that Michaels had dropped in from space. It's understandable why. It was, after all, the impending launch of a satellite that drew him there.

It was known as AUSSAT. A promotional poster from the time offers an airbrushed artist's impression of it spinning against a navy-blue, star-studded expanse, the iconic scatter of the Southern Cross glowing brightest of all. It's the epitome of cutting-edge innovation, built by the Hughes Aircraft Company in Culver City, California: a sleek canister braided with blinking lights, a foil-wrapped dish extending from one end. In the image it beams its transmission down towards Earth, neatly covering the entirety of the Australian continent.

The satellite was first championed in 1977 by the media mogul Kerry Packer, who had been frustrated by his failure to secure national coverage for the cricket. The government soon came on board, taking majority co-ownership of the pending service with Telecom, the national telecommunications provider. But not everyone was immediately taken by the idea. AUSSAT was set to provide television and other content to a vast swathe of previously cut-off territory. Culture comes hard on the heels of such initiatives, and in Aboriginal communities all too familiar

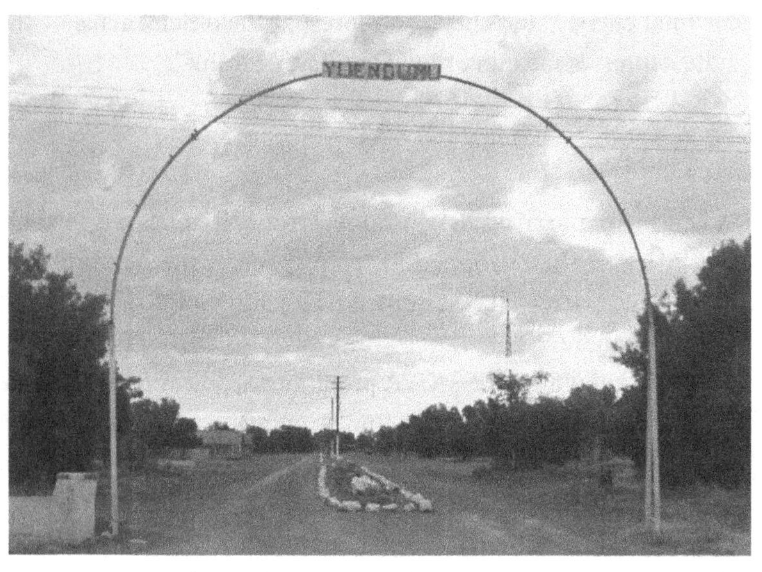

Yuendumu c. 1985

with a barrage of unwanted influence from elsewhere, there were soon dissenting voices.

Such communities were many, for the most part a scatter of outstations and former mission settlements that traced the region's haphazard history of white arrival. Their names were unfamiliar to all but the most attentive settler-Australians: Papunya, Kintore, Kiwirrkurra, Balgo. All would be affected in one way or another, and although the satellite represented an inevitable development – one step on a steady march towards global connectivity – the prospect, no matter how often it was couched in terms of 'breaking the tyranny of distance' between the populated 'centres' and the 'remote outback', was daunting. For who could control the content – the programmes and music that would soon arrive unbidden, the mediated images of non-Aboriginal life in all its apparent wealth and prosperity? Twenty-two separate Aboriginal language groups lay in the satellite's central footprint, some of them precipitously fragile.

The Australian Broadcasting Tribunal's inquiry into Satellite Program Services was soon established, and a cascade of meetings held across the region. The tribunal visited Kintore, a new Pintupi settlement to the west of Alice Springs, in 1984, a little over a year before AUSSAT was launched. That day, the Warlpiri Elder Darby Jampijinpa Ross was among those to make the stakes for Aboriginal peoples clear. Ross was from Yuendumu and a revered Law Man. Born around 1910, he had grown up in the nomadic lifestyle that had sustained his people for generations before white arrival. He'd seen unimaginable changes, and understood the risk at hand all too clearly.

'In the olden days, Aboriginal people didn't have satellites,' he explained to the visitors. 'Now people are chasing after them with satellites to interrupt their tribal law ... That's why we got the land back, to keep away from European things.'

Such a sentiment was not at all unusual at the time. It was at one level a perfect illustration of some of the underlying aspirations of self-determination, the broad name given to policies first embraced by the Whitlam Labor government in the 1970s. This shift had already led to the establishment of a network of smaller outstations and homelands throughout Aboriginal Australia: places where, it was hoped, dedicated cultural maintenance could occur free from Western intervention. Such initiatives had met some resistance under the subsequent Fraser-led Coalition, but with the election of the Hawke government in 1983, the self-determination era was soon climbing towards its optimistic height. Ross's vision was shared widely by Aboriginal peoples, as well as with the many enthusiastic non-Aboriginal figures who saw themselves as advocates and allies for the Aboriginal cause. From this perspective, the 'tyranny of distance' was not something to be overcome at all: it needed to be maintained.

It's against this emerging backdrop that Michaels successfully applied for a three-year fellowship from the Australian Institute of Aboriginal Studies in Canberra, its almost impossibly broad brief to 'assess the impact of television on remote Aboriginal communities'. He was living in Austin, Texas, where he was eking out a post-dissertation living by applying for project grants and writing a pithy and wide-ranging culture column for *The Daily Texan*, the student newspaper of the University of Texas. He welcomed the news of his fellowship by sitting down at his typewriter and banging out a characteristically hyperbolic note:

> What I will remember about this week will be that I got a particular telegram from Canberra. And that will claim its space in the autobiography which that telegram now makes a plausible undertaking for my declining years.

In an earlier era, Michaels may have found himself deeply at odds with a place like Alice: an outspoken American set like a whirlwind among a small Australian backwater. But by the early 1980s the town was undergoing something of a renaissance. It had always been a fluctuating community – an influx of military personnel during World War II had, for instance, briefly grown the population by as many as 8000 – but this time it was different. It was an era-defining shift that Michaels was part of: the town was booming with a new generation of largely white workers drawn to the burgeoning 'Aboriginal industry', buoyed in turn by the newfound energies of self-determination.

Those who were there typically remember it as an optimistic time. Funding for community initiatives was comparatively plentiful. In step, a now-familiar support structure was being established: community organisations that focused on Aboriginal health, legal aid, land rights and housing. At this intersection there was often a relatively easy bonhomie between Aboriginal and non-Aboriginal peoples: new points of contact, new kinds of relationships to be had. Parties were common, and often ran all night, soundtracked by local Aboriginal bands. The white go-betweens – the mediators, brokers, translators and allies – who clustered around these events, among whom Michaels would be counted, were many. Theirs was a presence mostly untethered from the ideologies that had driven their most obvious forebears: the missionaries, with their scripture targeted at saving the Aboriginal 'heathens', or the 'white socks brigade', named for their tendency to appear suddenly in groups, their khaki shorts and white socks identifying them as government administrators.

Although there were plenty of figures with rapacious interests among this influx (the carpetbaggers who would soon rise up around the desert art industry come to mind), for those like Michaels, self-determination provided something like a mantra.

Previous policies had sought coercive assimilation (in more veiled terms, 'integration'), but self-determination was intended to place Aboriginal-led decision-making at the foreground of Indigenous policy. Michaels aligned himself with a local community outfit that was in perfect step with this shift: the Central Australian Aboriginal Media Association (CAAMA), which had been established in Alice only two years before. Its manager and co-founder was Philip Batty, an east-coast émigré who had recently spent three years in the community of Papunya, a remote community some 250 kilometres to the west, as an art teacher. The two became fast friends: it was Batty who suggested Michaels focus the fellowship on one case study and turn his attention to Yuendumu, where a small, TAFE-supported grassroots media project was already being administered by the community's adult educator, Peter Toyne.

Years later, Batty would describe to me how the rhetoric of self-determination in those days seemed to enliven the world around them, bringing with it a charge of promise. He readily included himself among the 'signed-up' set of self-appointed 'white saviours', and recalled watching as his new friend fit into the same mould. 'It's like, you're going to do anything to save Aboriginal people from this wretched colonial imposition,' Batty said. 'We were all there to overthrow the old colonial ways, the welfare department, the policies that had kept people down.' He found Michaels to be a unique mix of romantic and cynic, as well as an incorrigible intellectual: Batty once took him to coastal Wollongong for a beach break and watched as he read his way through a volume of Foucault. When that was done, Michaels reached into his backpack and brought out Heidegger.

Michaels's arrival in Alice was attended by faintly outlandish rumours, many of which proved true. He had been something of a wunderkind back home, showing early promise as an honour-roll student before majoring in English at Philadelphia's Temple University. Upon graduation he ranged broadly. He joined a commune in New Mexico, where he enthusiastically dabbled in free love. It was there that he recognised his homosexuality, he later wrote. Afterwards, he held an editorial position at the notorious sex rag *Screw*, and briefly helped run an experimental art gallery. Batty would recall a story in which Michaels presided over an art performance that consisted of a truckload of wet concrete being poured from a height over the gallery's pristine floor.

One can't help but imagine that anthropology presented a logical choice for someone so interested in the countercultural margins. Although he was yet to come out to his family, Michaels had written his honours thesis on the division of property between gay lovers; his doctoral dissertation, which he titled 'TV Tribes' – an early example of his gift for deft and incisive titles – examined the use of television among evangelical religious groups in Texas. He was never an artist himself, but he drew close to artists throughout his career. In the early 1980s, just prior to his arrival in the Australian desert, he met the pioneering Chilean video artist Juan Downey at a conference, and the two collaborated on a study of the Amazonian Yanomami people. It resulted in Michaels's 1982 essay 'How to Look at Us Looking at the Yanomami Looking at Us' – the title alone a perfect illustration of his creative approach. In line with the leading edge of ethnographic practice, he was as interested in his own presence as he was in that of his presumed subject. There was an entire emergent academic theory around the approach, 'self-reflexivity' – a tangle of argument that Michaels would soon happily add to himself – but as with so much of his thinking, he would later distil it in his diary to a kind of essential essence. 'All of us,' he would write, looking back over his short life, 'ultimately create the tribes we study.'

Michaels and his kind were not anthropologists or ethnographers in their more classical manifestation as dispassionate observers of the lives of others. They proceeded with an awareness not only of their own presence, but also of how that presence unavoidably inflected everything they might record. Much of the resulting writing was weighted with a new kind of self-awareness: ethics had become a key consideration, as well as the unequal balance of power between ethnographer and subject. Earlier practitioners had been guided by the ideology of the 'salvage anthropology' that was a legacy of the colonial period: the careful observation and recording of social practices that, it was believed, would soon be lost to the seemingly inexorable spread of Western ways. This is where the figure of the heroic anthropologist had formed in the popular imagination: the lone researcher who sets out to 'save' a culture from the destructive force of history.

But such myths were not for Michaels. If the arrival of television and other forms of new media presented a threat to Aboriginal ways of life in central Australia, it was surely an opportunity too. He believed it might unthread misguided notions of authenticity and instead knit together new forms of representation that, in keeping with the ideals of self-determination, would not weaken local culture, but strengthen it.

After meeting in Alice with several Warlpiri already participating in the TAFE program, Michaels began to visit Yuendumu in April 1983. It was a return journey of some 600 kilometres on largely unsealed road: bone-shakingly rough if it was dry, and treacherously boggy after rain. Just getting to Yuendumu could take as long as five hours. I imagine that as he drove, he began to formulate the kinds of project-shaping questions he later spelt out in his fellowship report 'The Aboriginal Invention of Television', which was published in 1986: how do Aboriginal viewers use and interpret television and film? How does this usage influence their way of life? What problems does mass media pose for a largely oral tradition based on face-to-face interaction?

On his earliest visits, he met with Kurt Japanangka Granites, a voluble Warlpiri man in his late twenties who had already been filming sports and other events as part of the TAFE program. Granites, who Michaels soon employed as a research assistant, extended him the official community invitation that would allow the fellowship project to begin in earnest, and in August, Michaels relocated to Yuendumu. His initial intent was simply to put time and resources into growing the existing program by offering basic instruction and access to equipment, and to see what resulted. In this, he was influenced by the pioneering work of the American anthropologists Sol Worth and John Adair. In the early 1970s they had provided six members of the Navajo nation with 8mm equipment and enough training to create films, their intent being to prove that a distinctively 'Navajo' way of constructing the world existed (and would be apparent in the resulting footage). But Michaels was also guided by a more pragmatic desire. He would explain in 'The Aboriginal Invention of Television' that he simply wanted to hang back from any direct practical involvement: in his early days in the community he didn't want to be pigeonholed as 'the video-maker', and thus stake an unnecessary claim upon the activity he was ultimately there to observe.

In an expropriated schoolroom that was otherwise used by the visiting dental hygienist, Michaels set to work. First came a survey of how commercial videotapes were passed around the community through networks of kinship obligation, but a much broader objective – one that would ultimately define the scope of his fellowship – quickly emerged. With the additional equipment he'd brought with him, video production stepped up, and they'd soon amassed hundreds of hours of footage. This covered everything from local football and basketball games, bush trips and school parties, to ceremonies, cultural storytelling and the making of traditional artefacts. The logical next step was a means to transmit it, and by early 1984 the goal was a fully-fledged broadcast station. This was unveiled a year later, partly funded by $8000 profit from the community store, and built with mostly Warlpiri labour.

The first pirate broadcast from what was by then known as the Warlpiri Media Association went live on 1 April 1985. The moment was perhaps best captured by Granites in a video produced at the time: 'The satellite was a threat to the Aboriginals,' he said. 'But now we have our own TV and video: we can put our things on too. We can fight fire with fire.'

—

Michaels had already begun publishing the series of essays that would make his name, but it would be in 'The Aboriginal Invention of Television' where he most clearly articulated his approach to his research. In a short preface, he quickly dispatched his obvious forebears:

> Early Australian anthropologists believed that the Aboriginie was doomed, and they acted, at best, as collectors and protectors of Aboriginal culture, assuming that otherwise nothing at all would be left for future generations.
>
> They were wrong. (...) it cannot be doubted that a cultural autonomy persists and is fiercely and ingeniously maintained. This must affect how we conduct and report research now, for we must come to terms somehow with the contemporary aspirations and struggle of [Aboriginal] people.

He describes his own method in simple terms, breaking it down into three distinct approaches. The first two he conducted sparingly. Field interviews were something he generally shied away from due to their unreliability among tradition-minded Aboriginal people – he notes that direct questioning can easily be construed as rude and that specific custodial responsibilities, or lack thereof, meant 'for many questions, an individual will refuse to admit knowledge'. He also occasionally 'inserted small "experiments" into daily events to test out propositions or see whether a rule has been properly understood', but found this risked undermining the trust and rapport that was so essential to his work. The third, and most revealing considering his call for research that comes to terms with the contemporary aspirations and struggles of Aboriginal people, was a practice that might be best characterised as 'being there': 'Most of what I know,' he wrote, 'came from working alongside Aboriginal people and sharing in activity with them.' This included the video work, but it also meant 'hunting trips, attending ceremonies, running errands, going to community dances and participating in meetings'.

No surprise, then, that it wasn't only the Warlpiri's use of television and other media that drew his attention. A decade earlier, what would eventually be recognised as the Western Desert Aboriginal Art Movement had begun in Papunya and spread outwards. After a slow beginning in Yuendumu, it was now taking root. Alongside the artists, this was due to the efforts of another anthropologist, Françoise Dussart, who was undertaking fieldwork towards a PhD at the Australian National University. Michaels, who had developed friendships with a number of the older male painters, was watching carefully. He recognised that, just as television was being re-tooled to local ends through the media project, so too was the Western tradition of painting on canvas. But with the paintings so readily marketable to Western art collectors, a series of bracing contradictions were immediately clear to him, not least among them the stark contrast between the rough-as-guts community in which the art was being made and the high-end city galleries in which it was exhibited. In Dussart, Michaels clearly saw a competitor, and perhaps for this reason took to deconstructing the nascent painting movement with something approaching glee. It's here where his tendency to play the iconoclast rings most clear.

In his now-famous essay about Aboriginal painting, the provocatively titled 'Bad Aboriginal Art', which was first published in 1988, he looks back on these early developments. It includes what for me is one of his classic scenes. As he watched the old men painting, he arrived at a simple question. To what extent, he wondered, were the brushes and paints that were provided to the painters responsible for the specific aesthetic qualities of their work? By which he meant, how much of the celebrated aesthetic of Warlpiri painting was arbitrary?

Most field researchers would proceed carefully, observing developments with this question in mind, hoping for an answer to present itself in the data they collected. Not Eric. He came up with a more direct approach. Finding himself alone in the studio one afternoon, he took a length of unstretched canvas, selected some brushes and paints, and invented his own approximation of a Tjukurrpa (Dreaming) story 'based on a favorite locale from home', in Midwest America. The result held little charm – in his assessment it failed to look much like a Warlpiri painting at all – and he abandoned it, his question about technique only partially answered.

That would have been the end of the matter if, soon afterwards, the canvas had not turned up for sale at the Yuendumu store where artists working independently of the local art centre would sell their wares from time to time. But there it was – Michaels's painting, already circulating as a piece of 'authentic' Aboriginal art. If the question he had begun with was relatively simple, those that followed were far more elaborate.

'Not only,' he wrote, 'was nobody particularly fussed by the fact that this Dreaming, and its author, were unidentified, even unidentifiable, but the painting had been completed – the dotting filled in – by some old men in my absence.'

The power of this story lies less in its ability to show something of the revelatory contradictions of cultural translation (although it does do this, in spades) and more in its playful showmanship. There's much in his approach that we might call 'unethical' or 'culturally transgressive', especially in hindsight, but it nonetheless provides him a perfect means by which to rupture the misguided notion that Aboriginal art's enthusiastic Western interpreters are somehow removed from the processes that create it.

It's for this reason that Michaels's reading of the Warlpiri painting movement remains compelling, but the movement was for him only ever a counterpoint to what he found so compelling about video production. Unlike painting, which was turning the iconography of long-held traditional practices to new ends, video had no obvious prior claim to 'authenticity'. Yes, painting on canvas was new to the Warlpiri, but the intricate arrays of dotting and pictographic symbols the artists used showed long-held ways of viewing the world that refused to conform to Western ways of seeing; that was why in the white art world the paintings readily became shorthand for an often vaguely understood spirituality. It was work ripe for romanticisation, and at one level betrayed the kind of thinking that had driven salvage anthropologists: Indigenous culture was conceived of as at constant threat of compromise and loss. As inaccurate as this perception might have been, by the mid-1980s it had already become the painting movement's leitmotif. Michaels was instantly jaded by this tendency, which he read as not only an expression of enduring myths of cultural demise, but as a kind of failure of the historical imagination.

Here he is at the opening of 'Bad Aboriginal Art', describing an expedition to Yuendumu by a group of professional art enthusiasts: two anthropologists, a French ethnographer, a journalist and 'an "important" art curator from an unfamiliar but nonetheless New York gallery': 'These clever sorts,' he writes, 'managed to discover a whole tribe of Picassos in the desert, presumably a mysterious result of spontaneous cultural combustion. (...) The tedious descriptor of painting as the desert's new cash crop is trucked out once again.'

Yet when it came to the video project, his romantic side swamped any cynicism. As he saw it, video repelled the painting movement's tendency to replay certain stereotypes about Aboriginal cultural identity. For one, video footage didn't look 'Aboriginal' in the way that paintings did. Nor was it a form yet adapted to the demands of the Western art world, which is to say there was no market ready to fetishise it.

Even as media production seemed to be opening up an entirely new kind of expression, it was also enabling Michaels to apprehend the Warlpiri world more fully. He began to see video as a medium that in Walpiri hands could meet the world on uniquely Warlpiri terms. It achieved this in ways not bound by an external demand, implicit or otherwise, for a certain 'look' or 'style'. Whereas the art market lauded the individual, filmmaking was by its very nature collective. This far more closely reflected the reality of remote community life and its roots in pre-contact clan organisation.

There was also another revealing difference: whereas the most celebrated painters were often Elders, it was usually younger figures – many of them enthusiastic consumers of 1980s pop culture – who took the reins of media production. Michaels's description of his Warlpiri friend and co-conspirator Francis Jupurrurla Kelly, who replaced Kurt Japanangka Granites as the project's research assistant in late 1984, provides one example:

> (...) Jupurrurla, in Bob Marley T-shirt and Adidas runners, armed with his video portapak, resists identification as a savage updating some archaic technology to produce curiosities of primitive tradition for the jaded modern gaze. Jupurrurla is indisputably a sophisticated cultural broker who employs videotape and electronic technology to express and resolve political, theological, and aesthetic contradictions that arise in uniquely contemporary circumstances.

It's a stark contrast to the image of the 'senior desert seer' so enjoyed by the art market, and embodies Michaels's argument that the medium of video was uniquely able to communicate a contemporary Warlpiri worldview, one premised on resilience rather than loss.

The above passage is taken from another of Michaels's well-known essays, *For a Cultural Future: Francis Jupurrurla Makes TV in Yuendumu*, published as a slim volume by the Sydney gallery Artspace in 1987. It's perhaps his most fully realised work, not counting the diaries, and as close as he gets to an overarching theory of Warlpiri media. It's also – oddly, given his enthusiasm for a self-reflexive approach to ethnographic writing, for folding the form back upon itself – reminiscent of the more conventional ethnographic writing he so enjoyed railing against elsewhere. Although Michaels is present in the tone of the writing, and at times employs the first person, he nonetheless retains an unmistakeable observational distance.

This is most apparent in one of the videos he chooses to discuss, from the hundreds that had by then been produced since Michaels had arrived in Yuendumu. It was an account of the 1929 Coniston massacre – one of the last known massacres of First Nations peoples in Australia – titled *Coniston Story*. This film took shape largely as a response to his own frustration about the more passive mode that his Warlpiri collaborators were using: he suggested they make something 'just for the video' (rather than filming a real event like a football game or a performance), and Jupurrurla took the idea and ran with it.

From there, Michaels reads the resulting production in detail. He describes how the number of Warlpiri participants quickly ballooned to include those responsible for the correct telling of the story; how the kirda ('bosses') for that story took centre stage; how the kurdungurlu ('helpers' or 'managers') held back; how Jupurrurla's seemingly aimless camerawork was in fact an attempt to capture the ancestral presences that activated the landscape around them. From this evidence Michaels argues for the continuity of cultural production across different media. Such production was premised upon 'an essential oral form' that underwrote what it was, in his mind at least, to *be* Warlpiri. The argument 'is not meant to be romantic', he notes, but the fact he then frames the stakes in strikingly dramatic terms betrays his hand immediately. 'TV can be an instrument of salvation or destruction,' he writes. 'Its potential force is greater than guns, or grog, or even the insidious paternalisms that seek to claim it.'

It's a bravura performance, and because of this it's easy to ignore that he glosses over his own role in the production. It's almost as if after setting the whole thing in motion he then retracts completely, relegating himself to a place beyond his own enquiry. From this vantage he arrives at what will eventually become the argument he's often remembered by. In what he named the 'confrontation between Dreamtime and Our-time', he pictured only two possible futures for his Warlpiri friends and collaborators. One was a much-diminished 'lifestyle future' – a fate in which he saw the Warlpiri losing their distinctive cultural character, in part through the destructive force of new media – and the other a 'cultural future', in which new forms like television and video would sustain the 'privileged authority' of tradition. This in turn would be engaged to political ends. Michaels was taking the goal of self-determination and running with it: in this light, his presence was necessarily transitory, obsolete as soon as Aboriginal people moved into roles of self-governance and, in relation to media in particular, self-representation.

Melinda Hinkson, an anthropologist of the following generation who undertook fieldwork in Yuendumu in the early 1990s and similarly took media studies as her subject, was among those to respond to this sense of moral urgency. As a student she had been deeply enthused by Michaels's writing, but she soon found things were not so clear-cut as he presented them. When she first arrived in the community, the reality she experienced was very different.

'The intercultural scene of life pervaded everything,' she told me, when we spoke about Michaels's work. He had argued that only autonomy would enable Warlpiri culture to endure, but Hinkson soon understood that this didn't take into account the 'highly intercultural politicking' that bound the community together, and that so firmly underpinned an organisation like the Warlpiri Media Association.

As far as Hinkson saw it, Michaels was working within a 'self-determination imaginary': a kind of embodiment of its first-wave aspirations, unreconstructed by subsequent history. For many who have since engaged with remote Aboriginal life in similar contexts, including me, the idea that Aboriginal people would take complete control of community organisations like the Warlpiri Media Association seems to cut against the grain of remote community life: an ideal imposed from outside rather than an aspiration expressed from within.

In a clear-eyed appraisal of Michaels's work published in the media studies journal *Continuum* in 2002, Hinkson argues for a more nuanced understanding. Places like Yuendumu, she reminds us, have always been deeply intercultural in character: they are built as much on Western conventions of social organisation and governance as on their local counterparts. In fact, it's exactly this split that at times makes life there so confounding for Aboriginal and non-Aboriginal people alike: the question of who should take ownership of the interstices is rarely fully resolved. Michaels's reading of the nascent remote art industry turned on exactly this – its popular interpretation was wilfully blind to both its history and its contemporary reality – but in constructing a theory of media production, and anticipating its ultimate value in stridently political terms, he downplayed the very same.

It's an intriguing oversight, but in acknowledging it we should also remember this: Michaels would not live long enough to shift, or even moderate, his perspective. No matter how densely argued much of his work is, there's something almost appealingly simple about it: it harks back to the certainties of an earlier time. To read him now is to turn to thinking that was never required to adapt to subsequent policy developments in Aboriginal Australia: to the widely accepted failures of the self-determination era, for instance, or to the space such failures opened for conservative governments to strike down its more radical and visionary propositions.

All this for the most part happened after his death: for this reason, we can of course only imagine where Michaels as a writer and a thinker might have taken us.

—

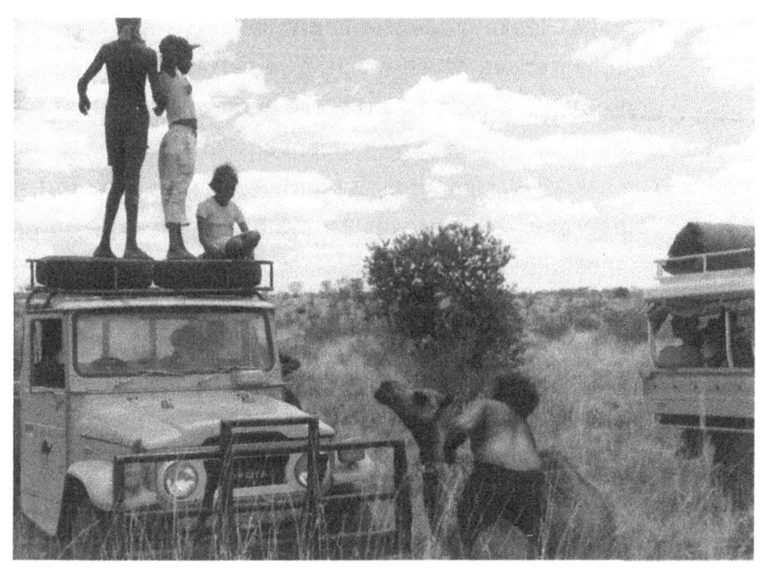

Near Yuendumu c. 1985

> *September 9, 1987*
> I watched these spots on my legs announce themselves over a period of weeks, taking them as some sort of morphemes, arising out of the strange uncertainties of the past few years to declare, finally, a scenario. As if these quite harmless-looking cancers might, when strung together, form sentences which would give narrative trajectory, a plot outline, at last, to a disease and a scenario that had been all too vague. (...) A moment's relief: it's come to this. The narrative, clear and insistent. Automatic pilot. But, of course, this relief proves always a false and premature dispensation.

One thread that binds much of what's been published on Michaels since his passing is the acknowledgement of his wide-ranging disciplinary interests. It seems one cannot write on him without noting the peripatetic quality of his thinking.

'The work of Eric Michaels straddles both anthropology and cultural criticism,' the Aboriginal activist and academic Marcia Langton, who knew Michaels in Alice Springs, wrote in her introduction to the posthumous collection *Bad Aboriginal Art: Tradition, Media, and Technological Horizons.* Compared to media theorist Dick Hebdige's foreword in the same volume, Langton's is a welcome simplification – anthropology, aesthetics, art criticism and theory, epistemology, semiotics and queer studies are just some of the academic disciplines in which Hebdige locates the likely impact of Michaels's contribution. 'Where exactly, then, in which section of the library, should the name "Eric Michaels" belong?' Hebdige asks, before proposing 'at least three possible locations'.

All this attests to Michaels's skill as a thinker, but few mention his considerable skill as a writer. Perhaps that's because for the most part it remains hidden: his best passages, in my mind at least, exist not because of his sometimes-aggressive restlessness ('He always 'wrote furiously', that is, in a ferociously interrogative mood,' Hebdige noted) but despite it. In the diaries, which were first published in 1990, everything is stripped back. Brevity is inherent to the form, of course, but one also senses the pressure, both physical and psychological, of looming death. It colours everything, even the many small humorous asides, with a touch of poignancy. He recounts petty conflicts with his neighbours (for instance, he made 'the ultimate Oz faux pas' of using the communal clothesline on Christmas Day; the yard had already been cordoned for celebrations), and reflects on his vanished sex drive with a certain detached resignation ('Yesterday, I found myself finally unable to jerk off at all – after two days of trying, after nearly a week of not bothering.') His entry for 14 April 1988 consists of just two short sentences: 'If I continue to live much longer, I will have to learn to read French, speak Warlpiri, and spell English. There are arguments both ways.'

But the poignancy also comes from the fact that Michaels is so clearly using the diaries to think beyond his own death, and in doing so, urging his reader to do the same. Perhaps if he'd lived, he would have eventually managed to settle his furious mind and reflect more gently upon his experiences in the desert. Maybe then, the autobiography – the one he'd not-so-winkingly flagged as a late-life undertaking when he'd received notice of his fellowship all those years earlier – would have been real.

As it stands, there are only hints. 'I've been working on another Aboriginal art essay,' he wrote only a few days after the two-sentence entry above. He was preparing for a conference in Melbourne that his illness will ultimately preclude him from attending. The essay, he continued, is intended to 'explain' the last two, but there's a catch: 'I again don't know what the purpose is (although I'll need something to read in Melbourne and elsewhere next month; it seems one has to keep producing these things to get around).' It's relatively anodyne as far as a critique of the limits of academic writing goes – that as a form it provides little more than access to the academy's echo chamber – but he gestures further: 'I am also seeking a grammar and poetics that will let me render things more clearly,' he writes.

One can picture him staring at the blank walls of Wattlebrae, going back in his mind over the work he's done, worrying away at its potential shortcomings, returning time and again to this passage or that. When a newly bound copy of *For A Cultural Future* arrives, he can't help but 'rush by sentences which seem too dense for sense on first reading ...' He decides that he's unsure if academic writing needs to be complex in execution or not.

By now, what will become his best-known essays have been published, many of them in the pioneering Australian art magazine *Art & Text*. He has become close with the magazine's mercurial editor, Paul Foss. Foss, who knows his friend's time is near, has been visiting regularly ('Paul arrived for a three-day jaunt. We spent the afternoon characteristically dishing and working.') Unbeknown to either of them, they are clearing the ground for Michaels's posthumous legacy to take root: working on the publication of the diaries, for which Michaels has set aside his meagre savings, and selecting the essays that will be collected in *Bad Aboriginal Art*. It's this publication, along with his fellowship report 'The Aboriginal Invention of Television', that a subsequent generation of aspiring cross-cultural media scholars and community workers will often bring with them, clutched to their chests, as they arrive in Yuendumu for the first time. By then, a stubborn post-self-determination pattern will have established itself: the turnover of idealistic white workers in Aboriginal communities, and the local frustration at the seeming inability to keep them there.

But all that, for now, is in the future.

As Michaels lies dying, he's still reaching for a way to render things more clearly. It's hard not to think that the diaries have prompted this, for the clarity and directness one assumes he is referring to is exactly what animates them. But lest we oversimplify things by arguing that one form allows for something another does not, it's worth noting that a similar quality also runs like quicksilver through his academic texts. Usually, it comes in brief passages threaded between others far denser. They act like short blasts of oxygen: *Breathe,* he seems to be saying in these moments, to himself as much as to his reader.

Such passages could be read as peripheral to the main game, but there's another way to see them too. I imagine them strung together into softer, more elusive texts – a counterpoint to his 'harder' academic output. We even might imagine it's here that Michaels's unrealised project as a writer, as opposed to a theorist, draws most clearly into focus.

Three years earlier, well before his diagnosis, he wrote a short essay for a publication on what are known as the Yuendumu Doors – a series of schoolhouse doors that a group of senior Warlpiri men had taken it upon themselves to paint with desert designs: roundels and dotting, representations of sinuous ancestral figures carving their way through the landscape.

The doors are now a subject of exhibition and study, and for decades have formed a core part of the collection of the South Australian Museum. But when Michaels sat down to write his essay they were largely unknown, at least to Western eyes. Although he was hard at work on the media project, they had proven too fascinating to ignore. On the page he takes to them as another would to high conceptual art. The resulting essay is circuitous and dense, characteristically so, but partway through he changes tack entirely. After spending most of his energy establishing the postmodern bona fides of his subject, Michaels turns to his own experience of the landscape.

For a few glorious paragraphs, he lets the oxygen rush in.

He recalls what it had been like to arrive in the middle of the desert in early 1983; how he had at first been left to his own devices, at times driving out from the community alone and navigating his vehicle along the narrow sand tracks that lead, seemingly aimlessly, into the landscape. Anyone who's been to Yuendumu, or to any of the desert communities like it, will recognise the feeling: the sense that the edges of the community – the last tin houses, the point where the sealed roads peter into dirt – mark a kind of threshold between one world and another. At first Michaels knew no one – he was yet to meet his great friend Francis Jupurrurla – so could only guess at the significance such a threshold offered. But he had quickly established the kinds of pragmatic kin relations that fill up one's Toyota with company on even the most incidental of journeys. In this way, the unfamiliar desert expanses slowly revealed themselves to him. Narratives big and small were laid bare: '... where we broke down last time, where we found Jupurrurla walking at night, where Japanangka jumped off the truck, the back way to Mount Allen, and, occasionally, the place where the ancestors came, or where water is, or bush tomatoes'.

At first, the landscape appeared to him among the oldest he'd ever seen – 'the mountains were worn down to craggy hills, the valleys flat with millennia of settled sand' – but as his familiarity with it grew, he found himself wondering if the opposite were possible. A persistent question began to rise within him on every trip: what if this landscape flagged a beginning, rather than an end?

'I played a game,' he wrote, 'and told myself that this was a new continent, that these hills were mountains just beginning to grow, that the mulga and spinifex were the first steps towards a forest, that time would build this landscape up, not wear it down.'

He admitted that he could never quite make the picture stick in his mind, but if he ever described it to his Warlpiri friends they would surely have recognised it. The Tjukurrpa (Dreaming) sets all things in constant motion: time is not linear; the furthest past exists in the present. As he and his companions made their way into the landscape, everything around them – the secret waterholes, the hills thrown up by the ancestors' epic travels, the plants and animals – was in the process of making and remaking itself: all of it was always becoming. Whether by accident or design, Michaels had imagined himself into the centre of desert consciousness, perhaps even out of time.

Coda

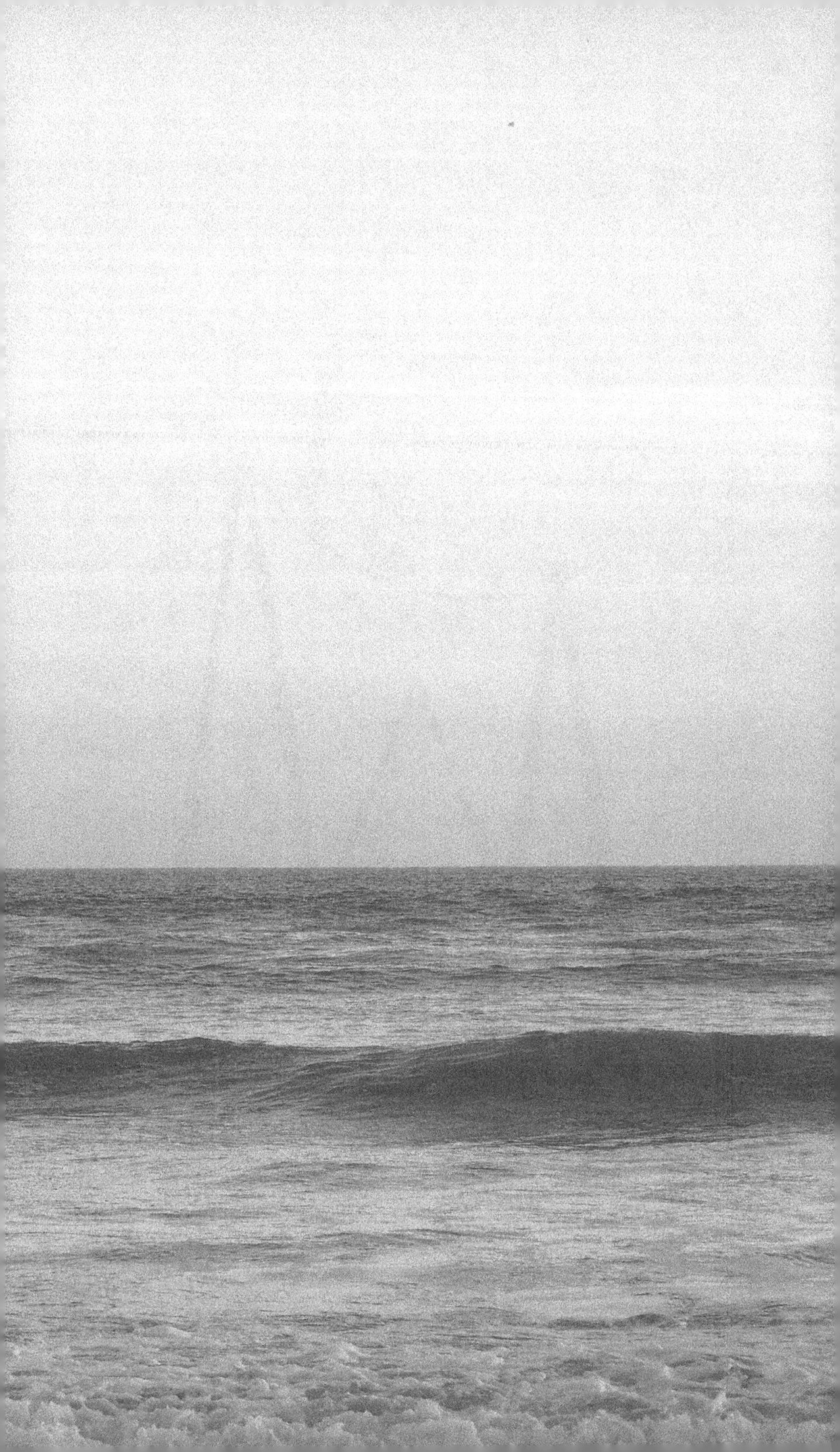

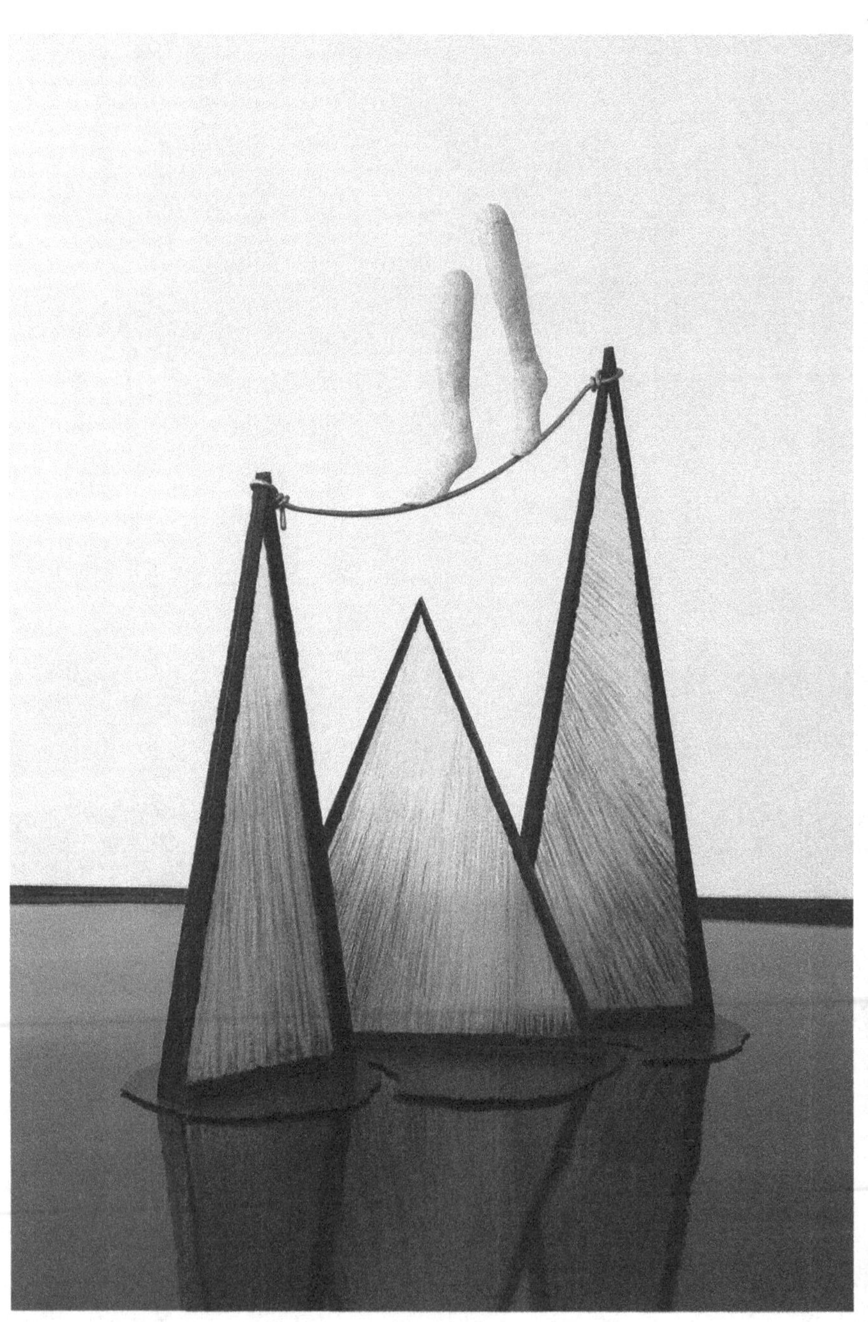

Benjamin Armstrong *Midday* 2024–2025

Dear Ben

Dear Ben,
A memory recently returned to me, unbidden, of the two of us picking blackberries together in the rain. Quite a way to start a letter, I know, but let's dispense with any pleasantries and pursue this image, which is what has prompted me to write. At first I was unsure of its accuracy, but it soon drew more and more sharply into focus: you and I working intently to extract the sweet black fruit from amid the tangles of thorns, soaked after only a short while in the soft yet steady drift of rain.

I could look up the exact date, but I'll settle simply on writing that it was 2010 or 2011. It was late spring or early summer, warm enough that we'd swum earlier that day in the river. The gentle rain did not hint at the torrential downpours that would hit that same region only a few months later and cause the catastrophic floods that washed away the blackberry bushes, along with various trees and sections of the riverbank.

I was at a hinge point, remember? Picking myself up from a failed relationship, attempting a foothold between one world and the next. We had already met, a couple of years earlier, when you'd visited the islands where I'd been living, but we hadn't stayed in touch. We crossed paths again and spent several days together at the block you were housesitting – talking, swimming in the river, bushwalking and making blackberry jam. I recall thinking, *Who would have thought life could be so simple and yet so alive?*

I wanted to say thank you, although I know that's not necessary. Mainly, though, I wanted to recall a drawing of yours you showed me during that visit, which I've since thought about often, but we haven't ever mentioned again.

I would hesitate to say it was among your best works, but memory has a way of rendering such judgements untrustworthy anyway, so take that as you will. I don't even know if you exhibited it. I could probably search this online, but I'd rather rely upon the image I have of it in my mind, no matter how inaccurate. For the moment, this seems more suitable – the outline of an artwork seen more than a decade ago, as imperfect and indistinct as the memories that surround it.

A man's face fills the picture frame, close up, looking outwards, a turbulent ocean behind him. It's rendered in thin washes of ink, light greys that transition to not-quite-blacks, here and there rushing and pooling together in discrete sections, a material equivalence of the water itself. The greyness of the ink washes the image out, leaving it – to initial appearance, at least – deadened, like a bright day suddenly dulled by clouds. The work's only touch of colour comes via the orange waterproof parka that is cinched tight around the man's face, doing what little it can to protect him from what one imagines as lashing wind and rain. The mess of white-topped waves behind him makes clear he's in the middle of whatever body of ocean he has chosen, for whatever reason, to traverse, and is adrift in a small watercraft. He stares at us. Or, more accurately, stares beyond us, at the ocean only he can see ahead. He looks terrified.

As you explained when you showed me this work, the image is of Andrew McAuley, the Australian who in 2007 tried and failed to cross the Tasman Sea in his kayak. We agreed his story was horrible, yet undeniably compelling. McAuley was no naif: he had a long, awarded history as a mountaineer and all-round adventurer, and by the time he embarked on his fateful voyage he had already clocked up thousands of kilometres kayaking on open ocean. That's not to mention his first attempt at the 1600-kilometre Tasman crossing, which he'd aborted soon after he'd begun because he found it impossible to stay warm in his kayak's simple berth. And he had to stay warm: as well as being fraught with vessel-dwarfing swells, 100-kilometre-an-hour winds and freak waves the size of municipal buildings, the Tasman is treacherously cold.

When your drawing first prompted me to think about McAuley, who I then only knew of as the unlucky subject of brief news attention, I had just one experience through which I could attempt to put his into perspective: a kayaking holiday I'd taken to Port Davey, on the far southwest coast of Tasmania. My three companions and I reached the mouth of the port by paying the skipper of a lobster boat to ferry us overnight around Tasmania's southern coast, from east to west. Don't get me wrong: although I'm sure our passage was not without its dangers, it holds nothing but the faintest comparison to departing that same southeast coast alone, as McAuley did, and paddling due east. But there was this: at some point during that long night we hit rough seas, and I dragged myself from our cramped, below-deck quarters and sat with the skipper. Or, more accurately, sat just behind him, as he held the ship's wheel and steered up and over what to me seemed immense walls of water rolling in from the surrounding darkness. One after another they came, and as the boat rose vertiginously upon each peak and then dropped into the deep trough that followed, floods of water crashed over the deck and shook the glass-walled cabin. It was bracing, but the skipper's apparent ease dulled any fear I may have otherwise felt: he had music blasting away and was singing along at the top of his lungs to Cat Stevens's maudlin version of the classic, 'Cat's in the Cradle'.

When I thought about your drawing, and tried to picture the seas that Andrew McAuley had faced, I returned to this moment, sans Stevens, and then worked backwards. *Shrink the vessel,* I thought, *by a factor of ten; grow the waves by the same.* Even now, my mind at this point goes blank, struggling to comprehend the immensity of it. McAuley's boat was retrofitted to purpose, bristling with various instruments and tools to help him meet the challenge before him, but in the end it could only provide the thinnest of membranes between body and ocean. At night, and during the worst storm conditions, he could let out a stabilising drift anchor, duck down inside the boat and pull a rounded hatch shut behind him. This was fitted with a ventilator that let in air but not water, and the boat was weighted in such a way that if capsized, as it surely would be again and again, it would right itself. At that point I can't believe that what McAuley was doing was much about skill, or even bravery. At that point – trussed up in a buoyant, tight-fitting container, holding on for dear life as the freezing ocean marauds its unfeeling way from horizon to horizon – surely the only thing that matters is a capacity to somehow live with, and in, terrible fear. Who can say if this capacity served him right up until the end, when, after thirty days at sea and only thirty nautical miles from the New Zealand coast, McAuley sent out a garbled distress call. A search-and-rescue team located his kayak twenty-four hours later, drifting at sea. His body was never recovered.

The question that follows immediately on the heels of stories like McAuley's is, of course, the simplest: why? It's one thing to be placed in such a situation by awful chance – plunged into a survive-or-perish scenario after the sinking of a passenger boat or the downing of an aircraft – and another entirely to go through months, or even years, of careful planning to engineer the same. There's one school of thought that the disposition of adventurers like McAuley can be explained by genetics, that through some quirk of their design they feel fear less keenly, or at the very least have a far higher tolerance for it, than the rest of us. But there's surely more personal reasons too. McAuley articulates one in *Solo*, a 2008 documentary about him by Jennifer Peedom and David Michôd:

'I *am* scared about this trip,' he says, just two months before the sea would claim him. 'I feel fear. But I don't necessarily fear being afraid. Because, being afraid, you really face your demons, you know? You're taken places in your head that you just can't be taken in normal, everyday life.'

As he reflects on the likely horror to come, his commitment is astounding. So too is his bravery, especially in light of another scene filmed at the outset of his first, aborted attempt. He's saying goodbye to his wife and three-year-old son on a beach in southern Tasmania. They hug; he tells them he loves them. His son, who McAuley affectionately calls 'Googie-Egg', is too young to understand the gravity of what is happening, and appears to be simply revelling in the novelty of the moment – the rocky beach, the softly lapping waves, his dad's face painted in a mask of stark white zinc. This only makes the whole thing more painful. And then GoPro footage shows McAuley paddling towards open ocean, his painted face now ghoulish against the receding coastline. As he speaks to camera he begins to cry: 'I'm really worried I'm not going to see my wife again, and my little boy, and I'm scared. I'm wondering why I'm doing this, I really am. And I just don't know.' Soon, he's gasping for air, sobbing so hard he almost heaves. 'I have to make it,' he gulps. 'I have to.' Yet it's not fear alone one sees in this moment. There's also a vast, unexplainable cruelty, even violence – to himself as well as to his family; what may seem to some, perhaps, as a deep and equally unexplainable selfishness, and to others a profound compulsion.

Ben, I wonder now if you chose this image because it puts some of the risks of your chosen vocation into perspective. Of course, McAuley's story is so dramatic most all else can't help but pale in comparison, so I'm not equating one thing with another, at least not directly. But not so long before my visit, you and M had come back together after a brief separation. The next steps were just taking shape: two artists planning for a home and child amid the significant financial and emotional insecurities of two practices. There was no certainty, just a driving need to somehow keep art at the centre of your life, even as you opened space for those other, life-sustaining things to flourish too.

In those days we spent together I sensed that although we were at different points, you too were searching for something like a foothold. Art had been good to you (I'm thinking particularly of how your success would soon allow you to buy a small industrially zoned property and convert it to a house and double studio – a stellar achievement). And, although preceded by years of quiet labour, this initial flush had come relatively early. You'd hit all the right notes for a young artist: acclaim for your early exhibitions, support from the right collectors and benefactors, representation from a top commercial gallery and inclusion in a run of reputable institutional exhibitions and biennales.

You were smart, and guided well by older artists, not to mention an influential mentor. This, I suspect, was why you knew that regardless of the attention your work had garnered in the first decade or so of your career, you had to prepare for what inevitably follows for most, if not all, artists: the moment when the art world turns and looks to the next generation. The previously steady drumbeat of external validation quiets; decisions made in one's life and practice are cast for the first time in a light clear enough to grasp their lasting implications.

I recently read Musa Mayer's *Night Studio*, a memoir of her relationship with her late father, the great American painter Philip Guston. There's plenty of books on Guston, of course, some of which I know you have (I recall you had a recently published volume of his drawings at hand during my visit all those years ago), but most of them look upon the artist from the outside in. They are structured around deep readings of the work, or long interviews with Guston himself, a famously engaging and endlessly quotable interlocutor. *Night Studio*, by contrast, provides something close to the view from the inside. What was it like to live with someone so driven to create?

It's not like Mayer's book contains some major revelation that her father was a monster, or anything like that. Far from it: although he was a complex and outsized presence in his daughter's life, it's clear from her words that the two loved each other. Yet the book is filled with her regret for Guston's emotional absence. His family had to share him with his practice. His moods swung wildly, seemingly controlled by his painterly fortunes, the rise and fall of which could pull him away both physically and emotionally without even a moment's notice. And by 'fortunes' I don't mean the outside fortunes of the art world – whether his work was selling (it sometimes was, it sometimes wasn't), or receiving attention from critics or major museums (same), was not of primary importance to Guston. What I mean is the inner fortunes of the work itself. It was this that he constantly worried at, a worry he could only partially dull with the cigarettes and alcohol that contributed to the heart attack that killed him at sixty-six. Were his paintings working, or not? Were they still working now, in the depths of night, like they were in the light of late afternoon? What about now, when hung en masse for all to see? Were they for or against him, right or wrong?

As you know, after dinner Guston would often disappear into the simple cinder-block studio he had constructed beside the family home in Woodstock, New York, and not emerge until morning. From her upstairs bedroom a young Musa would see the light glowing there, listening to the quiet sounds as her mother, also called Musa, cleared up downstairs. She too had been an artist – one of great promise, if the early public mural commissions she had painted with her husband are anything to go by – but she had set her own practice aside in favour of her husband's compulsive, all-consuming drive. That compulsion had always lived with them, a presence so real that it fundamentally shaped Guston's family unit (just as McAuley's strange compulsion to put himself in harm's way surely shaped his).

Like many viewers, it's the bravery of Guston's work that I respond to – his capacity to bear witness to himself and the world around him, the almost brazen confidence with which he handles his chosen medium. But it's a bravery that demands to be understood in light of the sacrifices that enabled it – not only his own, but those of people who surrounded him. Good artists take what their work demands they must; they do this without knowing whether this taking will be justified by the results of their labours, whether the thing they're chasing is worth the price. Yet they keep at it. An underlying violence emerges, coupled with a deep selfishness – these too constitute the stuff of art. Understanding this adds texture to a practice, it complicates it. Productively so. It makes apparent what good artists put on the line when they enter whatever space it is that constitutes their studio and set to work.

Things have changed since Guston's time, of course. To have a dedicated practice now is not necessarily to cut oneself off to the detriment of those close to us. The house you built attests to this in its architecture: the central living quarters that rise over two floors to an open aperture above; the generous studios on either side, sheltered under the same roof. If it's likely your son loses each of his parents, at different times, to each of their studios, it's just as likely that he wanders freely between those working spaces, tracing a passage that renders the mystery of creative practice as familiar to him as any domestic ritual. But I still wonder: how and where do you cut away from the push and pull of everyday life and carve out even a small piece of the magnificent solitude a practice demands? At what point does one compromise the other?

Did the image of McAuley at sea catch your eye because his story is such a visceral warning of the dangers of compulsion? Or was it more about the testament it offered to risk – risk being the all-consuming preoccupation for an artist worth their salt? Don't feel you have to answer that. I admit again that the line I'm drawing here is tenuous. But yet: all these years later your ink drawing returns to me, forceful and direct. Such directness, I feel, matters. Surely the best art is that which strikes us face on, with a quiet force that shakes us, even just a touch, from the familiar rhythms of everyday life. Ideally it shows us what it is to hang beyond the edge of the familiar, even what it is to reach back and untether the rope that holds us.

We fall, and as we do, the world we believe we know so well is once again rendered strange and new.

Acknowledgements

This book would of not have been possible without the artists who opened their practices (and themselves) to writerly scrutiny: I hope I've returned your trust here by honouring what you do.

The manuscript has benefitted greatly from the support and expertise of Julia Carlomagno at Monash University Publishing, and its design and layout has been shaped beautifully by Ricardo Felipe and Andrew Darragh of Small Tasks. Thanks to Jane Novak for placing the book. Thanks also to my colleagues at the Drill Hall Gallery, as well as Geoff Hassall OAM, Jonathan Nichols and Bala Starr, Terence Maloon, Jeremy Bakker, Ben Armstrong and Moya McKenna, Simryn Gill (for the beautiful cover image), my current and former editors at *The Monthly*, and my family and friends. Finally, thanks to my father, Leslie – the first artist I knew.

The majority of essays here draw deeply on conversations with artists and others as their primary source. Most are also informed to greater and lesser degrees by secondary research. My introduction quotes Philip Guston, in Philip Guston, *I Paint What I Want to See*, Penguin, 2022, p. 253. 'The Nuclear Clock' quotes extensively from Stuart Ringholt, *Hashish Psychosis: What It's Like to Be Mentally Ill and Recover*, self-published, 2006. 'The Artist in Space' quotes from an untitled and unpublished 2012 text by Simryn Gill, quoted in Brian Massumi, 'Making Place: In the Artist's Words, Refracted', in Catherine de Zegher (ed.), *Here Art Grows on Trees: Simryn Gill*, Australia Council for the Arts, Sydney, and MER, Paper Kunsthalle, Gent, Belgium, 2013, pp. 185–225, and from an untitled essay by Simryn Gill in Tom Melick and Catherine de Zegher (eds), *Clearing*, Art Gallery of New South Wales and Stolon Press, Sydney, 2022, unpaged. 'Maps and Mazes' quotes a letter from Mike Parr to John Loane, dated 8 March 2002, which is held in the archives of the National Gallery of Victoria, Prints and Drawings Department; and 'Yes, Google Knew Immediately' quotes from Henry Miller, *The Air-Conditioned Nightmare*, New Directions, New York, 1945. 'The Extraordinary Mrs Gabori' is underpinned by recorded interviews with Nicholas Evans, Brett Evans and Beverly Knight. Community health and related statistics in that essay (pp. 114–15) are drawn from a 2013 Community Health Profile of Mornington Island and Bentinck Island prepared by Central and North West Queensland Medicare Local, and from 2011 National Census data, while details of art centre income (pp. 115–116) are drawn from the 2010 Miridiyan Gununa Annual Report. I also draw extensively from David McKnight, *From Hunting to Drinking: The Devastating Effects of Alcohol on an Australian Aboriginal Community*, Routledge, London, 2002, and quote from Nicholas Evans, 'The Eye of the Dolphin: Sally Gabori and the Kaiadilt Vision', in *Sally Gabori*, Fondation Cartier pour l'art Contemporain, Paris, pp. 11–32. 'Eric in the Desert and Elsewhere' draws from a number of publications by Eric Michaels: *Unbecoming*, Duke University Press, Durham, 1997; *Bad Aboriginal Art: Tradition, Media, and Technological Horizons*, University of Minnesota Press, Minneapolis, 1994; *The Aboriginal Invention of Television: Central Australia 1982–86*, Australian Institute of Aboriginal Studies, Canberra, 1986; and 'How to Look at Us Looking at the Yanomami Looking at Us', in *A Crack in the Mirror: Reflexive Perspectives in Anthropology*, ed. Jay Ruby, University of Philadelphia Press, Philadelphia, 1982, pp. 133–48. It also quotes from an essay by Melinda Hinkson, 'New Media Projects at Yuendumu: Inter-cultural Engagement and Self-determination in an Era of Accelerated Globalisation', *Continuum: Journal of Media & Cultural Studies* 16, no. 2, 2002, pp. 201–20. Further attributions, along with other more minor references to publications and interviews – recorded or otherwise – can be clearly inferred from the text. More specific reference details can be provided by contacting the publisher and/or author.

A number of essays in this collection have appeared elsewhere: an earlier version of 'The Artist in Space' appeared under the same title in *The Monthly*, December 2022 – January 2023; 'The Extraordinary Mrs Gabori' includes portions from two essays published in *The Monthly*, the first in March 2015 (under the same title) and the second in April 2022 ('Art Heist: The Landmark Conviction of an Aboriginal Art Centre's Manager'); an earlier version of 'The World Is Made of Layers' was included under the same title in *Vivienne Binns: On and Through the Surface*, co-published by the Monash University Museum of Art and the Museum of Contemporary Art Australia, 2022; 'The House at Glenorie' was published under the same title in *The Monthly*, October 2023; 'Surrender and Catch' was published in *The Monthly*, June 2024, as 'Surface Tensions'; an earlier version of 'The Horse Trotted Another Couple of Metres' was published in *The Monthly* (online) in January 2018 as 'Katharina Grosse's Riot of Colour'; and 'Eric, in the Desert and Elsewhere' includes portions of an essay titled 'Inventing Eric Michaels', published in *Discipline* in 2019.

Image Credits

front cover
Simryn Gill
Let them eat potatoes, 2014
Potato print with Louis Vuitton ink on Hahnemuhle paper
potato – Blau Annaleise,
ink – Bleu Rêveur
62 × 43 cm
© The artist

pp 2–3
Photo: the author

p 4
Philip Guston
Bad Habits, 1970
oil on canvas
185.5 × 198.2 cm
National Gallery of Australia, Canberra, purchased 1980
© The Estate of Philip Guston, courtesy Hauser & Wirth, New York

p 18
Stuart Ringholt
Untitled (Clock), 2014
Clockwork, tubular bells, world globe, steel, glass, electronics
280 × 202 × 100 cm
Museum of Contemporary Art Australia, purchased with funds provided by the MCA Foundation, 2014
© The artist

p 44
Simryn Gill
Pawn #2, 2019/2022
C-type print
20.4 × 25.4 cm
Art Gallery of New South Wales, Sydney, Gift of the artist, 2022
© The artist

p 60
Mike Parr working at Viridian Press, Olinda, c. 1997
Photo: John Loane

p 82
Ken Whisson
A part of the forest, 2006
brush and ink on paper
50 × 64 cm
Private collection
Photo: Silversalt
© Ken Whisson Estate, courtesy Niagara Galleries

p 94
Gathering on Bentinck Island, 1934
Collection: State Library of Queensland, Brisbane

p 122
Vivienne Binns working on *Minding Squares* in her Canberra studio, with the company of Harriet (left) and Bosco (right), 2011
Photo: Daniel Shipp
© Daniel Shipp

p 133
Vivienne Binns
Surfacing in the Pacific, 1993
acrylic on canvas
170 × 159 cm
Parliament House Collection, Department of Parliamentary Services, Canberra, purchased 1997
© The artist

p 144
Ball–Eastaway House, Glenorie, 2023
Photo: Quentin Sprague

p 161
Lynne Eastaway
Blue, 2021
acrylic and gouache on linen
30.5 × 25.7 cm
© The artist, courtesy Gallery 9

p 166
Helen Maudsley
Renewal, to find permission, 1989
oil on canvas
205 × 153.2 cm
National Gallery of Victoria, Melbourne
Gift of the artist through the Australian Government's Cultural Gifts Program, 2014
© H. Maudsley
Courtesy National Gallery of Victoria, Melbourne

p 184
Brent Harris
Grotesquerie (le regarder), 2002
oil on linen
191 × 183 cm
© The artist, courtesy Tolarno Galleries

p 196
Martin Kantor, *Portrait of Brent Harris*, 1989
Courtesy Julie Kantor

p 202
Karl Wiebke
Buildings B/11, 2004–2008
acrylic on wood
34 × 28 cm
© The artist, courtesy Liverpool Street Gallery

p 218
Karl Wiebke painting in his Fremantle garden, 1995
Photo: Richard Woldendorp

p 222
Katharina Grosse
The Horse Trotted Another Couple of Metres, Then It Stopped, 2017
Installation view, Carriageworks, Sydney
Photo: Zan Wimberley
© Katharina Grosse. VG Bild-Kunst/ Copyright Agency, 2025

p 230
Eric Michaels, Yuendumu, c. 1985
Photographer unknown

p 238
Yuendumu, c. 1985
Photo: Eric Michaels

p 255
Near Yuendumu, c. 1985
Photo: Eric Michaels

pp 264–65
Photo: the author

p 266
Benjamin Armstrong
Midday, 2024–2025
encaustic, glass, paint, silicone, steel, timber
162.5 × 128 × 76 cm
Photo: Christian Capurro
© The artist, courtesy the artist and Tolarno Galleries

inside back cover
Photo: Ross Coulter